PORTRAIT OF A NATION
A History of
the United States

Volume I

Portrait of a Nation

A HISTORY OF THE UNITED STATES

MORTON BORDEN

OTIS L. GRAHAM, JR.

WITH RODERICK W. NASH

RICHARD E. OGLESBY

University of California, Santa Barbara

D. C. HEATH AND COMPANY
Lexington, Massachusetts Toronto London

PREFACE

"History is bunk," Henry Ford once announced, and our experience as teachers suggests that the sentiment is not entirely dead. Studied as a compilation of dry facts to be memorized and quickly forgotten, history is painful. Twisted to serve particular causes, it is dishonest. Taught as a patriotic exercise, it is dangerous. We have tried to avoid these abuses—which does not mean we have not committed others. Obviously, historians must be selective. Selectivity means subjectivity, and subjectivity means that interpretations of the past will often conflict. Were it otherwise, history would be an antiquarian discipline, the work of recorders rather than scholars.

Portrait of a Nation is highly selective. It is intended to be an introduction and a guide to college students in American history survey courses. Its purpose is more to evoke questions than to answer them, more to stimulate interest than to cover topics in exhaustive detail. Not everyone will be satisfied with its emphasis; but today students have at their disposal an enormous variety of paperback books from which they can select appropriate supplementary readings.

Two of our colleagues at the University of California, Santa Barbara, have written parts of this text. Richard Oglesby is the author of chapter 1 and Roderick Nash of chapter 3 in volume two. We owe them a considerable debt, as we do our wives, children, and editors, who, for different reasons, urged us to complete these volumes.

MORTON BORDEN

OTIS L. GRAHAM, JR.

CONTENTS

COLONIAL FOUNDATIONS
To 1763

1

GOD OR GOLD

"Let us rejoice," Christopher Columbus proclaimed after his initial voyage, "as well on account of the exaltation of our faith, as on account of the increase of our temporal prosperity." The words were really a boast to mask his failure. Instead of treasure and spices Columbus had found only frightened Indians and lush vegetation. Three times more he led expeditions without ever discovering the fabled wealth of the Indies, without ever realizing that he was touching the fringes of a vast, unknown hemisphere. Nevertheless, in that one sentence Columbus combined what were to become the twin motivating forces for European expansion: the spiritual and the secular. In the coming centuries men ventured into strange lands either to enrich king and country or to escape them; either to proselytize for Christianity or to practice it undisturbed; either to earn a livelihood or to make a fortune. Some went unwillingly as prisoners or slaves, and others from a sense of adventure. But two major impulses predominated for most explorers

1

and settlers, and who can now tell which was the stronger—God or gold?

THE IBERIAN EMPIRES

Portugal had been the first western European country to create an overseas empire. Before the voyages of Columbus, Portuguese mariners had ventured into the Atlantic, explored the western coast and rounded the southern tip of the African continent. By the early 1500's Portugal had established numerous trading posts in Ceylon, India, and the East Indies. Spices in Asia were cheap and plentiful, and could be easily transported because of their small bulk. In addition, prices on the European market were so high that each successful voyage yielded enormous profits. Portugal's population, however, was inadequate to colonize and defend its widely distributed commercial stations. European competitors gradually seized the most lucrative sites.

Spain's disappointment at the comparatively meager wealth of the

A series of voyages begun in 1497 convinced Amerigo Vespucci that the newly discovered lands were not a part of Asia, as Columbus had thought, but rather a "New World." In 1507 a map showing Vespucci and the New World first used the term "America." (Courtesy of New York Public Library)

Caribbean changed abruptly after the conquests of the Aztecs by Hernando Cortez and the Incas by Francisco Pizarro. So much gold and, especially, silver poured into Spain from the mines of Mexico and Peru that the sudden influx of wealth touched off an inflationary spiral that affected every aspect of European life. Outside the Iberian Peninsula inflation aided capitalistic development, which in turn helped to erode medieval institutions. In Spain and Portugal, paradoxically, the treasure of Asia and America served to freeze the rigid social structure of the past. Spain used its wealth to gild church altars, wasted it on courtly extravagance, and dissipated it in fighting holy wars against northern Protestants. The Iberian nations started poor —and ended poor.

SPANISH POWER

At first glance the Spanish empire appeared too bloated to defend itself. Buccaneers intercepted and seized Spanish galleons loaded with bullion, and carried out daring raids on Spanish colonial ports. Sir Francis Drake, on the *Golden Hynd*, brought back so much Spanish treasure in 1580 that Queen Elizabeth's portion was sufficient to pay off all England's foreign debts and to balance the national budget. Other shareholders in the venture realized a profit of 4,600 per cent. Some 50 years later the Dutch admiral Piet Hein captured an entire Spanish treasure fleet off the Cuban coast. The prize amounted to nearly $10 million.

Nevertheless, Spain was quite capable of defending its colonial possessions. The attempts made by the Dutch, the English, and the French to whittle away at the Spanish-American empire during the sixteenth century failed. Competitors established colonial posts from Florida to Canada, but none of them lasted for more than a few years. French settlers in Florida and South Carolina were slaughtered by the Spaniards. English settlers in North Carolina disappeared without a trace. To this day the fate of Sir Walter Raleigh's "Lost Colony" remains an enigma. Even the defeat of the Spanish Armada in 1588, contrary to legend, did not signify the twilight of Spanish power. The central parts of Spain's imperial domain remained impregnable throughout the colonial era.

FOUNDATIONS OF ENGLISH POWER

Not until 1607, at Jamestown, Virginia, did an English seed take permanent root in the New World. The settlement seemed totally inconsequential to the Spanish monarch. After all, the Spaniards controlled an area which stretched from Texas to Tierra del Fuego. The English, moreover, who yearned to duplicate Spanish triumphs, discovered neither gold, silver, nor precious stones. Rather, they encountered malaria and hostile tribes of Indians. In Virginia, and elsewhere on the North American continent, English explorers were frustrated in still another respect. They expected to locate a water route through the continent to the Pacific, and thus to the Orient. Sir Humphrey Gilbert had composed a *Discourse on the Northwest Passage* to prove that such a route existed. Despite repeated failures and mounting geographic evidence to the contrary, the belief and the fruitless search long persisted.

None could foresee that from such an unpropitious and unrewarding beginning the English would create a mighty empire. A small island nation, torn by religious dissent and political unrest, without colonies to provide easy windfalls of bullion or spices, England nevertheless emerged as an international power to rival and then to surpass Spain. How was it possible? What were the special ingredients which contributed to this remarkable achievement?

First, after Jamestown the English literally swarmed across the Atlantic in an unprecedented mass migration. In less than four decades some 70,000 came, not only to Plymouth and Massachusetts Bay, fanning out into New England, but also to the Chesapeake region, and to Bermuda, Barbados, and other West Indian islands. The men who ruled England were delighted. At one stroke, they reasoned, the homeland would be rid of unemployed vagabonds, incorrigible jailbirds, potential rebels, and religious malcontents like the Puritans. Ironically, the foundations of English imperial power were based in part on the work of these fugitives, who found conditions at home intolerable.

Second, overseas expansion was made possible by an extension of burgeoning capitalism in England. As the Spanish noble had wasted, the English capitalist had accumulated. The British made a virtue of necessity by extolling thrift and exalting business. Entrepreneurs who made fortunes in coal mining and iron manufacturing, in the glass and textile industries, or in trade and agriculture, invested some of their surplus capital in colonial experiments which they hoped would yield even greater profits. Of course, settlers had to be willing to make the journey across the Atlantic; but they also had to be equipped, transported, and maintained. The costs of colonization were often financed by groups of capitalists who formed joint stock companies under royal charters.

These companies proved to be a poor investment for the individual speculator. In Latin America, Indians mined silver for the Spaniards; in Canada, they gathered furs for the French. In between, there was no quick way to instant wealth. The land was virtually free, but hard work and patience were necessary to make it self-sustaining and profitable. (The English colonist came to venerate productive labor and to sneer at "indolent" foreigners—a prejudice many Americans still possess.) Eventually the colonies did produce money crops: tobacco from Virginia, sugar from the West Indies, rice and indigo from Carolina, flax and wheat from Pennsylvania, and lumber and fish from New England. The colonists flourished and England as a whole prospered, but the original investor was usually wiped out.

VIRGINIA (1607)

The history of Virginia's growth provides an excellent illustration of how a colony progressed economically while its backers failed. The company responsible for sending the first expedition to Virginia was directed by men of great wealth and distinction: financiers like Sir Thomas Smythe and Sir Ferdinando Gorges, the Earl of Warwick, the Lord Chief Justice Francis Popham, Lord Thomas de la Warr (later to become governor of Virginia), and others. In 1609 and again in 1612 their royal charter was revised to give the company more land, more authority, and the opportunity to raise more money. In addition to the considerable investments made by these men, other individuals and groups purchased smaller numbers of shares. But still more capital was needed. When the investors' confidence faltered, the company conducted a series of lotteries. Some members of Parliament complained, however, that the lotteries "do beggar" the motherland. "Let Virginia lose rather than England." King James I agreed, and the lotteries were suspended—a fatal blow to the company.

The settlers in Virginia were so ill-prepared for the hardships of the American frontier that the death rate was appalling. Within the first six months 50 per cent died. Nor did this percentage decrease. A later investigation concluded that between 1607 and 1623, of some 5,000 persons who emigrated to Virginia, about 4,000 had perished! On one occasion, when relief ships dispatched by the company failed to arrive, settlers were reduced to eating snails, snakes, and whatever animals they could find, and one man was reported to have killed and devoured his wife. On another occasion the relief ships, commanded by Lord de la Warr, arrived just as the remnants were abandoning the colony and sailing down the James River.

Supplies from England kept Virginia alive, but tobacco was its

Nova Britannia.

OFFERING MOST

Excellent fruites by Planting in
VIRGINIA.

Exciting all such as be well affected
to further the same.

An ad for Virginia from a 1609 booklet promoting emigration. In that year a "great fleet" of 9 ships, carrying some 600 men, women, and children set sail for Virginia. Seven vessels, with 400 aboard, arrived in Jamestown to find not "excellent fruites" but less than a hundred bedraggled settlers without adequate housing, food, or leadership. (Courtesy of Rare Book Division, New York Public Library, Astor, Lenox and Tilden Foundations)

LONDON
Printed for SAMVEL MACHAM, and are to be sold at
his Shop in Pauls Church-yard, at the
Signe of the Bul-head.
1 6 0 9.

true salvation. John Rolfe, who married the Indian princess Pocahontas, grew the first crop in 1612. By importing West Indian seed and crossing it with local Indian tobacco, he obtained a strain that sold for an excellent price in England. Thereafter Virginians went tobacco mad. They planted it everywhere they thought it might grow, even on the streets of Jamestown. They grew it so exclusively, neglecting other crops, that food shortages continued. By 1618 Virginia had shipped 50,000 pounds of tobacco to England. But whatever income accrued to the Virginia company did not meet its debts or expenses. Sir Thomas Smythe was ousted as head of the company and replaced by another financier, Sir Edwin Sandys. Sandys tried to institute a number of progressive measures—to no avail. In 1624 the company's charter was revoked and Virginia became a royal colony. By that time it had spent well over £160,000 on Virginia. No dividend was ever paid.

THE PILGRIM SETTLEMENT (1620)

Before its dissolution the Virginia company had agreed to permit a group of Pilgrims to settle within its colony. Permission was far from signifying approval of Pilgrim beliefs. The Pilgrims were regarded as an obnoxious minor sect of self-righteous religious extremists, holding views which threatened the established Anglican church as well as the monarchy. Like all the "Reformed" followers of Calvin, the Pilgrims believed they were among the elite whom God had predestined to heaven while scoffers (including Catholics, Jews, Lutherans, Anglicans, and heathen) were foredoomed to hell. Moreover, the Pilgrims refused to recognize the dictates of any higher ecclesiastical authority. Each of their congregations selected its own minister and formed its own church polity.

Persecuted in England, a number of Pilgrims had fled to Holland in 1608, where they expected to live in theological harmony with the Reformed Dutch. After a decade they were discouraged, for they found life in an alien land hard and unpromising. Despite their labors, they were still poor. Some of their children had taken to the sea and drifted away from the true faith. Their small community seemed to be aging and disintegrating. After considerable debate and soul-searching, the majority of the Pilgrims voted to migrate to America. "It was granted the dangers were great," one of the Pilgrim leaders, William Bradford, later recorded in his *History of Plymouth Plantation*, "but

One of the illustrations from John Smith's Generall Historie *(1624) shows Captain Smith taking an Indian chief prisoner during his exploration of the Chesapeake Bay in 1608. A professional adventurer, Smith had previously fought in Turkey and the Balkans. His strong leadership had much to do with the survival of the Jamestown colony. (Courtesy of Rare Book Division, New York Public Library, Astor, Lenox and Tilden Foundations)*

not desperate; the difficulties were many, but not invincible." The Virginia company would benefit by having its lands populated and productive. The Pilgrims would benefit by an opportunity to create their own Zion in the wilderness.

Pilgrims from both Holland and England came on the *Mayflower* in 1620, though not to Virginia. Perhaps by accident, possibly by design, they decided to locate permanently at Plymouth on Cape Cod Bay. The climate there was severe. They had few supplies. Disease struck, wiping out half their members. Only a few, Miles Standish among them, were strong enough to move about and to nurse the sick. Friendly Indians helped, but it was their unswerving faith and determination that sustained the Pilgrims through the first bitter winter. By April 1621, when the *Mayflower* sailed back, no Pilgrim elected to return to England; and in October the survivors shared a thanksgiving feast with the Indians. They had mastered a hostile frontier, created a government, erected their churches, and they worshipped as they pleased—which might not have been the case in Virginia. In time the Pilgrims obtained a patent to their land. They also renegotiated and repaid their collective indebtedness to the English backers who had financed their voyage.

Statistically the number of Pilgrims was insignificant, and Plymouth was never a major colony. The Pilgrims loom large in American history, however, because of their indomitable spirit and remarkable accomplishment. William Bradford wrote, with justifiable pride: "All great and honorable actions are accompanied with great difficulties, and must be overcome with answerable courage." His words were meant as a legacy to all Americans.

MASSACHUSETTS BAY (1630)

Another group of Reformed Calvinists, the Puritans, had remained within the Church of England, hoping to shape its policy and alter its form to accord with their beliefs—in short, to rid Anglicanism of certain Catholic vestiges. The Stuart kings and their appointed bishops, on the other hand, resisted these attempts. King James I stated that he would have "one doctrine, one discipline, one religion in substance and ceremony," and that it would not be contaminated by Puritan practices. Persecution of the Puritans grew increasingly severe, particularly during the reign of Charles I. To cite but one extreme example, a Puritan preacher was fined £10,000, flogged, pilloried, his ears were lopped, his nose slit, his cheeks branded "S S" (Sower of Sedition), and he was sentenced to long imprisonment. Thousands of Puritans

"We shall be as a City upon a Hill," John Winthrop, the Puritan leader, told his fellow passengers on their voyage to America, "the eyes of all people are upon us; so that if we shall deal falsely with our god in this work we have undertaken and so cause him to withdraw his present help from us, we shall be made a story and a byword through the world." The burden was great, and Winthrop's portrait reveals the gravity and dignity, the sober intelligence of a Puritan steward faced with the sacred duty of leading his people upon this great venture. The first governor of Massachusetts, Winthrop held that post, except for brief intervals, until his death in 1649. (Courtesy of the Rare Books Department, Boston Public Library)

decided to follow the Pilgrims' example and escape to America. Those that remained in England ultimately precipitated a rebellion—the Puritan Revolution—which overthrew the monarchy.

The Puritans who settled at Massachusetts Bay in 1630 were far superior to their Pilgrim neighbors in education, social status, and economic position. In numbers alone they dwarfed the Pilgrim settlement. But both shared a common purpose: to create a community dedicated to the glorification of God, at least the God which fitted their Reformed prescriptions. Puritan leaders took extensive precautions to insure the achievement of their goals.

First, by prearrangement they carried the charter of the Massachusetts Bay Company with them to Boston. The step was as audacious as it was unprecedented. It meant that control of the company could not fall into the hands of the Puritans' English enemies. King Charles I tried legal action to recover the charter, but the Puritans ignored the rulings of the royal court. He then ordered an expedition to seize the charter by force. The vessel designated to carry new officers to Massachusetts broke on launching and never sailed. For 50 years the Puritans ruled fairly unfettered by royal interference before the charter was revoked and Massachusetts became a royal colony.

Second, the Puritan elders cleverly converted the company charter into a frame of government, and so interpreted its clauses as to maintain their power. Thus, as the instrument of a commercial organization, the charter stated that all stockholders were freemen who could vote and participate in company affairs. As the constitution of a commonwealth, however, the definition was radically and illegally altered. Only members of the Puritan churches were considered freemen who could vote and participate in political affairs.

Third, the Puritans were as intolerant of dissenters as the Stuart kings were of them. Roger Williams, for example, though a famous Puritan minister, was banished from Massachusetts Bay for his heretical teachings. (He became the founder of Rhode Island.) Quakers who insisted upon preaching anti-Puritan doctrines in Boston were candidates for martyrdom. Many were brutally whipped, and some of the more zealous offenders were hanged.

For all their emphasis upon religious orthodoxy, the Puritan's legacy to America was secular and practical rather than spiritual and theological. Although Calvinism was given new life in the revival movements—the "Great Awakening"—of the eighteenth century, it could not resist the inroads of rationalism and economic progress. The New Englander metamorphosed from Puritan stalwart to Yankee merchant. The typical American continued to attend church but came to scoff at the doctrines of original sin and predestination. Puritans are remembered largely for their belief in devils, their witch trials, their Sabbath laws, and their strict moral imperatives. But their practical contributions were also great. They founded Harvard College, passed laws to establish grammar schools, and set up the first printing press in the English colonies. The earliest general treatise on medicine in North America was written by Cotton Mather, a Puritan divine. To be sure, the Puritans considered education and science as adjuncts of religion—as tools to help men read the Bible, master the catechism, train for the ministry, and understand God's arrangement of the universe. Nevertheless, the American emphasis on education is derived from these Puritan antecedents.

THE FEUDAL EXPERIMENTS

The Virginian dream of riches and the Puritan dream of a biblical commonwealth were altered by the realities of frontier existence. Other Englishmen had other dreams for America, but none worked out precisely as planned. The colonies of Maryland and Carolina, owned and established by proprietors rather than by companies, represented two different blueprints for creating feudal systems. In each the ideal had to be sacrificed to the practical.

Maryland. Sir George Calvert—the first Lord Baltimore, renowned as an entrepreneur, courtier, and convert to Catholicism—sought land in the New World which could serve as a Catholic refuge and, at the same time, be developed into a vast medieval estate to enhance the fortunes and prestige of the Calvert family. Though he died before the royal charter for Maryland was issued in 1632, his two sons carried forward the task of colonization. The charter granted to the Calverts over 10 million acres of what had been northern Virginia. Once a year the proprietors were to present to the king of England a symbolic payment of two Indian arrows, and—as specified in every charter— one fifth of the gold and silver found within the colony. Laws were to be enacted with the advice and consent of freeholders, and could not be repugnant to the laws of England. Aside from these restrictions, the Calverts enjoyed absolute power.

They were never able to convert the Maryland wilderness into a medieval palatinate, however. Some 60 manors were created, but there were no vassals bound to lords by feudal obligations. Few Englishmen in the seventeenth century would willingly turn themselves into serfs. Emigrants who came with funds insisted upon freehold land tenure, which the Calverts granted in order to attract settlers. Emigrants without funds came as indentured servants, contracting to work a specified number of years to repay their transportation costs. When this contract was satisfactorily completed, the indentured servant was given 50 acres of land and, at the same time, all the privileges and prerogatives of other property owners.

Most servants and freeholders in Maryland were Protestant. Conflicts with Catholic settlers were inevitable in an age of pronounced religious bigotry. Yet, the Calverts ruled Maryland fairly and judiciously, and remarkably little blood was spilled. Some Jesuits, for example, who proved to be a disruptive influence, were recalled to England at the request of the Calverts. Overzealous Protestants, who wished to make Anglicanism the official religion, were thwarted by Maryland's so-called Toleration Act of 1649. The law protected the Catholic minority by guaranteeing religious freedom to all who accepted the trinitarian creed. Marylanders did attempt to overthrow the proprietary government—five times between 1660 and 1689—but their major grievances were basically economic and political, not religious. The Calverts temporarily lost political control of Maryland for several decades, but they regained power in 1715 and never relinquished it until the American Revolution.

Carolina. With all its problems, Maryland proved so lucrative an investment that other Englishmen decided to emulate the Calverts. Eight of the richest and most renowned Englishmen—including the Earl of Clarendon, the Duke of Albemarle, and Lord Ashley Cooper—in 1663 were granted a charter, patterned after that of Maryland, to the vast Carolina area which lay between Virginia and Florida. Here the joint proprietors envisioned a colonial society neatly balanced between feudal nobility and freemen. They planned to hold one fifth of the land for themselves and their heirs, as seigniors exercising feudal jurisdiction over a race of hereditary tenants. Another fifth of the land would be formed into baronies. The remaining three fifths would be apportioned among freeholders, who would pay quitrents to the proprietors. The details of their grandiose scheme were meticulously worked out in the "Fundamental Constitutions." Drafted by John Locke and adopted by the proprietory board in 1669, it was neither accepted by the Carolina colonists nor effectively enforced by the proprietors.

From the beginning there were two Carolinas, with separate governments, contrasting economies, and divergent social patterns. The northern part was settled initially by Virginians, some of whom had located around Albemarle Sound a decade before the proprietors received their charter. Without good harbors, North Carolina lacked both major ports and bustling commercial centers. In fact, it had no town until after 1700. The people were more dispersed and isolated, culturally cruder, and less affluent than those in neighboring colonies. Most settlers lived on small farms with a few slaves and grew subsistence crops and tobacco. Even after the plantation economy developed in the eighteenth century, the ratio of slaves to owners was smaller in North Carolina than anywhere else in the South.

South Carolina early attracted a heterogeneous lot of emigrants, and imported so many slaves that by 1708 the black and white populations were about equal in size. Charleston, named Charles Town after King Charles II, quickly became the focus of a thriving triangular trade. South Carolinians shipped their cattle, lumber, and grains for sale to Barbados; there vessels reloaded with cargoes of sugar for markets in England; and then returned to Charleston carrying English manufactured goods. Like upstate New York, South Carolina also profited by an important traffic in deer skins and furs. But the money crops, first rice and then indigo, in time came to dominate the economy of South Carolina. The owners of plantations in the coastal region became the wealthiest class in all North America. Charleston developed into a social, political, and trading center for the planters, a gay and cosmopolitan capital.

Though the "Fundamental Constitutions" were formally renounced by the proprietors, relations with the settlers scarcely improved. Carolinians regarded the proprietors as too mercenary, their government as too autocratic. Colonists in all areas of Carolina resisted the

In South Carolina, before cotton became king, slaves were used to process indigo, a plant providing blue dyestuff. Eliza Lucas, who later married Charles Pinckney, marketed the first crop on the mainland in 1744. By 1754 South Carolina exported more than a million pounds of indigo. (From A Compleat History of Drugs, *1725)*

payment of quitrents, quarreled with officials over land titles, and despaired of receiving adequate military aid in fighting the Indians and Spaniards. Proprietary governors were often defied by the colonists, and sometimes forced out of office. In 1719 South Carolinians rebelled, deposed the governor, and seized the colony in the name of the king. Ten years later, having long since abandoned any dream of erecting a feudal paradise, and without realizing any profit from their venture, the proprietors sold their rights to the crown.

THE HOLY EXPERIMENT (1681)

Each colony was endowed with a distinctive character—a character long retained, even after statehood—which resulted from the interaction of its geographic circumstance, cultural inheritance, ethnic composition, economic structure, and, in an age of faith, its religious persuasion. Pennsylvania in particular was profoundly influenced by the theology of its founder, William Penn. The son and heir of an admiral in the royal navy, an aristocrat by birth as well as by inclination, Penn had nevertheless embraced a religion of the English lower classes. Indeed, Penn was probably the most illustrious member of that sect, the Society of Friends, disparagingly called Quakers because their leader, George Fox, had warned a hostile judge to "tremble at the word of the Lord." Quakers taught that all men were possessed of the Inner Light, the voice of God in the human soul. They believed that men needed neither books nor ceremonies nor priests to discover God, but only a pure heart and free conscience. They believed in social simplicity, religious toleration, peace, and brotherly love—tenets which antagonized the nobility, the clergy, and the military establishment of England.

To save his fellow Quakers from further persecution, Penn sought a charter from his friend, Charles II, to establish a proprietary colony for them in America. Charles was willing, but the court party was so hostile to the Quakers that he needed some excuse. One was found in an old financial debt owed by the crown to Penn's estate. The debt, which no one had ever expected would be repaid, was to be canceled in exchange for land in the New World. Penn received the charter in 1681. It was the last proprietary grant ever issued by the English government. Years later he explained that "the government at home was glad to be rid of us at so cheap a rate as a little parchment in a desert three thousand miles off."

Pennsylvania was a desert only in the metaphoric sense. From the beginning it prospered as thousands of English, Welsh, Scotch, Irish, Dutch, German, and other immigrants, attracted by Penn's pamphlets, flocked there to benefit from the liberal land allowances he offered. Pennsylvania became one of the most ethnically and religiously diverse of the American colonies. Its rate of economic growth outdistanced all others in the eighteenth century. Its toleration of non-Quaker Christian denominations and its degree of political democracy and personal freedom were scarcely equaled, except in Rhode Island. Slavery existed, but the institution was essentially repugnant to Quaker beliefs and the earliest movements for manumission originated in Pennsylvania.

Toleration, diversity, and material success did not ensure that Pennsylvanians lived in harmony. Indeed, the issues which divided colonists living in Penn's "Holy Experiment" were comparable to those which caused disturbances in the feudal experiments of Maryland and Carolina. First, the Quakers considered the heirs of William Penn too greedy in their collection of quitrents. A Quaker party attempted to thwart the proprietary governor through control of the colonial legislature. Second, Scotch-Irish settlers in the west were angered by the reluctance of the Quaker-dominated colonial legislature to appropriate funds to defend the frontier against Indian attacks. Third, the Quakers themselves eventually split into factions, as rural members found their Philadelphia brethren too wealthy and too worldly for their simple orthodox tastes.

For all these reasons politics in Pennsylvania was particularly muddled and stormy. By 1756, to regain and preserve the purity of their religious precepts, Quakers virtually abandoned their role in the government of Pennsylvania. Thereafter their energies were channeled into humanitarian rather than political efforts: building hospitals, improving conditions in prisons and insane asylums, working to end both the slave trade and slavery. The Quakers' concern for the whole human community, their pacifism, and their emphasis upon the right of dissent, then and in subsequent centuries, have served to stir the conscience of other citizens. No conscience is stirred without some irritation, which Americans have on occasion exhibited toward Quakers. But no other group has set a better example of democracy in action than the Quakers, a fact which Americans have recognized and of which they have proudly boasted.

GEORGIA (1732)

More than a century after Jamestown was first settled, when Boston, New York, Philadelphia, Baltimore, and Charleston were thriving communities, and half a million people lived along the seaboard, England established its thirteenth colony in America. In 1732 a group of

London philanthropists, led by Lord Percival and General James Ogle-thorpe, obtained a charter from King George II to the land south of Carolina, between the Savannah and Altahama rivers. Their settle-ment, to be known as Georgia, was conceived as a completely unique experiment. In form the venture was to be neither corporate, nor proprietary, nor royal, but was rather to be directed by a board of trustees. Its founders were motivated neither by material self-interest nor by sectarian impulse, but by a charitable desire to provide a liveli-hood for English paupers. While emigration was not restricted to the poor, those without funds were to receive free transportation, 50 acres of free land, and free rations until the colony was self-sustaining. The other colonies were financed, at least initially, by private venture capital. Georgia was the only one to receive a partial endowment from the English government. The other colonies had to guard against rivals and jealous detractors. Georgia enjoyed cordial endorsement every-where. No slavery was to be permitted. No strong liquor was allowed. No man could own more than 500 acres. The colony of Georgia was to give the impoverished a chance to start life anew; it would be popu-lated by sober and hardworking yeomen; it would produce silks and naval stores for England's benefit; and it would act as an effective buffer against Spanish domination on the colonies' southern frontier.

The fledgling colony did succeed in one of these objectives. Spanish forces were ambushed and routed at the Battle of Bloody Marsh, their morale destroyed, their menace forever removed. But in Georgia, as elsewhere in America, the realities of frontier life had a way of frus-trating the best intentions of English planners. The silk industry never developed as anticipated. Malaria took a heavy toll. The trustees badgered the colonists with paternalistic rules which were resented. Life was hard in the pine barrens, and Georgians, envious of their prosperous neighbors to the north, demanded rum, slaves, and espe-cially more land. At first the trustees resisted these pressures, but in time they acceded. By 1752, when Georgia became a royal colony, the ideals—and interest—of the founders had been abandoned. "It is a melancholy thing," Lord Percival remarked, "to see how zeal for a good thing abates when the novelty is over." Georgia soon followed Carolina's pattern with slaves, rice and indigo plantations, and even debtors and debtors' prisons.

SLAVERY IN THE COLONIES

The most persistent problem throughout the colonies was the shortage of labor. Indians refused to work for others and would not tolerate enslavement. Attempts to persuade or to force labor upon them were abject failures. The system of indentured servants, while important to the colonial economy, was also unsatisfactory. The demand for such servants was always far greater than the supply; and when the period of indenture expired, replacements had to be found. "Help is scarce and hard to get, difficult to please, and uncertain," was a familiar complaint of American colonial society. Particularly in the southern colonies, with the development of plantations, the necessity of a steady and cheap labor supply became imperative. Since the red man would not work, and not enough white men could be hired, the solution was to enslave the blacks. The supply from Africa seemed inexhaustible; if a black man refused to work he could be chastised with an easier conscience than could a white man; if he tried to escape his color made it simple to identify him.

The first blacks brought to Jamestown in 1619, and those who came for several decades thereafter, were treated as servants rather than as slaves. According to Christian dogma only heathen could be enslaved, and many blacks were baptized. Those who completed their period of indenture were granted the stipulated amount of free land. By the middle of the century, however, economic necessity overcame religious scruples. Blacks were imported either without indenture, or as "personal servants." Their precise status was legally ambiguous until 1664, when slavery was legitimized by an act of the Maryland legislature which secured the title of their white masters. Three years later the Virginia assembly declared them to be slaves by virtue of their color. In time every colony adopted slave codes. The fact that many blacks had accepted Christianity became immaterial. "Baptism," the Virginia legislature decided, "does not alter the condition of the person as to his bondage or freedom."

Not until the eighteenth century, however, were slaves brought to the New World in large numbers. In 1700 there were no more than 25,000 slaves in the mainland colonies; by 1790 there were 700,000. An apologist for slavery could argue that everyone benefited. The expanding southern plantation economy received the labor supply it required. The New England merchants gained a fair share of the slave trade, which returned lucrative profits. The African was exposed to Western culture and his soul was saved by conversion to Christianity. A critic, on the other hand, could point to the slaves' frequent insurrections as an index of their misery, and to repressive laws as eloquent testimony of the whites' fears. The institution of slavery may have created a leisure class of whites, giving them the time and wealth to build beautiful mansions, to educate their children abroad, to cultivate social graces, and to acquire the qualities of leadership which America needed. But slavery also had degrading effects upon whites as well as blacks. The black man was kept from participating in the American dream. The southern white often developed traits of callousness, ruthlessness, and profligacy. A Quaker visitor to Virginia in 1746, John Woolman, recognized the evil: "I saw in these southern provinces so many vices and corruptions increased by this trade and way of life, that it appeared to me as a dark gloominess hanging over the land."

REPRESENTATIVE GOVERNMENT IN AMERICA

While the Indian was being deprived of his land, and the black man of his freedom, white settlers were extending for themselves the political liberties they enjoyed as English citizens. In 1619, by order of the Virginia company, the first representative assembly was established at Jamestown. The acts of this assembly, the House of Burgesses, could be vetoed by the governor, or set aside by either the company or the crown. Nevertheless, the germ of self-government had been introduced, and when Virginia became a royal colony the House of Burgesses remained a part of the political structure. Eventually all 13 of the colonies possessed legislative assemblies, 12 of them bicameral, and one (Pennsylvania) unicameral.

Each colony had its own particular rules for voting and office holding. Usually women, slaves, indentured servants, propertyless individuals, and non-Christians were excluded from the suffrage. In the seventeenth century Rhode Island was the sole colony without a religious qualification for voting. The other New England settlements —Plymouth, Massachusetts Bay, Connecticut, and New Haven—all limited the suffrage to members of an approved Calvinist church. However, the major prerequisite for voting in most colonies was the ownership of a minimum amount of property. The amount required ranged from Pennsylvania, which had the lowest (either 50 acres of land or £50 in cash), to South Carolina, which instituted the highest by its franchise law of 1745 (either a cultivated plantation or 300 acres of undeveloped land). With certain exceptions, as the number of landholders increased the suffrage became more broadly based.

Gradually the colonial legislatures assumed greater prerogatives and powers, until they began to resemble the English House of Commons. Members debated without fear of arrest; they selected their own speaker; they won the right to initiate, not merely to ratify laws; and, above all, no taxes could be levied without their consent. Control of taxation gave the legislatures a degree of administrative power over public finances. They appointed public treasurers and audited the accounts of public officers. In a few colonies even the governors' salaries were dependent on the legislature. Supervision of the purse strings gave the assemblies in turn a major voice in military and judicial matters, in Indian relations, and in ecclesiastical policies. There were frequent bitter clashes with colonial governors over these issues. Particularly in the royal provinces, after the mother country began to exert its central authority, conflict was inevitable. The royal governor was the principal executive officer responsible for applying England's imperial decrees. Colonial resistance centered in the assembly, which, by 1763, had obtained a position of power it refused to relinquish.

THE OLD COLONIAL SYSTEM

According to English mercantilist theory, colonies were economic dependencies, indispensable in building and sustaining the strength of the motherland in at least four ways:

1. By supplying raw materials unavailable at home,
2. By providing a market for manufactured goods,
3. By serving as a dumping ground for what was thought to be excess population, thus alleviating unemployment, and
4. By stimulating trade, and thus adding to the royal revenues, primarily through customs duties.

But in the first half of the seventeenth century it became apparent that English colonists did not agree with these precepts. Dutch ships selling slaves and hardware, and carrying away sugar and tobacco, were welcomed in Virginia, the West Indies, and other English settlements. A series of royal decrees forbade this trade and ordered all American tobacco shipped directly to England, and only in English ships. In the 1640's, however, when England was preoccupied with its Puritan Revolution, the Dutch vessels returned to monopolize the colonial trade. So extensive was the commerce that Dutch currency became a common medium of exchange in New England. Dutch merchants even extended lines of credit to planters in Barbados and the Leeward Islands.

After Charles I was executed in 1649, and Oliver Cromwell took control of the government, Puritan merchants insisted that measures be taken to exclude the Dutch from commerce with England's colonies. Thus, in 1650–51, the first Navigation Acts were passed by Parliament. During the next century, other laws were enacted, and administrative agencies created, defining and regulating the economic relations of England with its colonies. The major contours of the colonial

The Humble
PETITION
AND
ADDRESS
Of the General Court fitting at
Boston in *New-England,*
UNTO
The High and Mighty
PRINCE
CHARLES
THE SECOND.

And prefented unto His Moft-Gracious
Majefty *Feb.* 11. 1660.

_____

Printed in the Year 1660.

*With the fall of Cromwell's govern-
ment, Charles II, the eldest son of
Charles I, was proclaimed king of
England. By announcing their loyalty
to Charles, the Massachusetts colonists hoped to appease the king for
having harbored the men who had
charged Charles I with high treason.
(Courtesy of Rare Book Division,
New York Public Library, Astor,
Lenox and Tilden Foundations)*

system can be traced in the following summaries of these acts
and agencies:

Act of 1650. The supremacy of Parliament over the colonies was un-
equivocally stated. Foreign ships were prohibited from trading with
any colonies except by special license.

Act of 1651. Decreed that goods brought from Asia, Africa, or America to England must be transported in English ships (which included,
by definition, vessels of the English colonies). Trade with and between
the colonies must also be carried in English ships.

Act of 1660. Passed after the restoration of the Stuart monarchy, this
act restated provisions of the 1651 law. It specified that sugar, tobacco,
and cotton—enumerated articles—could be sent only to England or to
another English colony. In the next century the enumerated list was
gradually extended to include everything from rice and copper ore to
whale fins, beaver skins, and coconuts.

Act of 1663. Declared that European goods for the American colonial
market, with a few exceptions, must be sent by way of England.

Act of 1673. Imposed export duties on enumerated products, to be paid at the colonial port. Necessitated stationing of royal customs officials in America.

1675. Lords of Trade—a committee of the Privy Council—was appointed to supervise colonial affairs.

1685. In an effort to consolidate England's control of the northern tier of colonies, the Dominion of New England was created by James II. It included New York, New Jersey, New Hampshire, Massachusetts, Rhode Island, Plymouth, and Connecticut, and was supposed to (but did not) cover Pennsylvania as well. No elected assemblies were to be permitted. England was to exercise direct authority through a royally appointed governor. The tactlessness of that governor, Edmund Andros, added to the natural hostility of many colonists to the Dominion. When James II was overthrown in 1688, the Dominion disintegrated.

1696. A 15-man Board of Trade, more representative of the merchant class, replaced the Lords of Trade as the supervisory agency for the colonies. It could recommend but not make or enforce laws.

Act of 1696. This was a comprehensive law which incorporated previous regulations governing trade with the colonies, and added several new provisions. All colonial governors were to take an oath promising to uphold these acts. A system of vice-admiralty courts, eventually 12 in number, was established within the colonies to hear cases involving violations of the acts of trade and navigation. By a ruling of the attorney general in 1702, jury trials in these courts were not permitted.

Woolens Act of 1699. This was the first legislation to limit a colonial industry that competed with the mother country. It did not prohibit local manufacture of woolens, but forbade their export from the colonies. The effect of the law was much greater in Ireland than in America, and spurred Irish immigration to the colonies.

Naval Stores Act of 1705. While restricting the growth of the woolen industry, England tried by this act to encourage the development of naval stores in the colonies. A substantial bounty was paid for the production of pitch, tar, turpentine, resin, hemp, ship timber, and masts, and these items were enumerated—to be sent only to England.

Hat Act of 1732. This act was comparable to the Woolens Act, forbidding the export of hats from any colony, and restricting each colonial hat-maker to a maximum of two apprentices.

Molasses Act of 1733. Imposed a high tariff on the colonial importation of non-English (French West Indian) sugar, molasses, and rum. The act obviously was meant to benefit English planters in the Caribbean at the expense of mainland colonies.

Iron Act of 1750. Encouraged colonial production of pig or bar iron by removing import duties on raw iron, and discouraged the colonial manufacture of finished iron products by forbidding the construction of any new mills, forges, or furnaces.

EFFECTS OF THE SYSTEM

Quite obviously, these laws were designed to benefit England's merchants and manufacturers. It does not follow, however, that the colonists were—or felt—subjected to economic tyranny. To be sure, the Hat Act ruined a young and flourishing industry, but not an important one. And Virginia planters were sometimes hurt by mercantilistic regulations governing tobacco, though there were also other reasons for the periodic low prices of tobacco on the English market. The Woolens Act, on the other hand, was not particularly detrimental to colonial economic growth. Since English woolens were cheaper and superior in quality, and since skilled textile workers were scarce in the colonies, it is doubtful if woolen manufacturing would have developed on a commercial scale in the eighteenth century.

In short, the Acts of Trade and Navigation did not seriously hinder —and in many ways they helped to accelerate—the thriving colonial economy. The manufacture of naval stores and indigo, for example, was stimulated by England's payment of bounties to producers. Ship-building became a major industry in New England once the Dutch were excluded and colonial trade restricted to English vessels.

Other potentially harmful laws were widely evaded by the colonists. Finished iron production in Pennsylvania increased substantially after 1750, as mills were built in open violation of the Iron Act. The smuggling of French molasses became a commonplace activity of colonial merchants, in defiance of the Molasses Act. Customs officers were frequently bribed. The administration of the empire was confused, inefficient, and corrupt. Governors, though instructed to disallow any colonial legislation contrary to the laws of England, were often intimidated or bribed into ignoring violations. The legislatures usually had the strongest voice in the concerns of their respective colonies. Under these conditions the colonists were economically prosperous and politically content in their relations with England. This situation would change after 1763.

COLONIAL CONCERNS

English imperial laws were not the most serious problem with which colonial America had to contend. All first-generation settlers, whether at Jamestown in 1607 or in Georgia more than a century later, faced the challenge of wilderness survival. Once a foothold in the New World was secured, a second concern was the production of a marketable commodity to use as a medium of exchange. America was not Asia. One could not profit by trading bells and beads to the Indians for precious gems. Each colony had to rely on staples it could export, and thus finance its purchases of essential goods from England. A third concern, which was a constant preoccupation, was the menace of Indian attacks and the pressures of foreign competitors for control of the American continent. The frontier had not only to be conquered, but also defended, and the necessity of defense forced colonists to cooperate. As early as 1643 New Haven, Connecticut, Plymouth, and Massachusetts joined in the New England Confederation, a "League of friendship and amytie for offense and defense, mutual advice and succor upon all just occasions."

Above all, colonists wanted land, the opportunity to prosper, and an orderly society. So long as England did not disturb these pursuits, the colonists remained loyal and dedicated subjects. Whatever main problems they encountered came from within, not without. They left England carrying certain preconceptions of the way in which society would function, but their institutions failed to develop quite as they had envisioned. And it was precisely in this zone between Old World anticipations and New World realities that colonial problems emerged. Puritanism did not mix well with capitalism and urbanization. Social stratification came into conflict with social mobility. Indians refused to follow the script prepared in England for their education and conversion. The hope of an orderly society was disturbed by internal political quarrels which at times spilled over into armed rebellions. The structural forms of colonial life in the seventeenth century, some of which are reviewed in the next chapter, grew erratically, painfully, yet inexorably, and it is there one must seek and begin to trace the antecedents of American culture.

SUGGESTED READINGS

James T. Adams, *Provincial Society*

*Charles M. Andrews, *The Colonial Period of American History*

*Bernard Bailyn, *The New England Merchants in the Seventeenth Century*

Daniel J. Boorstin, *The Americans: The Colonial Experience*

*John B. Brebner, *The Explorers of North America, 1492–1806*

Carl Bridenbaugh, *Cities in the Wilderness*

*Verner W. Crane, *Southern Frontier*

Wesley F. Craven, *The Southern Colonies in the Seventeenth Century*

Oliver M. Dickerson, *The Navigation Acts and the American Revolution*

Lawrence H. Gipson, *The British Empire Before the American Revolution*

Lawrence A. Harper, *The English Navigation Laws*

David Hawke, *The Colonial Experience*

Leonard W. Labaree, *Royal Government in America: A Study of the British Colonial System Before 1783*

*Leonard W. Levy, *Freedom of Speech and Press in Early American History: Legacy of Suppression*

*Perry Miller, *The New England Mind*

*Edmund S. Morgan, *The Puritan Dilemma*

Samuel E. Morison, *Admiral of the Ocean Sea*

*Richard B. Morris, *Government and Labor in Early America*

*Howard H. Peckham, *The Colonial Wars*

*Frederick B. Tolles, *Meeting House and Counting House*

*Carl Ubbelohde, *The American Colonies and the British Empire*

Thomas J. Wertenbaker, *The First Americans*

*George F. Willison, *Saints and Strangers*

*Louis B. Wright, *The Cultural Life of the American Colonies*

* Available in paperback

LIFE IN AMERICA
The Seventeenth Century

2

MIDDLE-CLASS ORIGINS

With some exceptions, neither the very rich nor the completely destitute of England came to America in the seventeenth century. The rich might speculate in colonial ventures, but they had no desire to abandon their elegant estates or luxurious living standards. The destitute, locked in a cycle of poverty for generations, had no ambition to leave the slums for the wilderness. The poor of England "live meanly," a contemporary noted, "and send their families to the parish to be relieved rather than [to undertake] a long journey to mend their condition." To its eternal good fortune, America was settled largely by the middle classes—farmers, artisans, professional men, unskilled workers, and small tradesmen. Within that broad category there were acute divisions, carefully graded social distinctions that were meticulously observed and enforced. Whatever their individual or collective reasons for emigration, these Englishmen brought with them rigidly constructed traditions of position and propriety. A world of difference existed between emigrants with capital, who arrived with family and furniture, cattle, and domestic help, and those without capital, who came as indentured servants.

Of course, social distinctions in America could never be quite the same as in England. "A plain soldier that can use a pickaxe and spade," John Smith commented on life in early Virginia, "is better than five knights." Military figures were esteemed by the first settlers for their leadership qualities. Fancy dress, high birth, and exalted rank meant less in a new environment in which the art of survival depended upon other talents. But the American frontier was slow to dissolve the pecking order of colonial society. Myth has it that the wilderness touched all who came with the wand of equality, leveled social differences, and transformed class-conscious Europeans into rugged individualists. The facts dispute this myth.

FEAR OF THE WILDERNESS

English settlers feared the forests of America, entered them reluctantly, and only of necessity. William Bradford noted that the Pilgrims stepped from the *Mayflower* into a "hideous and desolate wilderness." Reverend Michael Wigglesworth, a popular New England poet, called the forest a "Devil's Den,"

> Where none inhabited
> But hellish fiends and brutish men
> That devils worshipped.

The forests were rich with game and a variety of trees for the construction of homes and ships, but in those woods were savage Indians and wild beasts and unknown terrors. Cotton Mather, the famous Puritan divine, once described the "Dragons," "devils," and "fiery flying serpents" that lurked in the primeval forest. The beauty of the wilderness was best described by city writers. Those who lived on its rim thought otherwise. Roger Williams compared the wilderness to the world, a place "where greedy and furious men persecute and devour the harmless and innocent." Mary Rowlandson, captured by Indians on the Massachusetts frontier in the 1670's, wrote that she was taken "mourning and lamenting, leaving farther my own Country, and travelling into the vast and howling wilderness."

The wilderness, then, was not an enticing and romantic adventure which beckoned, but a formidable barrier against which colonists turned their backs. They clustered along the eastern coastline, and by the close of the seventeenth century the southern frontier had advanced no farther than Savannah, a small village of Indian traders. The northern frontier consisted of a ring of 11 towns in Massachusetts—York, Wells, Amesbury, Kittery, Haverhill, Dunstable, Chelmsford, Groton, Lancaster, Marlboro, and Deerfield—supplemented by settlements in Connecticut. Behind this protective screen the process of colonial growth proceeded at a rapid pace.

The fledgling colonies were appendages of England, tied to the mother country for supplies, for cultural sustenance, as well as for defense against foreign enemies. Their dress and fashions were English. Their manners and speech patterns were English. Their social system, though lacking a leisure class, was transposed from England.

FOUR RULES OF COLONIAL SOCIETY

Until the slow caustic effects of the New World eroded their traditional beliefs, the colonists looked to England and to past experience for guidance and wisdom. In this respect they were fundamentally conservative.

First, they believed that within all social groups there must exist a natural inequality. "God almighty, in His most holy and wise providence, has so disposed of the condition of mankind, as in all times some must be rich, some poor," John Winthrop wrote, "some high and eminent in power and dignity, others mean and in subjection." Since Puritan society placed its highest values upon spiritual salvation, clergymen were recognized and respected as holding the highest status. They lacked temporal authority. Their duty was to pray and preach, advise and admonish, but not govern. Nevertheless, together with important lay leaders, they formed the aristocracy which was squarely based upon the church. Within southern society, after tobacco culture had developed as the important money crop, and the criteria of social prominence depended upon the possession of land and slaves, plantation owners emerged as the ruling aristocracy. In the Puritan North, the aristocracy was based *on* the church; in the Anglican South, the aristocracy *led* the church.

Second, they believed that communities should be organized, controlled, and disciplined; society was an organism that functioned for a definite purpose, and each of its parts was subordinate to the whole. To Puritans the purpose was divine, the glorification of God, and their community covenants were designed, not only to lock out deviates and dissenters, but also to achieve an ideal of social perfection. Non-Puritan communities as well were concerned with social order. The

Quakers, for example, were indeed unique—they were called the "peculiar people"—in their contempt for rank and custom, and in their stress upon social simplicity. But even William Penn, their aristocratic leader, while opening his colony to all settlers, insisted upon orderly patterns of land development and upon firm lines of political authority so as to create a social state that would preserve the doctrines of Quakerism. Plans for feudal systems in Maryland, and later in Carolina, were attempts to structure society along the class lines that prevailed in medieval Europe. These efforts were doomed to fail. Nevertheless, a strict hierarchy existed in Maryland, at least initially, with a Catholic aristocracy predominating over lower-class Protestants. For Puritan, Quaker, Catholic, or Anglican settlements, the ideal was a social system based on peace, unity, order, and stability.

Third, if colonists believed in social gradations, they also held that differences in rank were not unalterable. Thus, the ebb and flow of power shifted from colony to colony, and varied in time with economic changes. There were significant differences in the kinds of aristocracies which existed. But it was expected that the elite would govern, and that they would follow a strict code of social conduct. In Virginia, in the first part of the seventeenth century, quite a number of settlers climbed the success ladder to attain the rank of gentry. The life style of the Virginia aristocracy was a conscious attempt to reproduce that of English country gentlemen, which meant owning a certain amount of land and a manor house, being an overseer of the poor, a dispenser of local justice, a church elder, and perhaps a member of the legislative assembly. Gentlemen were ordained to rule, they believed, but were not expected to wallow in luxury. The weight of public care rested squarely upon them. "In the greatest fortune," Richard Braithwaite noted in his book, *English Gentlemen*, published in 1630,

> there is the least liberty. . . . Such whose very persons should be examples or patterns of vigilancy, providence and industry must not sleep out their time under the fruitless shadow of security. Men in great place . . . are thrice servants—servants of the sovereign or state; servants of fame; and servants of business. So as they have no freedom, neither in their persons, nor in their actions, nor in their times.

In England the power of the landed aristocracy was somewhat checked by urban capitalists. In Virginia there were no cities of any substantial size, and no such checks existed. The power of the gentry was maintained and even augmented—and often abused—well into

LONDON'S VIRGINIA.

While the sun shone and blacks labored, gentlemen planters in Virginia could sit and smoke at leisure. The woodcut is from the label of a tobacco container, c. 1700. (Courtesy of The Granger Collection)

the eighteenth century. The result was a provincial, slave-owning, class-conscious leadership, but one that in time became public-spirited and dignified, with a keen sense of honor and responsibility. George Washington was its finest flower.

Fourth, while colonists undoubtedly enjoyed greater economic mobility than in England, yet they accepted the cultural restrictions that pertained to each class—and were punished if they did not. In fact, a correlation existed between one's rank and punishments meted out for infractions of the law. Rarely would a gentleman be whipped, though that sentence was usual for others. Josias Plastowe of Boston, for example, who was found guilty of "stealing four baskets of corn from the Indians," was ordered to "return them eight baskets, be fined 5 pounds, and hereafter to be called by the name of Josias and not Mr." His servants, however, who had participated in the theft, were severely flogged. Philip Ratliffe was fined, whipped, had his ears cut off, and banished from Boston for the crime of "uttering malicious and scandalous speeches against the government." Yet Roger Williams, the famous divine, was simply commanded to leave the colony for his "new and dangerous opinions against the authority of the magistrates." The sentence of death for capital crimes was carried out according to sex and rank in Maryland—women might be burned at the stake; lower-class men were to be hung, drawn, and quartered; and aristocrats were to be accorded a dignified beheading.

Class distinctions were maintained in matters of dress, in church, at the meeting house, in education, and, in fact, in most social institutions and relations. Graduates of Harvard and Yale were listed, not alphabetically, but by their "dignities." Church seating was by rank. The Massachusetts village of Woburn assigned its pews according to "estate, office, and age." Swansea divided its inhabitants into three classes, and Saco into seven classes, for purposes of seating. Only the gentry could wear silk or lace, gold or silver girdles, slashed sleeves, or embroidered capes. The authorities in Connecticut were so distressed at the practice of lower-class inhabitants wearing upper-class fashions that they enacted legislation to tax these upstarts as if their property amounted to 150 pounds. The first Virginia assembly provided for penalties against "excess in apparel." Even the Quakers, who made a fetish of plainness in "dress and address," displayed their concern by warning their Philadelphia brethren to cease wearing "long lapped sleeves, or coats gathered at the sides, or superfluous buttons, or broad ribbons about their hats, or long curled periwigs."

Seventeenth-century colonists aped English habits and copied English standards, which included a rigid application of class division. In 1674 a Virginia court fined a tailor for "having made a race for his mare to run with a horse belonging to Mr. Mathew Slader for two thousand pounds of tobacco, it being contrary to law for a laborer to make a race, it being a sport for Gentlemen." Nevertheless, despite these conscious attempts to duplicate the social forms of England, in time the forms degenerated. Authority was vested in personalities in the colonies, rather than in institutions. Wealth was a sure guide to power, but power was difficult for first-generation settlers to pass on to younger sons in a land without traditions. Colonists tried to fashion a pattern of social rules to fit the English mold, but life in America was too open and too flexible for the rules to be maintained. For that reason neither a native nobility nor a permanent aristocracy ever existed in the New World.

THE NEW ENGLAND WAY

Compared to the Virginia gentry, with their love of horse racing and fox hunting, balls, and renowned social hospitality, Puritan pleasures were somewhat restricted. Part of the reason was geographical: life was indeed hard and tedious, especially for women, during the long winters, when their monotonous round of drudgery could not be relieved by such simple communal activities as husking bees and house-raisings. And part of the reason was religious: the Calvinist code forbid wasteful idleness. But it is a mistake to portray the

Puritans, as so many popular illustrators have done, in somber grays and blacks, this apparel somehow characterizing a dour and repressed people. As a matter of fact Puritan clothes were brightly colored, and, with the passage of time and the increased secularization of the young—contrasted to the austere and primitive piety of their fathers —they began to enjoy a variety of recreational activities. "For a Christian to use recreation," Increase Mather noted in 1688, "is very lawful, and in some cases a great duty."

Gambling of any kind was always prohibited as "heinously sinful." The theatre, too, was devil's work. When a play was to be produced in Boston, Samuel Sewall objected. "Let not Christian Boston go beyond heathen Rome," he warned, "in the practise of shameful vanities." But the Puritans never were ascetics, and they came to permit many amusements and pastimes, including horse racing, fishing, fencing, chess, music, quoits, and even a limited amount of dancing, so long as these pleasures were not abused or performed on the Sabbath or a feast day. They preferred beer and ale to water, and drank hard cider, Madeira wines, rum, and other liquors, though in moderate amounts. In 1633 for the public offense of being intoxicated, Robert Coles was "fined 10 pounds and enjoined to stand with a white sheet of paper on his back, wherein a drunkard shall be written in great letters." Six months later, for a repetition of that crime, the court ordered that Coles "shall be disenfranchised, wear about his neck and so to hang upon his outward garment, a D, made of red cloth and set upon white; to continue this for a year, and not to leave it off when he comes amongst company." Neither the exhortations against intemperance, nor the penalties and social stigma which attached to that particular sin seemed to deter its commission. The number of alehouses and grogshops increased substantially. By the close of the century there were enough town drunks in Boston and Newport to draw complaints from sober citizens.

The frequency of their sexual transgressions, both premarital and extramarital, though not unduly great, indicates that the Puritan saints were as delinquent as other humans. The General Court of Massachusetts in 1631 ordered "that if any man shall have carnal copulation with another man's wife, they both shall be punished by death." In practice, however, the penalty for either adultery or fornication rarely was more severe than whipping. John Lee was so punished in 1634 for "abusing a maid of the Governor's, pretending love in the way of marriage, when himself professes he intended none; also for enticing her to go with him into the cornfield." Public repentance quickly restored a sinner to church membership; repetition, however, resulted in excommunication. The certainty of eternal suffering in the hereafter was no match for sexual impulse on earth, not even in Massachusetts. In 1668 the general court felt impelled to remark upon the large number of bastards in the colony.

THE PURITAN SABBATH

The Puritans worked hardest at being their brother's keepers in trying to preserve the Sabbath as a day of worship. Throughout the colonies the sacredness of the Sabbath was not to be defiled under penalty of the law, but none could compare in rigor with New England. Decade by decade the laws were added to—the Blue Laws—each circumscribing specific practices. No unnecessary travel. No play or recreation. No business transactions. No work. No gardening. No women could kiss their children. No eating mince pies. No smoking (in Plymouth) within two miles of the meetinghouse. No evidence to be taken at church trials. No frivolity. In some areas, no cooking, no bed making, no housecleaning. No idling outside church during services. No sleeping inside church during services. The Puritan Sabbath lasted from Saturday sundown until Monday morning, and the laws were imposed upon strangers as well as natives. One of the first blacks to visit Massachusetts, who happened to be Jewish, referred to in the court records as Solomon, "ye malata Jue," was prosecuted for travel on the Sabbath. Puritan reverence for the Lord's Day made it difficult at times to determine what conduct might or might not be considered desecration. On one occasion the citizens of Yarmouth seriously debated the problem of whether to dig out a man trapped in a well on the Sabbath, or whether to leave him there until Monday.

SCIENCE AND DEVILS IN NEW ENGLAND

Puritan theology left little room for toleration, and their colonies were not safe harbors for proselytizing Quakers, or disputatious dissenters, or for atheists, hedonists, or recidivists for that matter. But this does not mean that Puritans tried to crush intellectual and scientific inquiry. In Leipzig, Padua, Rome, Madrid, and other continental centers, new astronomical discoveries were being attacked by church censors. The lives and livelihoods of those who dared to study the stars were endangered, for their theories seemed to contradict scriptural interpretation, based upon the old Ptolemaic idea that the earth was the center of the universe. In the villages and towns of New England, however, there was a high proportion of educated men—many of them church-

Cafes of Confcience
Concerning evil
SPIRITS
Perfonating Men,
Witchcrafts, infallible Proofs of
Guilt in fuch as are accufed
with that Crime.

All Confidered according to the Scriptures,
Hiftory, Experience, and the Judgment
of many Learned men.

By Increafe Mather, Prefident of Harvard
Colledge at Cambridge, and Teacher of
a Church at BOSTON in New-England.

Prov. 22. 21. ---- *That thou mighteft Anfwer the
words of Truth, to them that fend unto thee.*

*Efficiunt Dæmones, ut quæ non funt, fic tamen, quafi
fint, confpicienda hominibus exhibeant. Lactantius Lib.
2. Inftit. Cap. 15. Diabolus Confulitur, cum ijs medijs
atimur aliquid Cognofcendi, quæ a Diabolo funt introducta.
Ames. Caf. Confc. L. 4. Cap. 23.*

BOSTON Printed, and Sold by *Benjamin
Harris* at the London Coffee-Houfe. 1693.

CRESCENTIUS MATHERUS.
Ætatis Suæ 49. 1688.

The Mathers, Increase and Cotton, were partly responsible for precipitating
the witchcraft hysteria in New England. As early as 1684 Increase Mather
had published his Essay for the Recording of Illustrious Providences, a
collection of what he believed were well-authenticated cases of witchery;
his son Cotton, five years later, published the Memorable Providences
which stated that anyone who disbelieved in witches was taking a step
towards atheism. After the death of some twenty alleged witches Increase
Mather was moved to remark: "It is better that ten suspected witches
should escape than one innocent person should be condemned." His belated advice helped save 150 of the accused who were in jail and awaiting
trial. Yet he insisted in Tales of Conscience Concerning Evil Spirits, published in 1693, that the execution of witches was correct, citing "Scriptures,
History, Experience, and the Judgment of many Learned Men." (Courtesy
of the Rare Books Department, Boston Public Library)

men—who readily accepted the stellar hypothesis of a solar universe. The findings of Copernicus, as refined by Kepler, Galileo, and others, confirmed rather than challenged their religious beliefs. The astronomers of Europe, wrote Samuel Cheever of Boston in his *Almanac for the Year of Our Lord 1661*, have "demonstrated the Copernican Hypothesis to be the most consentaneous to truth and ocular observations." John Winthrop, Jr., a founding member of the Royal Society of London for the Promotion of Natural Knowledge, was indefatigable in collecting and recording data and specimens which were dispatched from his home on the Connecticut frontier to excite the attention of English savants. Winthrop in 1672 donated a small telescope to Harvard College, which was later used so effectively by a young graduate, Thomas Brattle, that the precise astronomical information he sent to England was cited by Sir Isaac Newton in the monumental *Principia Mathematica*. To the Puritans the study of nature provided a tool to further explore the wonder of God's universe, a technique to expand man's understanding of God's laws. Science, a leading Puritan noted, "is no *enemy*, but a mighty and wondrous *incentive* to *religion*."

Nevertheless, for all their scientific enthusiasm, many of the most erudite seventeenth-century Puritans believed in omens, devils, pranks, occult signs, and psychic mysteries. Intellectually they were at midpoint between the superstitious terrors of the late medieval age and the scientific emphasis of the age of reason. Increase Mather, for example, who became president of Harvard, wrote a learned treatise in 1682, *Kometographia*, which explained the distinction between comets and planets. But Mather also held that comets were evil omens which affected human conduct, and he warned that their frequent appearance meant an impending calamity. Samuel Sewall also maintained a deep amateur interest in science: he took careful notes on extraordinary tides, comets, and eclipses, collected rare herbs, and once dissected the body of an Indian who had been executed. Both Mather and Sewall were members of a scientific club, the Philosophical Society of Boston, which met fortnightly to confer upon "Natural History." Yet Sewall was fully convinced that witches were loose in Salem during the famous hysteria of 1692, and he employed all his shrewdness to trap and exorcise the devil from Massachusetts.

Cotton Mather, the son of Increase, never doubted that the crazy fits, gibberish, and obscene displays of affected individuals were caused by black magic and diabolism. He had investigated a prior case of witchcraft as rigorously as he had studied the heavens, and he published what amounted to a laboratory report, *Memorable Providences*

Relating to Witchcraft and Possession. Reverend Samuel Willard, on the other hand, who was minister of the Old South Church in Boston and a member of the scientific club, distrusted the evidence of spectral phenomena that were exhibited at the Salem court cases. So did Thomas Brattle, who wrote an open letter censuring the entire proceedings. Twenty people were executed before the witch trials ran their course. Ultimately the mass fear and frenzy abated, and shame-faced participants—including Samuel Sewall—felt rather guilty about the excessive punishments and the possibility that some victims might have been innocent. Belief in witches hardly vanished, but in general sanity triumphed, and the Salem tragedy had a salutary impact upon New England, helping tip the balance away from the dead weight of inherited superstitions to the "enlightenment" philosophy of the coming century.

EDUCATION IN NEW ENGLAND

The Puritan accomplishment in education was remarkable by any standard, unprecedented in the colonial history of any nation. Other settlers were concerned; others established schools; others put a premium upon education lest their children grow up untutored and illiterate, and without institutional restraints, lapse into barbarism. The Dutch in New Netherland asked the States General in Holland for schools "so that the youth in so wild a country where there are so many dissolute people may first of all be well instructed and indoctrinated, not only in reading and writing, but also in the knowledge and fear of the Lord." Catholics in Maryland, equally avid to instil a heritage of religious and cultural values, opened schools on the Chesapeake frontier. Virginians were aided by collections of money subscribed in every English diocese for building schools. A number of planters donated or bequeathed land, cows, and books for the same purpose. William Penn's first Frame of Government specified the erection of public schools so that "all children . . . shall be taught some useful trade or skill, to the end that none may be idle, but the poor may work to live, and the rich, if they become poor, may not want."

If the Puritans possessed no monopoly in their concern for education, certainly their zeal in the cause, fed by their sense of urgency, was unparalleled. A large number of university graduates were among the first Puritan emigrants. Their cultural standards were high. Book dealers in Boston did a thriving and prosperous business importing and selling their wares throughout New England. To be sure, most of the works were theological, "devout and useful books," since Puritans believed that faith was a matter of intellectual comprehension as well as spiritual attainment. But their knowledge was hardly limited to biblical exegesis. Church and community survival depended upon leaders trained in Greek and Latin—a knowledge of Hebrew was also much esteemed—and in science, classical literature, and liberal arts. Without educated men, they believed their vision of creating a divine enterprise in the American wilderness would surely fail.

At first the Puritans relied upon traditional means to finance schools: contributions of money or land, tuition, private subscriptions, and with some limited help from the government. The results were disappointing. Harvard College, started in 1636, remained open, though on a somewhat shaky footing. So did the Boston Latin School, which began a year earlier. But many elementary and grammar schools in the colony met infrequently or failed altogether. A law in 1642, which fixed responsibility for education upon parents and masters, ordering them to teach children and servants to read, proved ineffec-

The founding of Harvard College is dated from 1636 when the General Court of Massachusetts appropriated four hundred pounds "towards a school or college." Within six years the first degrees were granted, though Harvard had no authority to do so. "The legal foundations of Harvard, the origins of its authority to grant degrees, and the question of whether, and in what legal sense, if at all, it is properly a "college" or a "university," writes one historian, "all these have remained uncertain and unresolved into the 20th century." From the beginning the president and trustees of Harvard capitalized upon this uncertainty. A later artist, H. R. Shurtleff, drew the above sketch of the initial buildings. (Courtesy of the Fogg Museum, Harvard University)

tive. Pioneer families, burdened with so many tasks, found it difficult, if not impossible, to comply with the law. Finally, in 1647, the General Court of Massachusetts enacted a bold measure to prevent "that old deluder, Satan," from keeping men "from the knowledge of the Scriptures." Every town of 50 or more families was to appoint someone "to teach all such children as shall resort to him to write and read"; every town of 100 or more families had to establish a Latin school where students "may be fitted for the university." Here was the beginning of public education in America. These schools were created by the state, not by the church. If their purpose was primarily religious in nature, it was not exclusively so, and clergymen did not dominate education in New England. The state, moreover, established standards for all schools, leaving matters of finance and management to the local community. Towns which would not comply with the law, either because of meager resources, or because their funds were exhausted in Indian wars, found the government of Massachusetts sympathetic yet firm—and fines were meted out equitably. As population increased, so did the number of schools. Massachusetts' example was soon copied, with some variations, by every other New England colony with the exception of Rhode Island.

RURAL NATURE OF AMERICAN LIFE

American colonial life was overwhelmingly rural, and any changes which occurred were gradual rather than sudden, dependent upon population growth and movement, capital accumulation, economic trial and error, and the slow shedding of inherited ideas. The similarities of day-to-day existence between colonies were as striking as the contrasts. In all regions the typical settler was a small farmer, and most farms were of necessity largely self-sustaining. The Massachusetts farmer might grow rye, the Pennsylvania farmer wheat, and the Virginia farmer tobacco, but all were likely to have an orchard, livestock, and a vegetable garden. All farmers supplemented their larder with fish and wild game. All adopted Indian dishes such as succotash, hominy, and roast corn. Corn, in fact, became the most basic of American foods from Maine to the Carolinas, prepared in a variety of ways, fed to cattle, converted to liquor, or even used as a medium of exchange. North or south, farm women aged quickly, exhausted from chores, and from bearing and raising large families. As in Europe, so in America, high death rates counteracted high birth rates, the results of medical ignorance, primitive sanitation, and frequent epidemics. But in Europe there were homeless unemployed roaming the countryside, or crowding the cities, sometimes existing on the verge of starvation, while in America the scarcity of labor provided substantially greater opportunities for work; in Europe the threat of famine periodically menaced entire regions, while in America such famines were virtually unknown; in Europe religious and dynastic wars killed considerably more than Indian wars did in the colonies.

NORTHERN COMMERCE

Inexorably, geography and climate shaped economic development in each section of America, and economic development shaped cultural patterns and political philosophies. The northern colonies, for example, raised mainly grain crops, and harvested the ocean for fish from Cape Cod to Newfoundland. Since they produced far too much for home consumption, and there was little demand in England or northern Europe, enterprising merchants sought markets in the West Indies and in southern Europe. From the forests of America a supply of apparently inexhaustible timber was available to build ships. Colonial vessels began to range over the entire Atlantic, selling grain, dried fish, and livestock to West Indian planters, taking on cargoes of sugar and molasses, which they transported to England, and returning home with manufactured goods sought by the colonists. This "triangular trade" took many forms. In the next century skippers of Yankee vessels carried molasses back from the West Indies, where it was converted to rum in New England distilleries; rum was then used to purchase slaves off the African coast, who were sold in American markets—at which point the trading process would begin again.

GROWTH OF NORTHERN TOWNS

Economically, then, it was somewhat inevitable that the northern colonies would spawn trading centers, seaport communities which might compete with those of England and Holland. By the end of the century there were four such towns—Boston, Newport, New York, and Philadelphia—each with its own characteristics.

Boston. Despite Puritan doubts about the moral problems that seemed to accompany economic progress, Boston grew to become the largest town in North America. Religious ideals and capitalist goals frequently proved mutually abrasive in the Puritan capital. "New England was originally a plantation of religion," Reverend John Higginson complained in 1663, "not a plantation of trade. Let merchants, and such as are increasing cent per cent remember this." His complaint proved fruitless. Boston became renowned for its shipbuilding and commercial zest, as well as for its strict Sabbaths. But try as they might to maintain an undefiled and rigorous Puritanism, secular standards began to intrude. The merchant was even then replacing the clergyman as the locus of power and prestige.

Newport. Newport had few conflicts between its material and spiritual pursuits. Founded by wealthy dissenters from Massachusetts, the town in its early years was an economic satellite of Boston. However, the fact that they were wealthy, and engaged in mercantile ventures, started Newport on the road to become a great slave-trading and commercial hub in its own right. And the fact that they tolerated religious dissent attracted groups of Quakers, Sephardic Jews, Catholics, and Seventh Day Baptists. Newport was a bustling, sophisticated center, far removed from the typical provincialism of the New England village.

New York. Surely the liveliest and most diversified center was New York. Even under Dutch rule, New York was notorious for the number of its taverns, its drunks, and its problems with law enforcement.

In 1650, fourteen years before New Amsterdam fell to the British, a water color of the harbor was painted by Laurens Block. Officially it was not a municipality, but a trading post of the Dutch West India Company. All vessels to New Netherland were obliged to stop there, unload their cargoes, and pay the requisite duties. The citizens complained that their subordination to the company throttled trade. But none could doubt the potential for economic growth; after the British took possession New Yorkers vied with Bostonians for commercial supremacy. (Courtesy of the New-York Historical Society)

A visitor reported in 1643 that one could hear 18 different languages spoken there. Official decrees had to be published in three languages (French, English, and Dutch). After the British took possession the number of crimes rose, mob violence often threatened, and ill-feeling among the heterogeneous population was a major concern.

Philadelphia. The Quaker capital, on the other hand, bore some resemblance to both Boston and New York. Its polyglot mixture of citizens resembled New York, and its tone of Quaker piety created a staid atmosphere somewhat akin to Boston. An early account, written by Gabriel Thomas, concluded that "the industrious (nay, indefatigable) inhabitants have built a noble and beautiful city, and called it Philadelphia. . . . In a very short space of time she will, in all probability, make a fine figure in the world, and be a most celebrated Emporium." So it happened. Settled in 1681, 50 years after the founding of Boston, Philadelphia in the next century surpassed all competitors to rank as America's foremost urban center. But none of the four towns ever dominated America, as Paris did France, or London did England.

Different as they were from one another, these seaboard communities had much in common. They were dependent upon foreign and coastal commerce for economic survival. They served as trading nuclei for the agricultural hinterland. They were funnels for European immigrants, gateways for European culture. Moreover, all shared the same urban problems—providing adequate water supplies, dealing with crime, fire, and health hazards, and caring for the destitute. Most important, the commercial society which developed in each of these towns shared a set of mutual interests—interests which were distinct from those who worked the land. Resentment between the two periodically flared into open hostility over many issues, particularly when the question of taxation was involved. "The merchants are for land taxes," Edward Randolph wrote in 1686, "but . . . others who have got very large tracts of land are for laying all upon the trading party." This antagonism between town and country would continue through the course of American history.

LACK OF SOUTHERN TOWNS

South of Philadelphia, for a distance of 750 miles, there were sleepy hamlets, but no towns of any size until one reached Charleston. Virginia and Maryland were without commercial centers throughout the colonial period, a fact which disturbed those who equated the maintenance of effective social order with urbanization. English officials favored towns since settlers were easier controlled and regulated when congregated rather than dispersed. Moreover, many Virginians sorely missed the social life and cultural opportunities which towns afforded. But those who wanted an urban Virginia discovered that towns could not be created artificially. They could not be formed by legislative fiat. In 1680, for example, the governor of Virginia, Thomas Lord Culpeper, convinced the assembly to pass a law requiring each county (there were 20) to build warehouses and a town on a navigable waterway, through which all trade would be required to pass. The law, called the Cohabitation Act, was impractical, never enforced, and quickly suspended by the king. Other royal governors tried to produce cities in the wilderness—to no avail. As late as 1705 the assembly attempted unsuccessfully to bribe towns into existence by exempting urban dwellers from paying three fourths of their taxes.

The explanation for the failure of commercial towns to develop is to be sought in the particular river systems and tobacco economy of the upper South. Four major rivers, the Potomac, the Rappahannock, the York, and the James, and a network of tributary streams, which flowed from them into the lowlands, were avenues of trade

A visitor to the tobacco plantations of Virginia and Maryland in the midseventeenth century—sailing up the James or York, or one of the many tidal streams of Chesapeake Bay— would find cultivated lands interspersed with primeval forests. Every few miles there would be a wharf, as pictured here, from which planters could ship their tobacco directly to Britain. This meant that vessels had to call at every wharf rather than at one central location. It was convenient for planters but, wrote the Reverend John Clayton in 1688, "an impediment to the advance of the country." (Copyright © 1937 by Charles Scribner's Sons)

which served the early tidewater plantations. To be sure, the plantation economy was not yet a dominant southern institution in the seventeenth century, but tobacco culture was. In 1628 some 500,000 pounds of colonial tobacco were shipped to England; by 1670 the figure was over 9,000,000 pounds; by 1700, it had risen to more than 35,000,000 pounds. In effect, each tobacco planter was his own merchant; each private dock was his own port of entry. Up these waterways came ships carrying slaves, supplies, household furnishings, or other goods ordered from English factories, which were unloaded directly at the plantation wharf, and then reloaded with hogsheads of tobacco to be carried to England. "Most houses are built near some landing-place," the Reverend Hugh Jones noted, "[and] anything may be delivered to a Gentleman there from London . . . with less trouble and cost than to one living five miles in the country in England." Little wonder that in Virginia, as well as in Maryland, commercial towns were not only superfluous, but also a positive danger to the interests of tobacco growers.

In fact, the antiurban sentiment of these planters grew until, by the following century, it became an integral part of their political faith. To them, rural life was best, and towns were regarded as centers of immorality, of slums, of devastating fires, or annual visits of the plague; and of a propertyless class, a people without a stake in orderly government, easily led and deceived by demagogues, who existed as leeches upon the landed part of society. "When we get piled upon one another in large cities, as in Europe," Jefferson once predicted, "we shall become corrupt as in Europe, and go to eating one another as they do there." Such militant hatred of town growth was shared by many, part of a larger current of conservative western thought; but for Southerners the hatred received added impetus, developing as a philosophical rationalization to protect the economic and political power of the landed aristocracy.

ANGLICANISM IN VIRGINIA

These two facts—that there were no sizeable communities, but rather a rural scattered population in Virginia, and that tobacco was so crucial a crop as to merit Virginia's description as "a colony founded on smoke"—serve to explain some of its distinctive cultural characteristics.

Most Virginians were Anglican, and proud of it. They were not religious refugees, such as Pilgrims, Puritans, Quakers, or Roman Catholics, nor did they have any theological quarrels with the estab-

lished Church of England. Instead of a zealous spirit of dissent, theirs
was a quiet piety, practical, moderate, and pervasive. But, as in so
many other cases, New World conditions transformed Old World
institutions. The parishes were too large, the roads too poor, the country too crude, and the problems too different for the Church of England to survive its transatlantic voyage unchanged. If a parish was too
small in size, there were not enough families to support the pastor; if
it was too extensive, as most of them were, then the religious needs of
the flock often were neglected. "Sometimes after I have travelled fifty
miles to preach," one minister reported, "the weather happening to
prove bad, on the day of our meeting very few or none have met; or
else being hindered by rivers and swamps rendered impassable with
much rain, I have returned with doing of nothing to their benefit or
mine own satisfaction." The environment forced compromises in religious practice, if not in religious faith. Virginians took to burying
their dead in private cemeteries, a violation of Anglican rites, which
stipulated burial in consecrated ground. In the vast spaces of Virginia,
however, it was both inconvenient and expensive to carry the dead
long distances to church grounds. Similarly, it became a common practice for marriage ceremonies to be solemnized in private homes rather
than in churches. Sticklers for proper ritual were shocked at occasional
deviations—the absence of a proper font for baptizing, or the lack of
a surplice for the minister conducting services.

In England, the Anglican church was, by ancient tradition, hier-
archically structured, with ultimate control vested in powerful
bishops; the Virginia church had no bishops throughout the colonial
period. In England matters of dogma were shaped, decided, and enforced by the bishops, synods, and other councils of the clerical elite;
in Virginia there was no central ecclesiastical authority, and the
leading laymen of each parish more or less decided upon religious
matters as local circumstances dictated. In England ministers were
appointed by the bishop, and not generally accountable to the parish-
ioners; in Virginia the tenure of clergymen was on a year-to-year
basis, at the pleasure of the vestrymen. Though proportionately few
ministers were actually dismissed, many resigned because of inadequate compensation. Their salary was fixed by law in 1695 at 16,000
pounds of tobacco. Thus the money value each received depended
upon the quality of the tobacco grown in that parish, and the market
price it fetched. There were always clerical vacancies, more in parishes
that grew the cheaper and cruder "oranoco" than in those that specialized in milder and preferred "sweet scented." Clergymen who
wished to retain a "sweet scented" parish would not challenge the

vestry. Thus it was, and rather ironically, that the Anglican church in Virginia took on congregational forms—which is precisely what the Puritans had been contending for in England.

EDUCATION IN VIRGINIA

Colonies such as Virginia and Maryland experienced the utmost difficulty in establishing schools. "I thank God we have not free schools nor printing," said Sir William Berkeley, governor of Virginia for over three decades, "and I hope we shall not have these hundred years. For learning has brought disobedience and heresy and sects into the world; and printing has divulged them and libels against the government. God keep us from both." Berkeley's attitude did not help matters, but the main obstacle was geographical. Unlike New England, which had the advantage of a compact town life, the southern colonies could not surmount the problem of a widely dispersed population. A few free schools existed in Virginia, the result of bequests from planters such as Benjamin Symnes, Thomas Eaton, and Richard Russel. Some operated in Maryland, such as King William's school in Annapolis, the result of legislative enactment. Nevertheless, they could not duplicate the New England system. In 1723, for example, a Maryland law ordered the founding of at least one school in every county. It was ignored.

"Good education of children is almost impossible," complained William Fitzhugh, a wealthy Virginia planter, "and better be never born than ill-bred. But that which bears the greatest weight with me . . . is the want of spiritual helps and comforts." The perennial shortage of Anglican ministers and the lack of proper educational facilities so disturbed the House of Burgesses that they dispatched James Blair to England to solicit a charter for a college. Issued in 1693, the charter for William and Mary College stipulated its intent to be "a seminary for ministers of the Gospel where youths may be piously educated in good letters and manners; a certain place of universal study, or perpetual college of divinity, philosophy, languages, and other good arts and sciences."

Primary and secondary education in the tobacco colonies, of necessity, was a private matter, left almost entirely in the hands of parents—and, as such, it became virtually a prerogative of the aristocracy. At the bottom of the social scale, poor farmers could do little or nothing in the way of teaching their children. In fact, nearly half of the white male inhabitants of Virginia in the seventeenth century were illiterate. At the top of the social scale, rich planters hired teachers, or shared the cost with a few neighbors. It was cheaper, however, and the practice was common, for planters to procure an indentured servant, versed in grammar and Latin, to serve as a household tutor. Only the affluent could afford private libraries. Only they could afford to send their scions to England or the Continent for legal training or business experience or university work—a procedure generally continued long after the College of William and Mary was founded.

EDUCATING THE INDIANS

For Englishmen, as for most Europeans, the seventeenth century was a *saeculum theologicum*. Christians might disagree with one another about the true path to salvation, yet all felt bound by biblical injunction to convert the heathen. But how to teach the word of God, when Indians in the New World were divided into thousands of tribes, each with a different language or dialect? Like the Spanish and French, English clerics attempted various methods of proselytizing, but they were unique in trying to educate Indians by giving them a college education. The aboriginals could thus be Christianized, civilized, and unified into colonial life. Their motive was charitable, the attempt genuine, and the results pathetic, yet from the first founding of Virginia to the American Revolution missionaries persisted in the delusion that Indians were willing and able to grasp Christian truth through university learning. One scholar has noted the tragedy of these Indian students, "toiling against every healthy instinct of their race to achieve that proficiency in the Seven Arts and Learned Tongues without which, so their white masters insisted, they could never qualify as purveyors of regenerating grace."

In fact, the first and most carefully planned effort in colonial education was directed not at the settlers, but at the Indians. According to the charter of the Virginia company, 10,000 acres were set apart as an endowment to build a university at Henrico "for the training up of the Children of those Infidels in true Religion, moral virtue and Civility, and for other godly uses." The bishops of England joined in the holy work by soliciting contributions, a project which stirred considerable attention in England. Gifts poured in: a communion set, a copy of St. Augustine's *City of God*, an anonymous bequest of £500 in gold, in all by 1620 more than £2000. Nothing came of it. There never was a University of Henrico, and in a few years Indian attacks upon Virginia settlements cooled the ardor of its promoters.

Benjamin Church, whose Indian follower killed King Philip, described the Indian leader as "a doleful great naked dirty beast . . . and for as much as he had caused many English to lie unburied and rot above ground, not one of his bones shall be buried." King Philip (or Metacomet, his Indian name) became surly when settlers' cattle drifted through his corn fields, when white bootleggers sold alcohol to his tribe, when he had to give up land for nonpayment of debts incurred in buying English clothes, and when on three separate occasions he was brought into colonial courts and fined. But when the Indian murderers of Sassamon were tried by a jury of whites, found guilty, and hung, his sense of outrage at this indignity could no longer be contained. So devastating was the war which ensued that twenty years passed before the destroyed villages could be rebuilt. (Courtesy of the Rare Books Department, Boston Public Library)

A second effort to educate Indians was instigated by President Henry Dunster of Harvard, who in 1651 requested that some missionary money be earmarked for an Indian College at Cambridge: Soon thereafter a building was erected, tutors were hired, and the initial students were in residence. One of the first to be enrolled, for training in divinity, John Sassamon, hoped to preach at John Eliot's famous settlement of Christian Indians at Natick. There were roughly 2,000 to 4,000 converted or "praying" Indians, living in or near Puritan communities. But even non-Christian Indians were forced to obey Puritan laws, and were harshly fined for violations. Indian resentment steadily mounted and ultimately culminated in a devastating war in 1675. Sassamon, serving as interpreter to Metacomet, or King

Philip as he was known to the Puritans, betrayed the plans of his chief to the English and was assassinated for this treachery. King Philip, in turn, was shot by a "praying" Indian. Before the war ended nearly a score of frontier villages were either annihilated or partially destroyed; a tenth of the adult white males were killed; Indian tribes took heavy casualties, and their leaders were executed or shipped off to the West Indies as slaves. The coming of peace did not remove the sting of memory or reduce the level of Anglo-Indian hatred. Naturally, the Indian school at Harvard languished. In all, perhaps a total of six Indians attended, and most of these before the war. But one, Caleb Cheeshahteaumauk, graduated—only to die of tuberculosis the following winter. Administrators realized the project was hopeless, and that their ends would be better served by preparing white missionaries. Gradually the Indian College building fell into disrepair, and in 1698 it was finally pulled down.

Nevertheless, the experiment continued elsewhere, and Indian students could be found at many new eighteenth-century colleges. Conrad Weiser, a renowned frontiersman and Indian trader, sent two Mohawks to the Philadelphia College (University of Pennsylvania) to be taught to read and write English. Within a year one died of smallpox. At William and Mary there was a resident Indian master and his students living at Brotherton House, named for the person who endowed it "with £200 a year for educating Indians in Christianity." A German visitor to the college reported that the Indian students "grasp . . . every opportunity of escaping from restraint and oversight, and joyfully return again to their inborn way of life—wild, rude, and careless." In time the College of William and Mary abandoned its Indian training as fruitless. Even Reverend Eleazar Wheelock, the most dedicated and persevering spokesman for Indian education, lost heart. Wheelock directed Moor's Indian Charity School in Connecticut for many years, and his experience led him to a gloomy appraisal: "The most melancholy part of the account I have to relate, and which has occasioned me the greatest weight of sorrow, has been the bad conduct and behavior of such as have been educated here after they have left the school." Wheelock accepted New Hampshire's offer to head a new school in that province, and in 1769 a royal charter was issued to establish "Dartmouth College for the education and instruction of Youth of the Indian Tribes in this Land for reading, writing and all parts of Learning which shall appear necessary and expedient for civilizing and christianizing Children of Pagans." Few Indians actually attended—Wheelock preferred to train white missionaries instead—and, whatever contributions Dartmouth has made, it rarely did so as a school that was chartered to spread "Christian Knowledge among the Savages."

DEFEATING THE INDIANS

English settlers never doubted that logic, right, equity, and morality were on their side in the conquest of America. They reasoned somewhat as follows:

1. The Indians were barbarians, wasteful wanderers, incapable of properly utilizing the natural resources of land and sea.
2. If England did not control North America, surely the French and Spanish would—and one consequence would be the conversion of the natives to Catholicism.
3. The continent was vast, thinly populated, with enough room for all, red man and white man.

If only the Indians could be convinced of the benefits of a better life which would accrue to them by cooperating with the English in a true community of interest—economic prosperity, spiritual salvation, and all the blessings of civilization—then the great work of expansion could proceed in peace and harmony. But, if Indians could not be convinced, then force would be justified. Early in the seventeenth century Richard Hakluyt advised the Virginia company that gentle measures with the heathen were preferable, but to rely on soldiers "to square and prepare them to our Preachers hands." Along with the cross, settlers brought the gun.

There were always some Englishmen troubled by the methods used to dispossess the Indians. Reverend John Gray in 1609 asked in a sermon "by what right or warrant we can enter into the land of these savages, take away their rightful inheritance from them, and plant ourselves in their places." There were always some who recognized and respected the dignity and individuality of the Indians and treated them honorably. Nevertheless, the vast majority of settlers—and their descendants to the twentieth century—regarded Indians as sly, lazy, dirty, and treacherous. But who, white or Indian, was more treacherous remains highly debatable. Examples of murders and massacres, of deceptions and cruelties, and of false promises and broken treaties abound on both sides. The Indians felt justified, for, once English intentions of conquest were evident, it was vital to fight relentlessly and mercilessly in defense of their homeland, to drive the invaders into the sea. The English felt justified, for like all racial conquerors they believed they possessed a divine injunction, and all means were permissible to replace a squalid lot of nomadic primitive savages with a civilized and Christian society.

War, disease, and starvation decimated Indian ranks. Far worse, however, was the cultural dependence that resulted from mixing with whites. Indians were convinced that their way of life was infinitely superior. They scorned weakness, tolerated eccentricity, abhorred routine, exalted nature, considered the concept of private property to be preposterous, and took pride in their freedom from any restraints imposed by others. They viewed the white man as bound by chains of discipline, leading a monotonous existence, and endlessly laboring for material acquisitions. Nevertheless, for all their abhorrence of white man's standards, they eagerly sought articles introduced by the enemy, such as cotton shirts, steel needles, metal pots, plus knives, guns, and alcohol. "The wonder is that the Indians resisted decadence as well as they did," Bernard De Voto has remarked, "preserved as much as they did, and fought the whites off so obstinately and so long."

INTERNAL CONFLICTS

If the colonies had to be alert to Indian attacks, especially along the western perimeter of settlements, there were other fermenting dangers at the very center of colonial society. Law and order was threatened by a series of internal political conflicts which occasionally broadened into outright rebellions. As early as 1634 a quarrel broke out when the governor's council in Virginia objected to the arbitrary power exercised by John Harvey, the royal governor. Harvey struck one council member with a cudgel, knocking out his teeth, and arrested another on "suspicion of treason to His Majesty." The council in April 1635 declared Harvey "thrust out of his government," and promptly shipped him back to England.

Disturbances of this sort were so common, one scholar notes, that one might say "a veritable anarchy seems to have prevailed" in seventeenth-century society. Two uprisings were particularly noteworthy. In 1676 the rebellion of Nathaniel Bacon wracked Virginia, and in 1689 Jacob Leisler captured and ruled New York for 20 months. These were not conflicts of poor against rich, or democrats against monarchists. Rather, they were uprisings caused by complex sectional and economic grievances, directed against the ruling classes—"the establishment"—of colonial society.

STRANGE NEWS

FROM

VIRGINIA;

Being a full and true

ACCOUNT

OF THE

LIFE and DEATH

OF

Nathanael Bacon Efquire,

Who was the only Caufe and Original of all the late
Troubles in that COUNTRY.

With a full Relation of all the Accidents which have
happened in the late War there between the
Chriftians and Indians.

LONDON,
Printed for *William Harris*, next door to the Turn-
Stile without *Moor-gate.* 1677.

Nathaniel Bacon, according to a Virginia contemporary, was "young, bold, active, of an inviting aspect, and powerful elocution." Trained in the Inns of Court in London, he came to America intent on wealth and power. A gift from his family enabled Bacon to purchase a respectable farm, and he soon sat on the governor's council. His uncle, the royal governor Sir William Berkeley, told him: "Gentlemen of your quality come very rarely into this country, and therefore when they do come are used by me with all respect." Before long the two quarreled and the rebellion which ensued spilled over into short-lived outbreaks of violence in Maryland and among settlers in the Albemarle Sound area. An account placing all blame upon Bacon was published in London in 1677. (Courtesy of The Granger Collection)

Bacon's Rebellion. In Virginia the popularity of the royal governor, Sir William Berkeley, declined as the price of tobacco fell in the 1660's. Berkeley was not to blame for the economic problems of tobacco growers—in fact, he had protested against the Navigation Acts —but there were other discontents for which he bore responsibility. No election to the House of Burgesses had been called for 14 years; a poll tax was being levied without the consent of freeholders; the governor's clique held the key administrative posts of the colony, and profited accordingly; rumor had it that Berkeley was planning to award a monopoly on fur trading to himself and his friends; most important, Berkeley's Indian policy was defensive rather than offensive. He agreed to build forts, but rebellious Virginians called them expensive "mousetraps," and complained that Berkeley "does not take a speedy course [to] destroy the Indians." The followers of Nathaniel

Bacon "swore to be true to him," but they could not foresee the extremes to which Bacon would carry the revolution. A new House of Burgesses passed "Bacon's Laws," in effect providing for a vigorous campaign against the Indians, requiring that sheriffs be rotated in office, and forbidding individuals to hold multiple offices. But, after being pardoned and released by Berkeley, Bacon turned his followers to violence. Berkeley was forced to flee, his mansion was captured, the rebels took an oath to resist even the royal navy, and Jamestown was burned to the ground.

What Bacon would have done next is unknown. He died of a fever contracted while fighting at Dragon Swamp against the Pamunkey Indians, and with his death the movement collapsed. Berkeley returned and summarily ordered the hanging of 23 rebels. "That old fool," Charles II remarked, "has hanged more men in that naked country than I did for the murder of my father." Berkeley was recalled, and Charles pardoned the rebels. But it was many decades before Virginia recovered from the devastating effects of civil war.

Leisler's Rebellion. Like Bacon, Jacob Leisler had reason to resent the colonial ruling classes. A German immigrant, Leisler had married into a prominent Dutch family and had amassed a fortune by trading in furs, wine, and tobacco. The power structure of New York, however, tried to exclude him from the fur trade by restricting the trading privilege to Albany merchants. Another similar law limited the bolting of grain to millers in New York City, placing Leisler's mill, located in Suffolk County, at a competitive disadvantage. When James II was overthrown in 1688, and the Dominion of New England fell, the ruling classes in New York declared their loyalty to James. Leisler sided with the vast majority of citizens, who wished to endorse Parliament's choice, the monarchy of William and Mary. A chance remark made by Lieutenant Governor Francis Nicholson while drunk, threatening to burn the city, touched off the revolution. Leisler, as captain of the local militia, seized the town fort, forced Nicholson to flee, and organized a provisional government.

That government functioned effectively, despite the opposition of aristocrats in New York City and Albany, and the threat of the French and their Indian allies. A legislative assembly was convened, taxes were collected, law and order was maintained, and the frontier was protected. Ironically and tragically, after this period of dedicated service, Leisler was arrested and ordered to be tried for treason by Governor Henry Sloughter, an appointee of William and Mary. The court was composed of Leisler's enemies, who had convinced the new governor that Leisler was a traitor and usurper. Leisler and his son-in-law were hanged, cut down while alive, their bowels ripped out and burned, and their bodies quartered. A decade later the injustice was recognized, and Leisler's heirs were granted an indemnity.

Rebellions such as Bacon's and Leisler's continued well into the eighteenth century, and are symptomatic of the social ferment that existed in America. Frontiersmen agitated for more liberal land laws, for a greater share of representation in the legislature, and for military aid against the Indians. Townsmen resented the special economic privileges awarded to favorites. As late as 1763 the "Paxton boys"—or "white savages," as Benjamin Franklin called them—marched on Philadelphia because the Quaker-dominated legislature had not voted enough funds to defend the frontier. Shortly before the American Revolution "Regulator" bands in North Carolina rose against the corrupt aristocratic government at New Bern. These cultural cleavages and colonial jealousies were difficult to surmount. But internal dissensions could not erode the unity created by a common heritage, or the incentive to cooperate created by common enemies. After the Dutch were expelled from New Netherland the major contenders for dominance were France and Spain, against whom England seemed to be constantly at war. Each time—in King William's War, Queen Anne's War, the War of Jenkin's Ear, King George's War, and the French and Indian or Seven Years' War—the colonists, as Englishmen, were involved. Whether they fought willingly or reluctantly is a subject scholars still debate. Nevertheless, these wars made it obvious that some form of intercolonial cooperation, some form of continental union, would be an indispensable part of America's future success.

SUGGESTED READINGS

*Bernard Bailyn, *Education in the Forming of American Society*
T. H. Breen, *The Character of the Good Ruler*
Philip A. Bruce, *The Virginia Plutarch*
Thomas J. Condon, *New York Beginnings*
Lawrence A. Cremin, *American Education: The Colonial Experience*
John I. Falconer and Percy Bidwell, *History of Agriculture in the Northern United States*

*Paul Goodman, *Essays in American Colonial History*

L. C. Gray, *History of Agriculture in the Southern United States*

*Kenneth Lockridge, *A New England Town: The First Hundred Years*

*Perry Miller, *The American Puritans*

*Edmund S. Morgan, *The Puritan Family*

Samuel E. Morison, *Harvard College in the Seventeenth Century*

*————, *The Intellectual Life of Colonial New England*

*Gary B. Nash, *Class and Society in Early America*

*Sumner C. Powell, *Puritan Village*

*Darrett B. Rutman, *Winthrop's Boston*

M. Eugene Sirmans, *Colonial South Carolina*

*James M. Smith, *Seventeenth-Century America*

Raymond P. Stearns, *Science in the British Colonies of America*

*Wilcomb E. Washburn, *The Governor and the Rebel: A History of Bacon's Rebellion*

Thomas J. Wertenbaker, *The Old South*

————, *Patrician and Plebeian in Virginia*

*Louis B. Wright, *First Gentlemen of Virginia*

Thomas G. Wright, *Literary Culture in Early New England*

* Available in paperback

EMPIRE AND REVOLUTION
1763/1789

3 COMPETITION FOR EMPIRE

It would hardly be appropriate to speak of the Seven Years' War as an imperialistic conflict between capitalist nations. These are nineteenth-century terms, not applicable to the motives of monarchs and nobles whose ideas were still rooted in the Middle Ages. The war was fought with muskets and arrows, in canoes and wooden sailing ships. Yet, in a very real sense it was a world war, fought in the Caribbean, in the Indian Ocean, on the North American frontier, and on the Asian and European continents. It was a war for empire, for political and economic supremacy.

The French were thoroughly and ignominiously defeated. They were not swept out of the Western Hemisphere completely, however. By the peace treaty signed in Paris in 1763, England allowed France to retain possession of her Caribbean islands, invaluable for their production of sugar. But on the North American continent, except for the islands of St. Pierre and Miquelon, France lost everything. England acquired Canada and all French lands east of the Mississippi; Spain, France's belated ally in the war, received New Orleans and all French lands west of the Mississippi as a consolation for giving up the Floridas to England.

FRENCH REACTION

The French never regarded the peace treaty of 1763 as conclusive. For more than a century, as part of a continuous struggle with Britain, they had sent a succession of explorers, settlers, Jesuit missionaries, and troops to seize and exploit America for the greater glory of France. France had invested too much treasure and blood to relinquish the dream of a Franco-American empire. The peace settlement of 1763 simply provided a breathing spell, a time to lick wounds and to culti-vate the acidulous emotions of hatred and vengeance.

COLONIAL REACTION

The British colonials rejoiced in the expulsion of French influence from the continent. Canada was Catholic, and the 13 colonies were largely Protestant. No one felt more self-righteous and infallible than a New England Calvinist attacking a French Catholic. A common Puritan term of opprobrium was "Jesuit!" With the French removed, the colo-nists hoped that Protestantism would spread over North America, Indian attacks would diminish, and Canadian land would be open to English settlement. The profits of the lucrative fur trade would fill the coffers of the victors. Even more fundamental, as a few foresaw, North America would derive its bases for law, education, government, and literature from the British rather than the French. In the place of Bour-bon militarism and despotism there would extend over America "the boon of rational and ordered liberty."

BRITISH REACTION

Although England was after 1763 the greatest imperial power in the world, British public opinion was critical of the peace settlement. Many believed that the West Indian islands were more valuable than the "frozen acres" of Canada, and that Britain had selected the wrong prize. Caribbean islands were easier to defend, cheaper to maintain, and quicker to yield a profit. The new empire, on the other hand, with its thousands of square miles of wilderness, imposed a heavy burden of responsibility and new problems which would test the abilities of British statesmen. What policies should be evolved concerning the western lands and the Indians? How should Canada, with its French population, be administered? What defensive measures would be necessary to protect the empire? How much would the costs of empire amount to, and who would pay them? These new expenses had to be added to an already astronomical national debt, the accumulated costs of four major wars which England had fought in 70 years. British taxpayers wanted relief from their intolerable burdens, not additions to them.

REVOLUTIONARY CONSEQUENCES

The same wars which saddled the British with an oppressive debt helped prepare the colonies for independence.

First, the experience of warfare convinced the colonials that their local militia was not inferior to regular troops. The colonials despised standing armies, regarded professional soldiers as sycophants and parasites, and thus placed their faith in the sturdy yeomanry of America. The wars had blooded the colonists, provided them with a knowledge of tactics and strategy, and left them filled with a feeling of pride and confidence in their own fighting capacities.

Second, the wars forced the colonists to join together to plan a common defense. In 1754, at an intercolonial meeting in Albany, Benjamin Franklin proposed a confederation to be governed by a president-general appointed by the king of England and a grand council elected by the legislatures of the colonies. The plan was never ratified. Seven colonies thought it gave England too much power over them: significant evidence that the colonists were used to a large measure of self-government, and that British authority, if stringently applied, would be resisted. Despite the defeat of Franklin's plan, the meeting showed that the wars had proved to the colonists that they shared mutual problems and that cooperation was indispensable.

Third, the peace which resulted from the wars led directly to the American Revolution. While France had remained a threat the colonists had to depend upon British military aid. Moreover, before the war the 13 colonies were comparatively unimportant to the British government and were therefore neglected. Now, additions to the empire were accompanied by imperial problems—raising money, governing Canada, distributing land, regulating commerce, guarding the frontiers, treating with Indians, dispensing justice—which bedeviled the British. They therefore enacted laws which spurred the colonists first to dissent, and ultimately to revolution.

The colonists were gradually becoming conscious of their separate identity as Americans. England was still the mother country, and the king's health was formally toasted at dinner parties and state occasions. But third- and fourth-generation colonists had little in common with Englishmen. During and following the Seven Years' War the Americans were discovering themselves, realizing the uniqueness of their continental interests, and reexamining their position within the British empire.

SUGAR AND STAMPS

After 1763 relations between the 13 colonies and England followed an uneven path of decay, improvement, further disintegration, slight recovery, and a final collapse. The British believed their colonial prescriptions were equitable. They believed that since the colonists benefited from the victory over France, it was only just and reasonable that America contribute to the costs of empire. George Grenville, the chancellor of the exchequer, was responsible for two acts designed to elicit this contribution. At his urging Parliament passed the Sugar Act (1764) and Stamp Act (1765). The Sugar Act actually lowered the tariff on imported sugar and molasses (used in the making of rum) but tightened the enforcement provisions to discourage the widespread smuggling by New England merchants. Violators of the Sugar Act were to be tried in Admiralty rather than in local courts, without the benefit of a jury. The Stamp Act required colonists to purchase specially stamped paper for virtually anything printed, be they newspapers, diplomas, land deeds, customs receipts, or playing cards. While the Sugar Act directly affected only shippers and importers, the Stamp Act touched all classes. Together, the Grenville duties aroused an uproar of protest in the colonies.

FEDERAL EMPIRE

The colonists responded with words and acts, the former to persuade and the latter to coerce Britain into withdrawing her legislation. British goods were boycotted and American manufacturing encouraged. The Sons of Liberty in Boston, urged on by the merchants, burned Admiralty court records and sacked the home of Lieutenant Governor Thomas Hutchinson. "Some of the principal ringleaders in the late riots," Hutchinson complained, "walk the streets with impunity; no officers dare attack them, no attorney general prosecute them, and no judge sit upon them." Boston was not the only scene of revolutionary activity. All across America colonial legislatures passed resolutions of

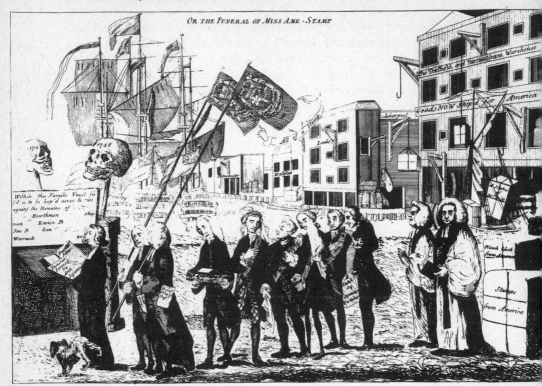

In a British cartoon satirizing the repeal of the Stamp Act, Grenville, who counseled against the repeal, is pictured cradling the dead act. Other mourners at the sparsely attended funeral are pamphleteers, lawyers, ministers, royal favorites, and bishops. Absent are British merchants who are too busy preparing for newly revived trade with America. (Courtesy of the New-York Historical Society)

protest, and royal officials and their supporters were intimidated by vigilante organizations. Nowhere could the Stamp Act be enforced.

Illegal actions of this nature require justification, and the colonists were quick to offer a theoretical defense. They maintained that they were not revolutionaries but good citizens upholding the traditional rights of Englishmen. By natural rights, by charter rights, by historic practice, and by the fundamental law of England, taxation without representation was a tyranny which they were bound to resist. Patrick Henry affirmed this belief in resolutions passed by the House of Burgesses in Virginia. The Stamp Act Congress, representing nine colonies, met in New York and affirmed it once again.

In effect, what the colonials were postulating was a federal empire in which authority was divisible. Parliament could legislate for the colonies but it could not tax them. The distinction seemed theoretically clear. Its application, even if the British accepted the definition, would be difficult.

DECLARATORY ACT

The colonists' theory was championed by several British spokesmen in Parliament, including the popular William Pitt. "The Americans have been wronged! They have been driven to madness by injustice! Will you punish them for the madness you have occasioned?" he asked. "No! Let this country be the first to resume its prudence and temper." The colonial boycott injured British merchants, who pressed petitions on Parliament calling for the repeal of the Grenville duties. Grenville fell from power. The tariff on molasses was substantially reduced, and the Stamp Act repealed by a vote of 275 to 167 in the House of Commons. The colonists had gained every point except one. For along with the repeal of the Stamp Act was passed the Declaratory Act (1766), which stated that Parliament had absolute authority to legislate for the colonies "in all cases whatsoever."

Parliament had lost a skirmish with the colonists but had refused to concede the battle. Only one of the conflicting views of the empire could ultimately prevail. Either the British government had to agree to a division of power, or the colonists had to accept the sovereignty of Parliament.

TOWNSHEND ACTS

Joy was exuberant but short-lived in the colonies. A new chancellor of the exchequer, Charles Townshend, acting in part on the basis of false information provided by Benjamin Franklin, offered another way for the colonists to pay a share of imperial expenses. Franklin, appearing before Parliament in the previous year, had unintentionally misrepresented the colonial position, testifying that their opposition was to internal taxes only. Townshend's scheme, which Parliament adopted in 1767, was to enact tariffs on colonial imports of certain British products—tea, paints, lead, paper, and glass—and to reorganize the collection of customs to minimize corruption. How could there be any objections? Did not Parliament have the right to regulate commerce within the empire? The House of Commons, convinced that

Townshend's plan would effectively increase revenues, also passed a law reducing the tax obligations of British landowners.

COLONIAL DISCONTENTS

The West. Although the turmoil in America in the late 1760's was due mainly to the Townshend duties, there were other objections to British rule. As early as 1763 England had offended potential settlers as well as land speculators by a proclamation temporarily forbidding settlement west of the Appalachian Mountains. The restriction had been precipitated by the uprising of the Indian chief Pontiac, and by Britain's need to consider her policy on the interrelated problems of the fur trade, Indians, land, and defense in the West. A later ministry, however, construed the proclamation as a permanent barrier. It proved unenforceable, and was openly violated by settlers. Then, in 1774, Parliament further exacerbated the western issue by passing the Quebec Act. The old Northwest, by this legislation, was annexed to the province of Quebec. French Catholics who lived there were to enjoy religious freedom. Anglo-Americans who lived there would be unrepresented, since autocratic Quebec had no legislative assembly. Worst of all, the Quebec Act automatically canceled the western land claims which several colonies derived from their original charters.

Currency. British merchants complained that some colonists were paying their debts in depreciated paper rather than in sterling. To correct this abuse, Parliament passed a Currency Act in 1764 which prohibited the colonies from issuing bills of credit as legal tender; moreover, bills of credit already issued were to be retired from circulation. The Currency Act was not a departure from previous practice but it was resented nonetheless. Franklin declared the currency problem to be a major cause of discontent. The scarcity of specie, added to the normal postwar economic contractions, hurt colonial debtors, who now had to pay their taxes and other obligations to the British in hard currency.

Troops. Contrary to colonial expectations, British troops were not removed at the close of the Seven Years' War. Their presence served as a constant irritant to Americans. Two Quartering Acts (1765–66) required the colonial governments to furnish housing and other necessities for the soldiers. Georgia at first refused to comply. But, when the British troops were withdrawn and the colony was exposed to

Indian attacks, the Georgia assembly voted the necessary funds. New York, site of the headquarters of the British army, was more adamant. The New York legislature, reflecting its changes in composition, refused all but the scantiest appropriations in 1766, approved expenditures for military housing in 1767, reversed itself in 1768, and yielded again at the close of 1769. So heated were the relations between British redcoats and the New York Sons of Liberty that several serious clashes and even riots occurred. When royal troops were moved to Massachusetts, the New Englanders inherited New York's problems. There, in 1770, a more famous incident occurred. A file of redcoats, their pride stung because of a beating British soldiers had received in a street fight several days before, and taunted by the jeers of a crowd, fired without warning. Five citizens died as a result of the Boston Massacre, and the event stirred Americans. Many colonists who had not yet become convinced of British perfidy changed their minds when the disagreements were expressed not in ink but in blood.

TOWNSHEND DUTIES REPEALED

By 1770 the British were ready to concede that force had not worked. On the contrary, it had served only to provoke the colonists to further denials of parliamentary authority and further exhibitions of defiance. John Dickinson's pamphlet, *Letters from a Farmer in Pennsylvania*, which was widely read, reiterated the American position: the colonies were unrepresented in Parliament and therefore Parliament could not pass legislation for the purpose of obtaining revenue, even in the guise of the Townshend duties. Other voices, using the same argument, questioned the right of Parliament to keep a standing army in the colonies and to deny jury trials. However, the British government was persuaded to retreat not by the logic of these arguments, but by a realistic appraisal of economic facts. Colonial boycotts of British goods were so effective that imports had declined some 40 per cent. The Townshend duties had failed to reap the desired harvest (as many had predicted). On the very day of the Boston Massacre, Lord North requested a repeal of almost all the Townshend duties, which Parliament later passed. Tea was the only product specifically excepted. Moreover, the Quartering Act was permitted to lapse. The colonists had gained another substantial victory. But once again the British insisted on the principle that Parliament's acts could not be limited and were the supreme law of the empire.

SAMUEL ADAMS

Political consistency was not a virtue of the colonists. With the partial repeal of the Townshend duties, relations with the mother country improved. As long as parliamentary legislation did not pinch American pockets too much, there were few murmurs of protest. The tariff on sugar and molasses continued to be collected. After 1770, the tariff on tea was paid. Both were clearly for the purpose of revenue. But, since American merchants were prospering, what reason was there to sustain the fight for abstract principles? These merchants wished to maintain the new status quo, and leadership of the anti-British movement devolved on more radical men.

Samuel Adams, one of the earliest revolutionaries to think in terms of total independence, stoked the fires of American discontent. His cousin John successfully defended the British soldiers tried for the Boston Massacre by winning them only a token punishment for man-

When the British revenue ship the Gaspee *ran aground near Providence, Rhode Island, on the night of June 9, 1772, eight boatloads of Providence patriots took possession of the boat and burned her. A special royal commission sent to investigate the affair was unable to collect evidence from the colonists to convict the culprits.* (Courtesy of New York Public Library)

BURNING OF THE GASPÉ

slaughter. But Samuel used the episode as a valuable propaganda weapon, pouring out a stream of inflammatory material. When England agreed to pay the salaries of royal governors and judges to free them from their economic dependence on the colonial legislatures, Adams aroused his fellow Americans to the danger. Perhaps his most valuable contribution to the cause of independence was the organization of the Committees of Correspondence. These committees, formed in towns throughout and even outside Massachusetts, could work quickly and in unity by interchanging letters to establish a common policy against Britain. And they could, by spreading propaganda, influence public opinion to subscribe to their radical viewpoint. Still, Adams could not have accomplished so much had it not been for two factors. First, many people were receptive to his propaganda. Second, the British—after a period of relative quiescence—committed another major blunder.

TEA ACT

The Tea Act (1773) was regarded by a large majority in Parliament as the mildest and most equitable law that could be enacted. By its provisions the British East India Company was permitted to sell and market tea directly to the American consumer and was given a monopoly of the American tea business. The anticipated results were to be mutually beneficial. Colonial tea drinkers could purchase the product at a lower price since it did not have to pass through England. In fact, they could purchase it cheaper than smuggled tea. Furthermore, the East India Company, a huge corporation by eighteenth-century standards, was to be rescued from near bankruptcy by the profits from tea sales on the American market. The purposes of the Tea Act were indeed meritorious. For that reason its consequences were not foreseen by the responsible British ministers.

BOSTON TEA PARTY

The Tea Act contained a greater threat to the profits of American merchants than any mere tax. By giving the East India Company import and marketing privileges, colonial competitors feared they would be driven out of business. If the monopoly took effect, predicted the merchants, the East India Company would raise the price of tea. If Parliament could grant a virtual monopoly in one product, they argued, they could do it with others. The scare was convincing enough to Americans, who took up the cries of "Monopoly" and "Tyranny" in every major port. Nowhere did they permit the tea to be sold. In most cases cargoes were simply returned to England. In Charleston the tea was unloaded and left to rot in a damp warehouse. In Boston some 50 men "dressed like Mohawks, of very grotesque appearance," boarded the company's ships and tossed 342 tea chests overboard. Although bands in America still played *God Save the King*, George III and the British ministers regarded the Boston Tea Party as something less than a patriotic act.

COERCIVE ACTS

Events now moved rapidly, almost inexorably, toward revolution. The number of the colonists' supporters in the House of Commons was reduced to a handful, and even they could not excuse actions so flagrantly treasonous. These few were not enough to block the punitive measures against Massachusetts which were rushed through Parliament in 1774. One bill closed the port of Boston and removed the capital of the colony to Salem. Another prohibited town meetings convened without the governor's approval, and gave the king sole power to appoint the Governor's Council. A third provided that persons charged with murder committed in support of the crown could be tried either in Nova Scotia or in England. The fourth, a quartering act, required housing for the troops which were to arrive in Boston with the new governor, General Thomas Gage.

The military occupation and coercion of Boston served to unite Americans of every class and section. Other cities offered their wharf facilities to Boston merchants. Collections were taken and sent to indigent Bostonians. Illegal town meetings were convoked. Radical resolutions were adopted. Nonimportation and nonconsumption of British products were resumed. Committees of correspondence actively seconded a call for a colonial congress "to deliberate and determine on wise and proper measures . . . for the restoration of union and harmony between Great Britain and America, which is most ardently desired by all good men."

FIRST CONTINENTAL CONGRESS

The "good men" assembled at the first Continental Congress in Philadelphia in September 1774 represented a wide variety of political persuasions. Some proposed to raise an army at once, attack the British forces under General Gage, and expel them from Boston. This position was much too extreme. The conservative end of the spectrum recommended conciliation with Britain. Joseph Galloway suggested a new version of Franklin's old plan of union: a president-general appointed by the king, and a colonial grand council to share power with Parliament, each to have a veto power over legislation. Galloway's plan narrowly failed, six colonies opposing to five in favor. (Had it been adopted there is little reason to assume Britain's approval.) Thereafter the more radical members, led by John and Samuel Adams, Patrick Henry, Richard Henry Lee, and Christopher Gadsden, controlled the congress.

The radicals had previously pushed through an endorsement of the Suffolk County, Massachusetts, resolutions, which categorically declared that "no obedience was due to either or any part of the recent acts of Parliament." The "Declaration of Rights" which Congress adopted went even further. It enumerated a long list of infringements and violations of colonial rights, including the Sugar Act, Stamp Act, Quartering Act, Tea Act, Quebec Act, and all the Coercive Acts. These rights, stated the declaration, were guaranteed "by the immutable laws of nature, the principles of the English Constitution, and the several charters or compacts." Now, in 1774, after a decade of attempting to construct an operative definition of their place in the British empire and being driven by parliamentary legislation to ever more radical positions, the leaders of the Continental Congress entirely repudiated Parliament's authority over them. However, to indicate their willingness to compromise in the "mutual interest of both countries," they promised to accept bona fide parliamentary regulation of external commerce.

PREPARATION FOR WAR

Even if Lord North had wanted to adopt a pacific policy, neither King George nor a majority of the cabinet had any intention of appeasing rebels—for Massachusetts was declared to be in a state of rebellion—and hostile action soon followed. At the beginning it took the form of economic sanctions. By the New England Restraining Act (1775), which prohibited New Englanders from trading with any country except Britain and the West Indies, and which also barred them from the Newfoundland fisheries, Parliament tried to coerce the colonists into obedience. Later these provisions were extended to five other colonies. The Americans reciprocated in kind. They created the intercolonial Continental (or American) Association, by which trade with Britain was gradually closed. Some loopholes existed, but the association's system of inspection proved remarkably effective. For example,

New York's imports of British goods fell from a value of £437,000 in 1774 to £1228 in 1775.

Meanwhile, the ill-feeling began to assume a distinctly military character. When General Gage called for 20,000 more troops, British ministers were shocked. They assured one another that the colonists could not stand against seasoned veterans, that only one or two battles would bring America to terms. The colonists began to mount cannon, cache arms, enlist officers, and train volunteers. Many read and took heart from Charles Lee's pamphlet, which concluded that the Americans could defeat the British and any mercenaries brought from Europe. Given the temper of both sides, one match could ignite the entire continent.

LEXINGTON AND CONCORD

That match was struck in the early morning of April 19, 1775, on the village green at Lexington. Coming up the road from Boston to arrest rebel leaders and to search out hidden arms, an advance guard of British soldiers was met by some 70 minutemen and militia. The colonists had been alerted at midnight by Paul Revere. Samuel Adams and John Hancock had fled certain capture and the minutemen stood ready to block the British. Who fired the first shot is uncertain—scholars disagree—yet the initial battle of the American Revolution was an unfortunate beginning for the patriots. Eight Americans were killed and 10 wounded, while only one redcoat suffered a slight injury. But the day was far from over. On the British went to Concord where the colonists, warned by Dr. Samuel Prescott, had had time to remove most of the military supplies. There an inconclusive skirmish occurred at North Bridge which forced the British to fall back into the village. That afternoon the 16-mile march back to Boston proved disastrous for the British. All along the route hundreds of colonial sharpshooters harried the royal troops, firing from behind trees and stone walls and barns with devastating effect. Gage wisely dispatched 1,200 men as a relief force to protect the retreating troops. Before the regulars found safety at Charlestown, there were 273 British and 95 American casualties. Who, asked Thomas Paine, could now talk of reconciliation with murderers?

THOMAS PAINE

More than a year was to elapse between the Battle of Lexington and adoption of the Declaration of Independence. During this period a series of military and political events made independence inevitable.

The rebels fought at Bunker Hill. George Washington was appointed commander in chief of the American forces. Fort Ticonderoga on Lake Champlain was taken by New Englanders led by Benedict Arnold. An invasion of Canada was launched but failed to achieve any of its key objectives. Some colonies expelled their royal governors; others permitted them to flee. All colonies began to undergo a constitutional metamorphosis into sovereign states. Still, many rebels did not consider themselves traitors. Although they felt that Parliament had no authority over them, they recognized fidelity to the king. In other words, by 1774–75 the Americans had arrived at a definition of the empire which other dominions would not achieve for more than a century: that each be completely sovereign, yet linked to the mother country by the mutual recognition of a common monarch.

The person most responsible for breaking that final link was

Amos Doolittle, a Connecticut militiaman, made this engraving of the Battle of Lexington, in which the British are depicted as "the party who first fired." Regardless of blame, news of the bloodletting swept the country. "This is a glorious day for America," Samuel Adams exclaimed, and the colonials began to gird for battle. Everywhere colonials were to be seen training for military duty, casting mortars, making firelocks, and manufacturing saltpeter. The shots at Lexington marked the beginning of the first anti-colonial war in history. (Courtesy of the Print Department, Boston Public Library)

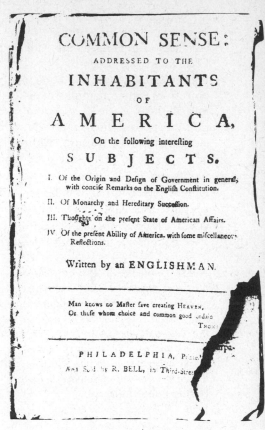

COMMON SENSE:

ADDRESSED TO THE

INHABITANTS

OF

AMERICA,

On the following interesting

SUBJECTS.

I. Of the Origin and Design of Government in general,
with concise Remarks on the English Constitution.

II. Of Monarchy and Hereditary Succession.

III. Thoughts on the present State of American Affairs.

IV. Of the present Ability of America. with some miscellaneous
Reflections.

Written by an ENGLISHMAN.

Man knows no Master save creating HEAVEN,
Or those whom choice and common good ordain
THOM

PHILADELPHIA, Pr

And Sold by R. BELL, in Third-Stre

Thomas Paine's pamphlet, Common
Sense, *denounced British legislation,
monarchical rule, and George III,
and called for separation from the
mother country. Written in language
the layman could understand, his
pamphlet helped transform the
struggle for redress of grievances
into a real war of revolution. (Courtesy of Thomas Paine National Museum)*

Thomas Paine. A recent immigrant, he had been in the colonies less
than two years when he wrote and anonymously published the pamphlet *Common Sense* (January 1776). Its reception was phenomenal.
In three months over 120,000 copies were distributed, and several
times that figure were eventually sold. Some contemporaries claimed
that the British prosecution of the war, not Paine's pamphlet, was the
determining factor in the break with England. John Adams later, and
typically, asserted that Paine offered no new arguments. True enough.
But if words and ideas can influence public opinion, Paine's pamphlet
was crucial.

"Can ye give to prostitution its former innocence?" asked Paine.
"Neither can ye reconcile Britain and America." He maintained that
the colonies gained nothing by being part of the empire, except involvement in Europe's wars. American food, wrote Paine, "will always
have a market while eating is the custom of Europe." He condemned
those who argued for friendship with Britain: "Whatever may be your

rank or title in life, you have the heart of a coward." Like most great revolutionaries, he was acutely conscious of history: "Now is the seedtime of continental union, faith and honor. The least fracture now will be like a name engraved with the point of a pin on the tender rind of a young oak; the wound would enlarge with the tree, and posterity read it in full grown characters." He excoriated George III, declared it against all reason for an island to govern a continent, and penned an eternal apostrophe to American freedom:

> O! Ye that love mankind! Ye that dare oppose not only the tyranny but the tyrant, stand forth! Every Freedom hath been hunted round the globe. Asia and Africa have long expelled her. Europe regards her like a stranger, and England hath given her warning to depart. O! Receive the fugitive, and prepare in time an asylum for mankind.

INDEPENDENCE

The second Continental Congress, like the first, had its conservative and radical wings. The final attempt of the conservatives to reunite the colonies to England, the "Olive Branch Petition," was written by John Dickinson. George III rejected it. Thereafter Congress was spurred to declaring independence by the influence of Paine's pamphlet, by the recommendations of George Washington and other officers, and by the authorizations of several states. Richard Henry Lee introduced a resolution calling for independence on June 7, and Congress approved it on July 2. However, a committee of five had been appointed to draft a more formal declaration, which Congress voted on July 4, 1776.

The Declaration of Independence was a combination of philosophical statement, political tract, and legal brief. Written by Thomas Jefferson, it reflected the belief in natural law held by most educated Anglo-Americans. Derived mainly from John Locke, this philosophy can be summarized as follows: First, all men are equally entitled to certain inherent and immutable rights, among the most important of which are "life, liberty, and the pursuit of happiness." Second, government is purposely created by men, contracting together, to safeguard these rights. Third, when government no longer fulfills this function—when, in fact, government is oppressive and destroys human freedom—then as a last resort the people have a right to revolution. Further, the declaration expressed an extreme of colonial federalist theory, denying that Parliament had ever had power over the colonists, and claiming that allegiance had been due solely to the king. Finally, the declaration cited a long list of abuses directly attributed to the king, thus providing justification for revolt. "With a firm reliance on the Protection of Divine Providence," Jefferson concluded, "we mutually pledge to each other our Lives, our Fortunes and our sacred Honor." The 56 representatives of 13 colonies then signed their names.

CAUSES OF REVOLUTION

Perhaps 30 to 35 per cent of all colonists remained Loyalists. These were concentrated mainly in New York City and its vicinity, portions of New Jersey and Maryland, Philadelphia and southeastern Pennsylvania, the Mohawk Valley, the southern part of Delaware, western Carolina, and Georgia. Rebels could be found everywhere, but their strength centered in New England and Virginia. Generally, the Revolution did not divide the colonists along class lines. Merchants and artisans, farmers and frontiersmen, as well as lawyers and speculators belonged to both sides. Why did some people remain loyal and others rebel? The answer is as complex as each local experience, as enigmatical as the personalities involved.

Two complementary tendencies should be noted: First, by the middle of the eighteenth century the American colonies had reached a level of economic growth which—in some cases—offered serious competition to that of Britain, or—in others—felt circumscribed by British regulations. When the colonies were an infant economy, participation in the British empire had seemed an asset; as a burgeoning giant of unlimited potential, they looked upon the same participation as restricting. Thus, a major cause of the Revolution was economic. Second, along with economic growth, the belief had gradually developed that the destiny of America was distinct from that of England and the Old World. Americans did not want their country to repeat the unhappy European pattern of kings, standing armies, wars, and established churches. For decades the colonies had elected their own assemblies and appointed their own courts, and the characteristics of self-reliance and political independence had become deeply ingrained. Even had there been no revolution against England, the impulse toward democracy would have continued, and would have caused serious internal conflicts between established authorities and liberal aspirants. The struggle with Britain provided a focus for demands for political freedom. Thus, a major cause of the Revolution was political. The eco-

In 1778 Baron von Steuben, a Prussian trained in Frederick the Great's military school, began to drill inexperienced soldiers at Valley Forge, proving himself to be an unorthodox but superb drillmaster. He would shriek at the troops in a mixture of French and English sprinkled with curses. "Mon ami, mon bon ami! Sacre! Goddam de gaucheries of dese badauts," he once shouted to an aide. "Je ne puis plus. I can curse dem no more." (Courtesy of Pennsylvania Historical and Museum Commission)

nomic and the political causes were closely linked. Property and liberty were synonymous to most colonists. British taxes therefore seemed as much a deprivation of liberty as a loss of property.

George III was not the tyrant pictured by the rebels. Nor was he guilty of the offenses Jefferson submitted "to a candid world." From a British point of view the acts of Parliament were neither unconstitutional nor unreasonable. But they were unwise. The ultimate failure of the king and Parliament stemmed from their rigidity and provincialism, their hopeless misunderstanding of the colonial mentality. In 13 years they had repeatedly demonstrated their inability to solve the problems of empire.

THE LONG WAR

They could solve the problems of war no better. The British expected a quick victory, but the Revolution did not end until the Battle of Yorktown in 1781, and a final peace treaty between the parties was not signed until 1783.

The British miscalculated by ignoring the effects of European politics. French agents had urged the colonists to independence and after 1776 French economic and military aid was extended, though unofficially. The astonishing defeat of "Gentleman Johnny" Burgoyne at Saratoga late in 1777 convinced the French to ally with the Americans by an open declaration of war against Britain. In 1778 France and America signed a treaty of alliance in which, among other stipulations, each party pledged not to make a separate peace with Britain and to continue fighting until American independence was assured. The following year Spain entered on the American side. Other northern European nations joined together in the anti-British "League of Armed Neutrality." British possessions in the Caribbean and the Mediterranean became vulnerable. Final victory was achieved with the aid of the French navy. At the Yorktown peninsula, where General Cornwallis was surrounded by American and French troops, the French fleet under Admiral De Grasse blocked the British navy from coming to the rescue. Cornwallis had no option but to surrender.

The long war doubled the British national debt and threatened the country with bankruptcy. As these problems mounted, political opposition to the king and his ministers rose ominously. The North ministry resigned and George III almost abdicated. By 1782 the British were desperate for peace. Only the final settlement was to be arranged.

WASHINGTON'S ROLE

If victory was due, in part, to French help and British miscalculation, the major architect of the American success was George Washington. Sometimes he moved so slowly, so cautiously, that his competence was questioned. A few critics suggested that he be replaced by General Horatio Gates. Nothing came of the idea, fortunately for the patriot cause. The essence of Washington's strategy was to adhere to a defensive position. Yorktown was the result of six years of patience and fortitude. When officers quarreled over rank and honors, when state governments were tardy or remiss in supplying food, clothing, and troop quotas, when men deserted, when currency became hopelessly inflated, when French naval support seemed an infinity away—Washington resisted the "apostles of rash offensives." The ultimate defeat of the British army was due to his prolonged reluctance to risk a major battle at unequal odds. "In strategy, as in land speculation," according to one of his biographers, "Washington habitually was a bargain hunter. He always sought the largest gain for the least gore."

THE PEACE TREATY

Three fears dominated the peace negotiations. Spain feared the colonies' westward expansion and wanted them contained. America feared that the French supported Spain's policy. Britain feared the Franco-American alliance.

The American representatives in Paris—Benjamin Franklin, John Jay, and John Adams—were under instructions to cooperate with the French. They soon suspected, however, that the French minister of foreign affairs, the Comte de Vergennes, was intent on pleasing the Spaniards. Various proposals were made which would have divested the United States of large land areas they claimed east of the Mississippi. The Americans therefore violated their instructions and met secretly with British representatives. The latter were pleased to drive a wedge between the allies, and a peace treaty was arranged. Although the Americans did not receive Canada, as they had requested, the terms were generous. The treaty secured the trans-Appalachian area as far as the Mississippi, and it even preserved American fishing privileges off Nova Scotia and Newfoundland. "The day is now come when the sun will raise on amirrica never to set," commented one rebel on hearing of the peace. "I look forward with pleasure to the happy days that our children will see."

QUESTIONS FOR AMERICA

The United States was the first revolutionary country to win independence, the first modern nation to reject monarchy, the first to predicate her government on the equality of mankind. Could she live up to these high ideals? American visionaries foresaw a nation without prejudice, free from corruption, seeking not domination but peace. Cynics sneered at the attempt, and others alternated between hope and despair. Could Americans put their vision into practice? Sectional and economic rivalries had to be surmounted. Could the colonies control the conflicting pluralisms and exist together as one people? Americans were still largely locally oriented. Could they learn to think in terms of continental interests? Their inheritance was revolutionary. Could they practice moderation? Radicals and conservatives disagreed on the nature of the central government. Could they discover the magic balance between liberty and order? Could they make federalism work? The French and British had failed to solve the problems of empire. Could the Americans do any better?

RATIFICATION OF THE ARTICLES OF CONFEDERATION

The beginning was inauspicious. As early as 1776 Americans were aware of the dire need for a permanent central government to replace the revolutionary Continental Congress. John Dickinson composed a draft of a constitution which was debated and considerably altered, yet five years elapsed before the Articles of Confederation were ratified. The delay was caused by an issue which had plagued Britain—the problem of western lands. Certain "landed" states, on the basis of their original colonial charters, claimed possession of territories between the Appalachians and the Mississippi. Other "landless" states, lacking such claims, demanded that these lands be given up voluntarily and ceded to the central government.

Virginia was the last (and the largest) of the "landed" states to refuse to cede its territory. Maryland was the last of the "landless" states to withhold approval of the Articles because of Virginia's obstinacy. Maryland's argument ran somewhat as follows: states without western lands would be dwarfed in size, wealth, and influence by mighty colossi like Virginia. Virginia could derive much of its income from the sale of western lands, but states without lands would have to rely entirely on taxes for revenue. Therefore, people would flock to the "landed" states, compounding the evil. Besides, the western lands should be considered as spoils of war, the common possession of all Americans, and should be administered in their behalf by Congress under the Articles of Confederation.

This patriotic argument, however, was presented by groups of land speculators—including some of the most prominent revolutionary leaders of the middle Atlantic states—who acted from less laudable motives. They had formed companies, invested capital, and purchased large tracts from the Indians. Virginia refused to confirm the validity of their titles. (Why should Virginia do so? After all, Virginia had her own land speculators!) If the Articles of Confederation provided for national control of the West, Congress might prove more amenable to the non-Virginian speculator's interests.

Virginians were well aware of the baser reasons for Maryland's dissent. But the need for unity in the war effort, a threat of British invasion, and the gradual recognition that the principle of national control of the West was right persuaded them to yield. The land northwest of the Ohio was ceded in January 1781, with two stipulations: that it ultimately be formed into states with "rights of sovereignty, freedom, and independence as the other States"; and that previous purchases of lands within the ceded territory from the Indians be considered invalid. Within two months Maryland ratified and the Articles of Confederation became effective.

CONFEDERATION WESTERN POLICIES

Despite this unpromising start and the continued bickerings and briberies of rival land speculators, one of the enduring achievements of the Confederation was its western legislation. The precedents established constituted the most progressive and successful colonial policy of any nation in modern history. Its major features derived from the liberal and farsighted thinking of Thomas Jefferson. The Ordinance of 1784, for example, reflected his belief that the western territories should be self-governing and, when they reached a certain stage of growth, should be admitted to the union as partners with the original 13 states. The famous Northwest Ordinance of 1787 was, in a sense, less democratic, since it placed the territories under more rigid controls of the national Congress. But the ordinance of 1787 did contain another democratic concept first advanced by Jefferson, which the law of 1784 had omitted: the prohibition of slavery in the Northwest Territory.

CRITICISM OF THE CONFEDERATION

The Confederation's accomplishments in other areas were less noteworthy, if only because Congress lacked coercive authority. Critics repeatedly pointed out the system's weaknesses. Congressional taxation could operate only by means of voluntary levies upon the states. When states neglected or only partly met their obligations, Congress was powerless. When Congress negotiated treaties, the states could and did ignore them. Britain barred all trade with her West Indian possessions to American ships or ships manned by American seamen; she placed heavy duties on imported American products, and at the same time dumped huge quantities of goods in America without fear of economic reprisal. Massachusetts did attempt to place a duty on British goods. But other states did not, and the loss of business forced Massachusetts to repeal the law.

Still other weaknesses of the Confederation were readily apparent. Contrary to the treaty of 1783, the British controlled and refused to abandon their northwest military posts. The Spaniards temporarily closed the port of New Orleans to Americans, a great hardship to

Westerners who floated their produce down the Mississippi for sale on the New Orleans market. Some members of Congress would have officially sanctioned the closure of New Orleans in return for a favorable commercial agreement with Spain, and the proposed Jay-Gardoqui Treaty was only narrowly defeated.

Critics of the Articles could point to a languishing economy, a depreciated currency, a burgeoning debt, a divided people, an impotent government, and national humiliation. Surely the Revolution should have resulted in something better. Unless the Confederation were strengthened quickly, they felt, the result would be anarchy, financial chaos, even civil war.

DEFENSE OF THE CONFEDERATION

These criticisms were rebutted by defenders of the Confederation. Many of the economic problems facing the country, they contended, were due not to the form of government, but to normal postwar economic dislocations. A recession was natural. New markets had to be found, and Americans were aggressively finding them. As commerce in the Caribbean was curtailed, trade in the Pacific was opened. The first American ship reached Canton in 1784 with a cargo of ginseng (an herb prized by the Chinese as an aphrodisiac) and exchanged it for tea. Another ship, in that same year, was the first to carry the American flag to St. Petersburg. True enough, the defenders argued, states had not met congressional appropriations, but only because they were at times unrealistically high. Revolutionary war debts remained vexatious but some states—through land sales, paper money issues, and redemptions of state obligations at market value—were paying off their state debts and even assuming part of their national debt. They felt that time alone would cure many of the young nation's economic headaches.

To endow the Confederation with unlimited power to regulate taxes and commerce, it was claimed, would amount to an admission that the Revolution had been fought in vain. Why free America from the despotism of the British government only to create a similar despotism in the United States? The Confederation was based on the idea of cooperation among, not coercion of, its members. With the states supreme, and Congress merely their agent, a national tyranny could never develop. No European country threatened invasion, despite nonpayment of debts. All the states lived in peace. The prediction of civil discord was looked on simply as the bugbear of a few pessimistic and overanxious creditors.

ANNAPOLIS CONVENTION

All the logic of the defenders of the Confederation could not erase one stubborn fact: the perennial shortage of funds in the national treasury. Money could be raised by territorial land sales, but the process was slow and uncertain, and the results insufficient; or by a tariff, but that required the approval of all the states, which was never received; or by levies upon the states, which increasingly yielded less, since many of the states had their own financial problems. In 1786 New Jersey flatly refused to pay any part of the national requisition. Time was running out.

At the instigation of Virginia, a convention was held in Annapolis to draft a uniform code of commercial regulations. Although all the states had been invited, only five sent delegates. Moreover, the authority of several delegates was hampered by instructions imposed on them by their respective states. Alexander Hamilton, James Madison, and John Dickinson, perhaps by prearrangement, argued that the issue of commercial regulations could not be separated from other vital questions, and that fundamental changes in the Confederation could hardly be decided by five states. Convinced, and despairing of achieving any reforms at Annapolis, the delegates agreed to adjourn, recommending a general convention to meet in Philadelphia in May 1787 for the purpose of revising the Articles of Confederation to render them "adequate to the exigencies of the Union."

There was little reason to anticipate a successful convention at Philadelphia. There was reason to doubt that it would meet at all. Many states were apathetic and some were hostile to the idea. Congress passed the recommendation to a committee of three, who referred it to a committee of 13, which was never appointed. Then came the news of a revolution in Massachusetts which—more than any other factor—gave life to the proposal.

SHAYS'S REBELLION

The farmers of western Massachusetts had no particular love for Boston and the state government. In addition to other iniquities, Boston was crowded with money-hungry lawyers. And, being a litigious people, Americans found the services of lawyers frequently necessary. Court procedures were slow. Costs were outrageously high. The wealthy lawyers had a considerable influence on the government. With other creditors, they had urged the state legislature to pass tax laws unbearable to the farmers. The income from these taxes was used to pay off the holders of state debts, not at the depreciated market value of the bonds but at par. For these reasons the farmers rebelled. Of their many leaders, a former revolutionary war captain, Daniel Shays, became known as the prime mover of the insurrection.

Local conventions were held. Petitions of grievance were drafted. Mobs of armed men stopped county courts from meeting at Concord, Taunton, Great Barrington, and Springfield. By September 1786 the Massachusetts government was inoperative west of Boston.

The state legislature had already enacted laws to lower taxes and modernize the court system. Now, at Governor James Bowdoin's request, other corrective legislation was passed to quench the discontent. But, like a fire out of control, the rebellion continued without reason or purpose. Although their grievances had been redressed, the insurgents still marched and drilled. Since they were paid, why should they

Farmers in western Massachusetts who were losing their farms through mortgage foreclosures and tax delinquencies rose in rebellion under the leadership of Daniel Shays. The farmers demanded cheap paper money, lighter taxes, and a suspension of mortgage foreclosures. Pictured is an engraving of Shays's insurgents preparing to attack troops defending a courthouse in Springfield. (From Springfield 1636–1886, *by Mason Green)*

go home? Their leaders schemed and wondered what to do next. But before they found an answer, the Bostonians raised an army by private subscription which marched to Springfield and on January 25, 1787, scattered Daniel Shays's forces with one volley.

Like many other rebellions, this one was misinterpreted by most contemporaries. Shays's forces were viewed as levelers, determined to hang every creditor, and dedicated to spreading anarchy. The tale grew with the telling, and the result was salutary: state after state decided to send delegates to Philadelphia for the national convention.

THE PHILADELPHIA CONVENTION

The Constitution of the United States was the work of an entire summer. Although the delegates met in secret, news leaked out in various ways. Defenders of the Confederation grew alarmed at the reports. First, the delegates violated their states' instructions, which authorized them only to suggest changes in the Articles of Confederation. Instead, they committed the revolutionary act of deciding to compose an entirely new document. Second, it was rumored that the new Constitution would be a drastic change from the Confederation, providing for a dangerous redistribution of sovereignty. Yet, little could be done either for or against the document until it was actually finished and submitted. Meanwhile, George Washington's presence as presiding officer of the convention served to allay the doubts of many Americans.

Solutions to the problems of the Confederation were not easy, for each question suggested another more difficult one. While the delegates were determined to build the new Constitution on a firm foundation, they were irresolute as to means. Conflicts between sectional interests, conflicts between those who favored greater or lesser national power, and even each individual's contradictory beliefs, all had to be resolved. Decisions were made, reversed, reintroduced, changed, settled, unmade again, and modified until the very last days of the convention.

For example, the Founding Fathers' political heritage was based on the belief that government's power derived solely from the people. But they were equally certain that the people could not be fully trusted. As Shays's Rebellion had illustrated, the majority could be as tyrannous as an individual. A New England minister expressed the dilemma as follows: "Let it stand as a principle that government originates from the people; but let the people be taught . . . that they are not able to govern themselves." How did one fashion a government which would solve the dilemma? Practical questions also divided the delegates. Small states were apprehensive of the big states' powers. Northerners raised the problem of slavery. Southerners feared that an export tariff might be inflicted. How was representation to be fairly apportioned? And taxes? Each point required time-consuming discussions. Most crucial, however, was the problem of how to give the government coercive strength. To vest it with the bald power to punish states for noncompliance with national laws would be unwise. The Constitution could never be ratified with such a provision. The states were too jealous of their sovereign prerogatives. Still, without it, the rest of the document would be worthless.

THE FEDERAL CONSTITUTION

The Constitution was preeminently a document of compromise reflecting a balancing of conflicting interests. Small states obtained equal representation in the upper house. Big states obtained representation based on population in the lower house. Three fifths of the slaves were to be counted for purposes of representation and taxation. The African slave trade was allowed to continue for 20 years. Congress could pass uniform commercial regulations, but could never tax exports. Money bills had to originate in the lower house. Treaties had to receive the consent of two thirds of the upper house.

The people were represented in the House of Representatives, but they were screened from too much participation in government in other ways: by an electoral college, responsible for the final selection of a president; by a Supreme Court, which had the power to strike down state laws yet was independent of the popular will; and by the Senate, which was to be appointed by state governments. The Confederation had not contained such devices to check popular rule. In fact, under the Confederation there was no separate executive or judiciary branch of government. But it does not necessarily follow that the Confederation was a more democratic form of government than that provided for by the Constitution. The Confederation was essentially a league of sovereign states, in which the people had no direct voice, and in which the central government had no power of coercion. It could be considered more democratic only if the state governments represented the people better than the federal government. This was not the case in many states. The Constitution, despite its distrust of the people, proceeded solely from them. Thus it solved the problem of coercion. For, by its own express declaration, the Constitution was the supreme law of the land, to which all public officials swore an oath of support, and which operated directly upon every citizen. In short, it created a new and superior sovereignty. The Constitution did not begin with the words "We the States," but rather "We the people." The distinction was crucial.

The Constitution challenged traditional concepts of government, best expressed in the writings of Montesquieu. It was an axiom of political philosophy that a republic could not exist over a large territory. History had shown that only in small contiguous regions could republicanism flourish; large areas required an emperor or military chief to control the people by force. When a small democratic state enlarged its boundaries (the Roman Republic's expansion was frequently cited), the government inevitably became despotic. Thus, the Constitution was a bold experiment. No one realized this fact more than James Madison, sometimes regarded as its chief creator. All governments, said Madison, are prone to the machinations of selfish men and special interests. Although republics may exist in smaller areas, in such countries it is easier for a faction to gain control and rule tyrannically. In a nation as large as the United States, with so many diverse interests—northern, southern, and western, landed, mercantile, and financial—he felt that it would be difficult for any one faction to seize and maintain control. The Constitution, therefore, by recognizing that mankind is in part dominated and directed by the passion for power, particularly economic power, turns evil into good by balancing faction against faction, and requiring a national consensus on each issue.

METHOD OF RATIFICATION

Of the 55 delegates assembled in Philadelphia, 39 signed the finished document. Few who signed considered it a perfect frame of government. All concurred, however, that the alternative was "anarchy and convulsion." The Constitution was submitted for ratification, not to the state legislatures, but to special popular conventions. The move was both wise and proper for two reasons. First, many of the state legislatures would have been hostile. Second, the Constitution was a compact not of the states, but of the people of the states. The Founding Fathers concluded that the Constitution could become operative if it was ratified by the people of nine states.

THE ANTI-FEDERALIST ARGUMENT

Proponents of the Constitution called themselves "Federalists" and labeled their opponents "anti-Federalists." The latter objected to these terms as inappropriate and misleading, and suggested that they would be more accurate if reversed. But they gained acceptance through wide repetition. The debate over the Constitution was waged primarily in the newspapers before and during the conventions in each state. Most of the journals were Federalist, and the anti-Federalists complained that they did not receive fair treatment; that the Federalists were pushing the Constitution to a vote too quickly and without the possibility of qualifying or conditional ratification; and that objections to it were so widespread that a second national convention should be called to consider them.

The anti-Federalists were at a disadvantage because they were unorganized and because they had no constructive alternative to offer except to retain the Confederation. Some, but by no means all, of their criticisms were:

1. The Constitution lacked a bill of rights.
2. Coercive authority would destroy individual liberty.
3. The form of the Constitution was federal, yet the effect was national. It would create a "consolidated" system. State sovereignty would be insignificant in contrast to national sovereignty.
4. The taxing power would bring down squads of collectors to harass the people.
5. The president would become an elected despot.
6. The Senate was too aristocratic.
7. There was no provision for future national conventions to review the basic law of the land periodically.
8. A standing army in peacetime was unnecessary and dangerous. It would be used as an engine of oppression.
9. The ratio of representatives to population in the lower house was too small; elections of representatives should be held annually.
10. The national courts would have the power of judicial review.

The anti-Federalists drew a picture of the supporters of the Constitution as propertied aristocrats, rich merchants, and men of great wealth motivated by the desire to protect their own economic interests. Even George Washington came under attack. "Notwithstanding he wielded the sword in defense of liberty," wrote one anti-Federalist, "yet at the same time [he] was, and is to this day, living upon the labors of several hundreds of miserable Africans; and some of them very likely, descended from parents who, in point of property and dignity in their own country, might cope with any man in America." The anti-Federalists portrayed themselves as simple agrarians, sturdy yeomen voicing the sentiment of the masses.

ACCEPTANCE OF THE CONSTITUTION

New Hampshire was the ninth state to ratify the Constitution in June 1788. Federalists in many regions heralded the event with fireworks, parades, and inspiring speeches. But some believed the celebrations to be premature. Without the participation of Virginia or New York,

Three states—Delaware, New Jersey, and Georgia—ratified the Constitution without a single dissenting vote. In Connecticut it passed by an overwhelming majority, 128 to 40; and in Pennsylvania by 46 to 23. Massachusetts was the sixth state to ratify by a vote of 187 to 168; followed by Maryland, 63 to 11; South Carolina, 149 to 73; and New Hampshire, 57 to 46. Technically the Constitution could go into effect at this point, but no one believed it could be successful without the approval of New York and Virginia. Virginia was the tenth state to ratify, 89 to 79, and New York then followed by the narrow margin of 30 to 27.

As each state ratified there were usually ceremonies marked by grand parades, the shooting of cannon, public dinners, and the inevitable patriotic speeches. Shown below is a contemporary drawing of the celebration in New York, with one of the floats labelled "Hamilton." (Courtesy of Culver Pictures, New York City)

neither of which had yet acted, the experiment could hardly hope to succeed.

The anti-Federalists in Virginia were championed by the popular Patrick Henry, an orator of incomparable ability, and by the highly respected George Mason, author of the Virginia Declaration of Rights. The Federalist phalanx was led by men of equal talent: Madison, George Wythe, and John Marshall. George Washington did not attend the ratifying convention in Richmond but his endorsement of the Constitution helped the Federalist cause immeasurably. Both sides claimed the vote of Thomas Jefferson, who was in France. Everyone expected Governor Edmund Randolph to come forward as an anti-Federalist leader, since along with Mason, he had refused to sign the Constitution in Philadelphia. But he switched to the Federalist position. Virginia ratified by the narrow margin of 89 to 79.

The news was relayed to Poughkeepsie—site of the New York ratifying convention—as soon as possible, for the Federalists there needed help. The governor of New York, George Clinton, was firmly opposed to the Constitution, and a majority of the convention seemed to agree with him. Alexander Hamilton had done everything possible to change the minds of the delegates. With Madison and John Jay, he had coauthored *The Federalist*, a series of brilliant essays explaining and defending the Constitution, which appeared in the New York press. Hamilton spoke publicly and "politicked" privately. He reasoned, cajoled, and threatened. Together with the impact of Virginia's decision, his efforts were barely enough: New York ratified on July 26, 1788, by a vote of 30 to 27. Sixteen months later North Carolina entered the union, followed by Rhode Island in May 1790.

America's hopes for the future were laced with fears. The problems were formidable. Britain had failed to solve them. The Confederation had failed. Another collapse might result in fragmentation and even civil war. Europe appeared indifferent, and England scornful. Both Federalists and anti-Federalists believed that America, the first to throw off the shackles of the Old World, was the last refuge of liberty. "Be of good cheer," Gouverneur Morris advised Hamilton. "My religion steps in where my understanding falters and I feel faith as I lose confidence. Things will yet go right but when and how I dare not predict."

SUGGESTED READINGS

Thomas P. Abernethy, *Western Lands and the American Revolution*

*John R. Alden, *The American Revolution*

Clarence W. Alvord, *The Mississippi Valley in British Politics*

*Charles A. Beard, *An Economic Interpretation of the Constitution of the United States*

*Carl Becker, *The Declaration of Independence*

*Morton and Penn Borden, *The American Tory*

Robert E. Brown, *Middle-Class Democracy and the Revolution in Massachusetts*

*Edmund C. Burnett, *The Continental Congress*

*Elisha P. Douglass, *Rebels and Democrats*

*Max Farrand, *The Framing of the Constitution of the United States*

Douglas S. Freeman, *George Washington*

*Merrill Jensen, *The Articles of Confederation: An Interpretation of the Social-Constitutional History of the American Revolution*

*————, *The New Nation: A History of the United States During the Confederation*

*Bernard Knollenberg, *Origin of the American Revolution: 1759–1766*, rev. ed.

*Forrest McDonald, *Formation of the American Republic 1776–1790*

*John C. Miller, *Triumph of Freedom: 1775–1783*

Lynn Montross, *The Reluctant Rebels*

*Edmund S. Morgan, *Birth of the Republic: 1763–89*

Richard B. Morris, *The Peacemakers*

*Howard H. Peckham, *The War for Independence: A Military History*

*Clinton Rossiter, *1787: The Grand Convention*

*Arthur M. Schlesinger, *Colonial Merchants and the American Revolution, 1763–1776*

Charles Warren, *The Making of the Constitution*

*Esmond Wright, *Fabric of Freedom: 1763–1800*

* Available in paperback

LIFE IN AMERICA
The Eighteenth Century

4

THE ELITE CLASSES

"The poor are destined to labor," John Adams wrote with customary certainty, "and the rich, by the advantages of education, independence, and leisure, are qualified for superior status." By the eighteenth century an aristocracy of great landholders and merchant princes dominated society. Judges and generals, legislators, governors, and diplomats, all were from the upper classes. Even the revolutionary army was commanded by a Virginia aristocrat, and directed strictly along class lines. "Take none but gentlemen," was Washington's advice about the recruitment of officers. On one occasion a captain was court-martialed and dismissed for associating socially with a wagonmaker in his brigade. Another officer was reprimanded for employing the services of an enlisted men's whore. Colleges depended upon the endowments of aristocrats, artists upon their patronage, and the indigent upon their contributions. If many were generous, they also paraded their wealth in other ways. Aristocratic weddings were ostentatious affairs; their funerals expensive displays. In 1736 Governor Jonathan Belcher of Massachusetts distributed 1,000 pairs of gloves to mourners in honor of his deceased wife; Peter Faneuil outdid him two years later by handing out 3,000 pairs at the funeral of his uncle. Their dinners were sumptuous feasts, served on Nankin or East India china over the finest damask cloth. Before 1776 English nobles visiting the colonies were handsomely feted in the richest homes, whose owners vied for their attendance. During the war French officers were similarly entertained. The Comte de Segur wrote with approval that "democracy has not banished luxury."

Society was more structured than in the seventeenth century—at least along the Atlantic seaboard. The American Revolution scarcely

The descendant of French Huguenots, Peter Faneuil was born in New Rochelle in 1700, and inherited a large fortune upon the death of an uncle in 1738. His gift of a building to the city of Boston, the famous Faneuil Hall, was narrowly accepted (367 to 360), since many doubted its necessity. (Courtesy of the Massachusetts Historical Society)

disturbed this structure. Class leveling did not occur. The range between rich and poor remained fairly constant. Revolutionary leaders "were not making war upon the principles of aristocracy," one scholar has remarked. "They expected . . . to achieve a safe and sane revolution of gentlemen, by gentlemen, and for gentlemen." However, class structure and class attitudes are not the same. The American Revolution directly, and the French Revolution indirectly, had a profound effect upon the latter.

First, rifts within the elite classes widened into deep divisions. All subscribed to the philosophy of the Declaration of Independence. All believed in upper-class rule because everyone believed that only the upper classes possessed the education and training to decide upon sophisticated political issues. But the more conservative equated wealth with wisdom, believed that form was as important as substance, and exhibited a profound distrust of the masses. "The mob begin to think and reason," wrote Gouverneur Morris contemptuously. "Poor reptiles! They bask in the sun, and ere noon they will bite, depend upon it. The gentry begin to fear this." Morris was a perfect representative of conservative aristocracy: he was accompanied in his travels by two French valets—he considered Westerners to be barbarians—and he wanted senators chosen for life. The more liberal aristocrat placed human values above property values, preferred intellectual attainments to social trappings, and assumed that the free choice of informed citizens would result in the election of natural leaders. Thomas Jefferson best articulated this position. He considered "an aristocracy of wealth of more harm than benefit to society," and he wished "to make an opening for the aristocracy of virtue and talent."

Second, there was a mounting difference in the attitudes held by the masses toward aristocratic rule. In 1700 that attitude was deferential, subservient, and unquestioning. By 1800 such deference was fast eroding. Titles of any kind were abhorred, and newspapers teemed with antiaristocratic denunciations. George Washington was berated for accepting the presidency of the Order of the Cincinnati, an exclusive society limited to revolutionary war officers and their descendants. Aedanus Burke of South Carolina published a widely read pamphlet on the society, "proving that it creates a race of hereditary patricians or nobility." Members of the Cincinnati, wrote an anonymous contributor to *The Boston Gazette*, together with "holders of public securities, men of great wealth, and expectations of public office, bankers and lawyers," were "greedy gudgeons" who "form the aristocratic combination." Yet if there was class consciousness, there was no class

Eighteenth-century townspeople took care of their own poor. The Philadelphia chimney sweeps pictured here could receive free schooling, medical attention, even food if necessary. To Americans poverty was a natural condition, and some welcomed the divine opportunity it afforded them to be charitable. (Courtesy of The Granger Collection)

conflict. The masses had been awakened to an interest in government, and a desire for political participation which in a few decades would directly challenge the aristocracy.

THE WORKING CLASSES

For skilled workers, white, and free of debt, all observers agreed that America was a land of unparalleled economic opportunity. "Here there are no beggars," the Maryland legislature boasted in 1699, "and they that are superannuated are reasonably well provided for." A Georgia settler reported that "industrious people live more comfortably here than in their native country." Wages were 30 to 100 per cent higher than in Great Britain. Colonies competed to attract workers with special skills by offering various inducements. Particular craftsmen were exempted from labor on roads as well as from militia training. Those who could set up desired manufacturing processes were rewarded with tax exemptions for a specified number of years, or with land grants, or loans without interest. In 1719, for example, New York City permitted William Dugdale and John Serle to use "certain lands as tenants at will" to erect a building for the making of rope. In England these skilled workers were employed as journeymen or workshop foremen; in America they became capitalists.

Life was not as good for other workers, either because they were unskilled, debt-ridden, or indentured. In seaboard communities, especially, the number of indigent rose in the eighteenth century. Boston, in 1687, counted 14 per cent of its adult males as indigent; by 1771, with the population doubled, 29 per cent were so classified. Poorer immigrants tended to collect in these cities, where employment was cyclical and uncertain, depending on the vagaries of the import trade. But poverty was not confined to cities.

The Marquis de Chastellux, traveling in Virginia, was shocked by the "wane looks," "ragged garments," and "miserable huts" of the rural poor. Indentured servants were so often mistreated that royal governors were instructed to have laws passed "restraining of any inhumane severity." Thousands of servants fled before their terms were completed. Court dockets were filled with complaints against the brutality of masters, whose offenses appeared to be the most flagrant in the tobacco colonies. "While it would be unfair to indict the whole planter class," one scholar concludes, "the fact remains that an impressive number of masters led drunken, dissolute lives and were brutal and sadistic toward their workmen."

To be sure, there were many rags-to-riches accounts in colonial history. William Byrd I began his family fortune by selling pots, pans, rum, and guns to the Indians. Robert Livingston utilized his position as town clerk in Albany to acquire 160,000 acres, which led the governor to comment sarcastically: "[From] his being a little bookkeeper, he has screwed himself into one of the most considerable estates in the province." Daniel Dulany and his two brothers came to America in 1703 as indentured servants: through perseverance, ability, clever real estate speculations, and astute marriages into wealthy families, an enormous fortune was amassed. But for every celebrated success, there were hundreds of silent failures. For every Benjamin Franklin, whose rise from poverty to affluence has become part of America's legend, there were countless vagabonds or habitual drifters. For every indentured servant who acquired property and advanced economically, there were four others who either died during their term of service, became landless workers, or returned to England.

People live by myths, however, as much as by facts, and Americans wholeheartedly adopted and apotheosized economic success—no matter how attained. "If there is one test of national genius universally accepted," Ralph Waldo Emerson wrote in 1847, "it is success." The same held true a century before, as it does today. The United States was the golden land of opportunity, and no set of statistics could convince Americans otherwise. Besides, all such judgments are comparative. The percentages for success were always more favorable in America than in England or Europe, where tradition was strong, chances limited, and the class structure rigid. "You may depend upon it," wrote Judge William Allen, "that this is one of the best poor man's countries in the world." Rich aristocrats in America were condemned for their haughtiness, their sense of superiority, their monopoly of power and position, but not their wealth. Indeed, wealth was the goal to which every citizen aspired.

SLAVERY

An indentured servant cost his master, on the average, two to four pounds per year during his service; a slave could be purchased for 18 to 30 pounds for a lifetime of service. Where slaves could be used effectively, they were cheaper than white labor, and inevitably replaced them.

Slavery in the North. At the time of the Revolution there were about 25,000 slaves in New England alone. But the institution never took hold in the North, primarily for economic reasons. Slavery was most profitable in large-scale enterprises, which required a considerable amount of unskilled gang labor. It was not suited to household industries, commerce, or small farming operations, all of which flourished in the North. The capital investment for a slave was simply too great unless his productivity could be fully utilized, which it could not be during the long northern winters when farm labor was minimal. Some slaves could be "hired out" by their masters. But when this was done white workers bitterly resented such black competition. John Adams flatly stated that the determination of free workers to oppose slavery was a significant reason for its abolition in the North. "If the gentlemen had been permitted to hold slaves," wrote Adams, "the common white people would have put the slaves to death, and their masters too, perhaps."

Except for the Quakers, few Northerners were much concerned with the issue of slavery until the American Revolution. But the philosophy of the Revolution, so clearly defined and so often reiterated, made hypocrites of Americans as long as the practice of slavery continued. "It always appeared a most iniquitous scheme to me," Abigail Adams told her husband, "to fight ourselves for what we are daily robbing and plundering from those who have as good a right to freedom as we have." Black leaders such as Prince Hall, Benjamin Banneker, Absalom Jones, and Richard Allen petitioned both the state and federal governments to outlaw slavery. In 1775 the first manumission society was organized in Pennsylvania, and the Quaker state was also the first (in 1780) to abolish slavery. Thereafter, either by constitutional provision, legislative enactment, or judicial decree, every northern state provided for emancipation.

Slavery in the South. Slavery became the South's "peculiar institution" because it proved vital to the commercialized agriculture of the plantation system, which required a large and stable labor supply to produce crops for export. One foreman could readily oversee the daily work of dozens of slaves. They could not leave after a few years, as did white servants, and their color made it more difficult for them to escape. Moreover, while the initial capital investment to purchase slaves was heavy, planters could increase their landholdings. All other variables being equal—soil fertility, transportation costs, and market prices—profits were greater in larger units which could be farmed more efficiently. Once cheap labor drove out expensive white labor in agriculture, the tendency for it to expand was irresistible. Skilled white labor preferred to go North. Those who remained protested vehemently, as did northern workers, against the use of slaves in their trades. For example, ship carpenters in Charleston in 1744 petitioned the legislature for relief, since slaves were hired out at lower wages. Pilots of vessels in North Carolina also petitioned to keep blacks, slave or free, from being licensed as pilots, especially since they were said to exhibit an "insolent and turbulent disposition." Restrictive laws to protect white workers were enacted, but to no avail. The laws were evaded or ignored. By 1790 black craftsmen hired out by their masters—who turned a tidy profit—became entrenched in virtually every trade. Since the immigration of indentured servants was discouraged, even small farmers in the South were forced to rely on slave labor. It is a statistical fact that most of the 700,000 slaves in America at the end of the eighteenth century were in the possession, not of rich planters, but of farmers who owned five or less.

Slavery was morally disturbing to the revolutionary generation, and by the close of the century even its economic value was being called into question by tobacco planters in Maryland and Virginia. Soil fertility was rapidly exhausted, exports had fallen, and tobacco prices were low. "Were it not then, that I am principled against selling negroes, as you would do cattle in the market," George Washington commented in 1794, "I would not, in twelve months from this date, be possessed of one. I shall be happily mistaken, if they are not found to be a very troublesome species of property 'ere many years pass over our heads." The Marquis de Chastellux, traveling in the Chesapeake region, reported that people "seem grieved at having slaves, and are constantly talking of abolishing slavery, and of seeking other means of exploiting their lands." Between 1782 and 1790 individual owners in Virginia freed approximately 10,000 blacks. Nevertheless, all legislative attempts in the southern states to emancipate slaves failed. The proslavery forces were too strong. In a few decades more the invention and wide application of the cotton gin resuscitated the slave system. As the price of slaves rose, the number of personal manumissions declined. From being a necessary evil, slavery to Southerners became a positive good.

A RACIST SOCIETY

Had slavery been abolished, the prospect of ever assimilating blacks into white society was unthinkable to most Americans of that period. No one can doubt that Jefferson regarded slaves as human rather than a species of property, or that he found slavery antithetical to American principles of liberty and equality. As a young lawyer he had once argued for a black's freedom on the grounds that "under the law of nature all men are born free." And though a slave owner himself, Jefferson had penned a "vehement philippic against negro slavery" in the Declaration of Independence, John Adams noted, a section which was struck before adoption because several deep Southerners objected to it. Nevertheless, when Jefferson spoke of the people, he had in mind whites, not blacks. When he spoke of American expansion across the continent, it was white Anglo-Saxon expansion he pictured. Blacks were not considered as constituent members of society. White racism was the common property of virtually all Americans. In fact, one might say that the American celebration of individual rights rested on a sense of supremacy over blacks. "It is not only the slave who is beneath his master," the Marquis de Chastellux observed, "it is the Negro who is beneath the white man. No act of enfranchisement can efface this unfortunate distinction." Blacks were judged to be inferior, an alien element, and the ultimate solution of the problem was to settle them elsewhere. Jefferson proposed colonization of

At the time of the American Civil War, the orator Wendell Phillips delivered a lecture on Toussaint L'Ouverture which was widely reprinted and circulated among the troops of the Union army. "The negro race," said Phillips, "instead of being that object of pity and contempt which we usually consider it, is entitled, judged by the facts of history, to a place close by the side of the Saxon. . . . Go to 50,000 graves of the best soldiers France ever had, and ask them what they think of the negro's sword. . . . Haiti, from the ruins of her colonial dependence, is become a civilized state. . . . Toussaint made her what she is." Of all authentic black heroes in the western hemisphere the greatest was the liberator of Haiti, who led his people to freedom and vanquished the forces of Napoleon. (Courtesy of the Library of Congress)

blacks in Africa or in the West Indies—"drawing off this part of our population, most advantageously for themselves, as well as for us." The prevailing attitude was expressed by a North Carolinian, J. C. Galloway: "It is impossible for us to be happy, if, after manumission, they are to remain among us."

The alternative to freedom for blacks, many Americans believed, was their rebellion—a prospect which was alarming to all whites. When the blacks in Santo Domingo rebelled against their masters in 1791, and a brutal slaughter ensued, the national government responded on racial grounds. Alexander Hamilton—a founding member of the New York Manumission Society—did not hesitate to commit $40,000 of federal funds to crush the uprising without first consulting the president. Washington gave his belated approval, ordered Secretary of War Henry Knox to send arms and ammunition, and informed the French ambassador that the United States would "render every aid in their power to . . . quell the alarming insurrection of the Negroes in Hispaniola." "Lamentable!" Washington told a friend, "to see such a spirit of revolt among the blacks. Where it will stop, is difficult to say."

A few Federalists were quick to point out that the Santo Domingo nightmare stemmed from French radicalism. "That malignant philosophy," John Marshall wrote to his wife, "which . . . can coolly and deliberately pursue, through oceans of blood, abstract systems for the attainment of some fancied untried good, were gathered in the French West Indies." Jefferson was both sympathetic to and scornful of the white French aristocrats who fled to the American continent. Their situation "cried aloud for pity and charity," and he urged the Virginia legislature to be "liberal" in its help. But he also suggested, rather sarcastically, that the monied aristocrats might be distributed among the Indians "who would teach them lessons of liberty and equality." Jefferson saw the Santo Domingo revolt as a frightening harbinger of what might happen in America unless slavery was abolished—"bloody scenes which our children certainly, and possibly ourselves (south of the Potomac), [will] have to wade through." His friend John Breckenridge put the matter succinctly: "I am against slavery. I hope the time is not far distant when not a slave will exist in this union. I fear our slaves will produce another Santo Domingo."

Opportunities for fundamental social reform in American history are rare, and even more rarely seized. They are present usually during times of mass economic crisis or emotional stress. The best chance to abolish slavery peacefully came during the postrevolutionary period, when the institution was temporarily languishing, natural law philosophy was strong, and the Santo Domingo revolt spurred numerous antislavery voices. But the psychological moment was missed, never to reoccur. To Northerners, the revolt confirmed the wisdom of their having freed the slaves. Southerners refused to follow that course. Instead of reform, they chose repression.

BLACKS AND WHITES

Laws of the colonial period prohibiting miscegenation are testimony of the white compulsion for racial purity. Yet miscegenation was a common practice. The two facts are not incompatible: conquering races usually exploit subject peoples both economically and sexually. White colonials mythologized the black woman as a dusky Venus, more erotically attractive and accomplished than white females. At one point eighteenth-century South Carolina newspapers openly discussed —what was usually a secret subject—the relative sexual merits of both races. Women of the planter class complained bitterly, to no avail. "We southern ladies are complimented with the names of wives," Dolly Madison's sister wrote, "but we are only the mistresses of seraglios." Some decades later Mary Chestnut, a planter's wife, noted in her diary: "Any lady is ready to tell you who is the father of all the mulatto children in everybody's household but her own. Those, she seems to think, drop from the clouds." In cities such as Charleston, Mobile, and New Orleans the habit of white men keeping black concubines was so widespread as to become almost socially acceptable.

One might think that the degree of miscegenation would, as a scholar worded it, dissolve bigotry "in the equalitarian crucible of sexual intimacy." There were numerous examples of interracial love affairs, and of penitent white masters displaying marked affection for their mulatto children. Robert Purvis, a nineteenth-century black abolitionist, the natural son of a Charleston merchant and free black woman, was educated at Amherst and left a considerable fortune by his father. Bishop James A. Healy, the first black priest in America, was born in Georgia, the child of an Irish planter and mulatto slave. Nevertheless, these examples were statistically rare. Sex did not break down racial barriers. Many slave women were coerced or intimidated, or submitted because of the prestige such a relationship would confer. Moreover, the laws stated that children of female slaves were slaves, whatever the color of the child's skin, and whites were not prone to disturb this arrangement. By the end of the Civil War, out of a total slave population of 3,900,000, there were 411,000 mulatto slaves.

BLACKS AND INDIANS

So pronounced has been the mixture of blacks and Indians in American history that whole Indian tribes, according to one sociologist, "became untraceably lost in the Negro population of the South." Whites, especially white planters, feared collusion between the two, and with good reason. Blacks often escaped into the surrounding forests, lived with the Indians, and united with them to fight their common foe. As early as 1658 black and Indian slaves rebelled in Hartford, Connecticut, destroying the homes of several whites during their fight for freedom. In 1727 fugitive blacks joined the Yamasee Indians in marauding attacks upon white outposts in Granville County, South Carolina. From bases in Florida, always a magnet for runaway slaves, blacks and Indians carried on guerrilla warfare against Georgia settlements. Many blacks rose to positions of leadership among the Indians —John Horse of the Seminoles, James Beckworth of the Crows, and

There were fewer and smaller maroon settlements in the United States than in Brazil, writes Carl Degler, since "the tropics . . . requires less substantial shelter and provides easier access to food for runaway [slaves]." Thus, it is no surprise that the most substantial colony of fugitive blacks and Indians was to be found in the Seminole villages of Florida (pictured below). In fact, the Seminole wars of the early nineteenth century can in part be considered a slave revolt, since Indian warriors and blacks fought side by side against whites. (Courtesy of Historical Pictures Service, Chicago)

Jim Boy of the Creeks, for example. In 1813 a tribe of Creeks attacked Fort Mims on the Alabama River and massacred only those with white skins. "The Master of Breath," explained the Creeks, "has ordered us not to kill any but white people and half-breeds."

Nevertheless, there never was any substantial military consolidation of black and Indians, or any sizeable forest hideaways for the blacks. In Brazil black fugitives established a community at Palmares, which numbered 20,000 inhabitants, and which endured for nearly a century against repeated assaults of government troops before it was demolished in 1698. No American maroon settlement could compare, except Florida, where blacks and Seminoles held out for seven years against the American army. The forests were too well settled by white pioneers during the eighteenth century to provide sanctuary for maroons. Whites were alert to destroy these hideaways—as Virginians did in 1729 in the Blue Ridge Mountains, leading the captured blacks back into bondage—lest their existence provide a dangerous example to others. Most important, black fugitives could never be certain of a friendly reception. Some Indian tribes kept them as slaves. And some, like the Notchees and Catawbas of South Carolina, returned them to slavery.

ETHNIC VARIETY IN AMERICA

If blacks and Indians were considered unassimilable, whites were not, regardless of their religion or country of origin. This does not mean that all whites were immediately and universally welcome in America. The impoverished Sephardic Jews who arrived in New Amsterdam in 1654 were harshly received by the Dutch leader, Peter Stuyvesant. A shipload of Scotch-Irish immigrants from Belfast and Londonderry was once prevented from landing by a Boston mob. On another occasion the Puritans of Worcester, Massachusetts, destroyed the Presbyterian church of Scotch-Irish settlers. These examples of intolerance did not halt the influx of non-English whites, who were to be found in every colony. A few Poles and Italians were residents of Virginia even before it became a royal colony. The Bronx, one of New York's boroughs, received its name from Jonas Bronck, a Dane. Germans were flocking into Pennsylvania. Swedish settlers colonized the Delaware region. French Huguenots, though heavily concentrated in South Carolina, were located throughout the seaboard. Scots and Welsh, Irish, Finns, and Swiss all added to the pluralism of white America. Nevertheless, until the eighteenth century, in terms of sheer numbers

Peter Stuyvesant, the fiery governor of New Netherland—pictured above railing at his burgomeisters—did not want any Jewish settlers in his colony. When a group of twenty-three impoverished Jews arrived in New Amsterdam in 1654 from Brazil, Stuyvesant asked the Dutch West India Company for permission to order their departure. "The deceitful race, such hateful enemies and blasphemers of the name of Christ," Stuyvesant warned, should "be not allowed further to infect and trouble this new colony." The Jews of Amsterdam came to the defense of their brethren, arguing that they should be permitted to remain. "Yonder land is extensive and spacious," they wrote. "The more of loyal people that go to live there, the better it is in regard to the population of the country." Peter Stuyvesant to the contrary, the Jews stayed in New Netherland. The earliest laws of that colony, copying those of Europe, forbade Jews from citizenship, from owning property, from guild membership, from retail trades, and from holding public religious services. But in time, though not without a struggle, the laws were either abrogated or ignored. (Courtesy of the Boston Public Library)

rather than variety, the non-English stock was not substantial enough to alter the basically English character of the colonies.

In the 1700's, however, hundreds of thousands of non-English immigrants swarmed across the Atlantic. By the time of the Revolution, south of New England, fully half the population was non-English. And by 1790, when the initial census was taken, analysis of the national origins of America's white inhabitants was as follows:

Per cent	National origin
60.9	English
14.3	Scotch and Scotch-Irish (Ulster)
8.7	German
5.4	Dutch, French, and Swedish
3.7	Irish
7.0	Miscellaneous

This massive migration profoundly changed colonial life. First, English ethnic homogeneity was decisively broken. Second, military defense against the French and Spanish, as well as the Indians, was enhanced as these colonials poured into the backcountry. Third, many brought with them, as a result of prior experience, a feeling of hostility toward Anglicanism, toward parliamentary rule, and toward political authority of any kind. Fourth, despite the cultural isolation some sects were determined to maintain, a considerable degree of assimilation and amalgamation took place. If America has not been quite the melting pot of legend, still few lived as did the Pennsylvania Amish: neither relating to nor being influenced by the New World. Except for the Germans, and even for many of them, aloofness gradually gave way to fusions, and intermarriage with other stocks was common. "I could point out to you," wrote Hector St. John de Crèvecoeur, "a man whose grandfather was an Englishman, whose wife was Dutch, whose son married a French woman, and whose present four sons have now four wives of different nations." Only in America, said Crèvecoeur, have "individuals of all nations . . . melted into a new race of men . . . which you will find in no other country."

GERMANS AND SCOTCH-IRISH: FRONTIER SETTLERS

Numerically the two most important non-English groups in America were the Germans and Scotch-Irish, far different from one another in religion and temperament, but similar in their hunger for land. "Both these sets [of people]," reported James Logan, "frequently sit down on any spot of vacant land they can find, without asking questions." They were destined to meet on the American frontier, acting as a protective buffer between the Indians and the seaboard settlements.

The Germans. So many of them crowded into Pennsylvania, according to Benjamin Franklin, that "unless the stream of importation could be turned from this to other colonies . . . they will soon outnumber us, [and] all the advantages we have, will in my opinion, be not able to preserve our language, and even our government will become precarious." The overflow of German colonists traveled by way of Lancaster down into the Shenandoah Valley, settling the western regions of Maryland, Virginia, and the Carolinas. They usually colonized by their denominational persuasions—pietistic sects from the Rhineland, such as the Dunkers and River Brethren, New Mooners and Mennonites; others from the Palatinate, usually poorer and chiefly Lutherans; and Moravians, who had fled first from Austria to Saxony, becoming the founders of "Wachovia" in North Carolina. As a stock they were industrious and thrifty, their well-tended farms easily recognized and frequently commended. "A German farm," Benjamin Rush noted, "may be distinguished from the farms of other citizens by . . . a general appearance of plenty and neatness in everything that belongs to them." A cautious people, both passive and pacific by nature, the Germans were not interested in politics or esteemed as Indian fighters. Yet they made solid contributions in the conquest of the West. German gunsmiths in Lancaster developed the long "Pennsylvania" rifle, forerunner of the "Kentucky" rifle, the indispensable companion of frontiersmen. With this weapon, more quickly and quietly reloaded than the cumbersome European guns, a skilled marksman could snuff a candle at 50 yards and behead a turkey at 80 yards. Germans also developed the sturdy Conestoga wagons, usually blue colored and covered with stretched canvas, the forerunner of the "prairie schooners" known to every western pioneer in the nineteenth century.

The Scotch-Irish. "Men who emigrate are, from the nature of the circumstances," wrote Arthur Young, who was thinking of the Scotch-Irish, "the most active, hardy, daring, bold and resolute spirits, and probably the most mischievous." Not to be confused either with the Scots (who rarely settled the frontier), or the Irish (who were Catholic), the Scotch-Irish should more properly be called Ulster Scots: people of Scottish descent who had been residents of northern Ireland since the early seventeenth century. Accustomed to border wars in

A visitor to a Scotch-Irish settlement in the Smoky Mountain range of the Appalachians wrote: "The clothes of the people consist of deer skins, their food of Johnny cakes, deer, and bear meat. A kind of white people are found there, who live like savages. Hunting is their chief occupation." (Courtesy of the Boston Public Library)

Ireland, tough and pugnacious, they tried at first to live among the inhabitants of Massachusetts, assuming—incorrectly—that their conservative Presbyterianism would mix well with Puritanism. Cotton Mather considered their residence another "formidable attempt of Satan and his Sons to unsettle us." When finding the best coastal lands occupied, streams of Scotch-Irish went to the frontiers of America: into New Hampshire, Vermont, and the far reaches of Maine, up the Hudson River into northern New York, across the Appalachians to western Pennsylvania, down the Shenandoah Valley, into the hinterlands of Georgia. Though fiercely defensive of their own rights, the Scotch-Irish had few qualms about possessing slaves, and none at all about dispossessing Indians. They fought Indian battles and political battles with equal zeal. Above all, the Scotch-Irish were people of fortitude, ready to endure enormous hardships in the wilderness to attain personal freedom. They represented the best and worst of American yeomanry: practical and humorless, independent and dogmatic, courageous and mercenary, and many of these qualities could be found in the long roster of distinguished statesmen descended from Scotch-Irish stock.

THE AMERICAN WEST

Shortly before the Revolution the royal governor of Virginia, Lord Dunmore, reported that New World inhabitants "forever imagine the lands further off are still better than those upon which they are already settled." The characteristic of geographic mobility, spurred by the desire for cheap and fresh lands, was indisputably American. Colonials in 1700 were still huddled along the coast, and the wilderness was considered a menacing barrier; by 1800 it was an exciting opportunity, attracting Yankees and foreigners, pioneers and speculators. Halted temporarily by the revolutionary war, the westward march resumed after independence in ever increasing numbers. "The woods are full of new settlers," wrote an observer in upstate New York. "Axes are resounding, and the trees literally falling about us as we pass." A traveler in Albany in 1797 counted 500 wagons on the western road in a single day. But this was a small stream compared to the torrent of migrants who, in sun or in snow, by wagon or by foot, passed through the Cumberland Gap. By the close of the century Tennessee numbered close to 80,000 people, and Kentucky more than 220,000.

Many Easterners either dismissed the West as an uncivilized place inhabited by the disorderly, or romanticized it as an agrarian paradise of democratic virtues. Some, like Gouverneur Morris, feared its potential. He warned that "if the western people get power into their hands, they will ruin the Atlantic interests." Others gloried in its promise. Philip Freneau visualized a West of "empires, kingdoms, powers and states." George Washington thought the West in time would become a "second land of promise" for "the poor, the needy, and oppressed of the earth." Americans in the eighteenth century had turned from the ocean to the interior, had pierced the Appalachian barrier, and had begun the colonization of the continent. The West as a specific region was born, set apart from the seaboard by different agricultural methods, racial compositions, political loyalties, and social standards. Frontiersmen, no matter what their country of origin, shared certain values, and exhibited certain common traits. "In the heart of the continent," wrote one scholar, "arose a new *homo Americanus* more easily identified by his mobility than by his habitat. He began to dominate the scene in the years between the American Revolution and the Civil War."

The West was a state of mind that reproduced itself throughout American history on every successive frontier—and lingers to this

very day. First, the Westerner was proud to the point of arrogance of
his skills and accomplishments. If some urban Easterners were patron-
izing or scornful of western settlers for their crude manners and lack
of formal education, the Westerner was equally contemptuous of eastern greenhorns to whom he felt distinctly superior. Second, the Westerner resented eastern economic and political control of the nation. To
many the tax collector was an agent of oppression and the territorial
judge an unwelcome representative of a distant power. Third, the
Westerner was more democratic than the Easterner in a social sense.
He judged individuals by their performance, not by their origins or
status—a refreshing and disconcerting experience to travelers. Fourth,
the Westerner was as litigious as his eastern forebears, but impatient
with bureaucracies, legal complexities, and the slow operations of government. Often, and of necessity, he fashioned his own law: simple,
quick, informal, and majoritarian. Fifth, the Westerner was incurably
optimistic, a community booster, who saw not the present scraggly
village, but the future great city. Enterprising publishers started newspapers to herald the coming economic greatness. A press, ink, type,
and paper were hauled over the mountains from Philadelphia to start
the Pittsburgh *Gazette* in 1786, when that village had no more than
300 inhabitants. The first issue of the *Kentucky Gazette,* in 1789, was
printed in a log cabin in Lexington. Cincinnati had its *Centinel of the
North-Western Territory* as early as 1793, when Indians still menaced
its settlers. In fact, the paper offered a bounty for "every scalp, having
the right ear appendant," of Indians killed in the vicinity of the town.

DEFEATING THE INDIANS

Not all Americans believed that only dead Indians were good Indians.
George Washington, for example, was never as callous as the British
general, Lord Jeffrey Amherst, who seriously thought of decimating
Indian tribes by infecting them with smallpox. A few blankets carrying the germ, it was suggested, would do the trick. Amherst's short-
sighted policies were largely to blame for the Indian uprising led by
the Ottawa chief, Pontiac, in 1763—a powerful and desperate attempt,
which almost succeeded, to drive the white men back across the Appalachians. Washington thought of himself as scrupulously fair in his
dealings with Indians. "Brothers," he told one tribe, "you do well to
wish to learn our arts and ways of life, and above all, the religion of
Jesus Christ. These will make make you a greater and happier people
than you are." Indians to Washington, as to most whites, were either
good or bad, depending on whether they were friendly or hostile,

which largely depended on whether they honored treaties abdicating their lands to settlers. Friendly Indians, Washington promised, would receive the protection of Congress. Hostile Indians would be suppressed by force.

After the American Revolution tribes of Indians ravaged settlements throughout the old Northwest. Urged on by the British and undeterred by previous defeats, Shawnees, Miamis, and Kickapoos plundered boats on the Wabash and Ohio rivers, and crossed over into Kentucky to continue their raids. Frontiersmen called upon George Rogers Clark to lead a punitive expedition in 1786, but the magic of his name was not enough—the expedition failed, Clark's militiamen first rebelling and then retreating in disorder. The Indians, more determined than ever, announced that all prior treaties with the white men were repudiated, and that henceforth "the Ohio shall be the boundary between them and the Big Knives." Such was the situation when George Washington was sworn in as America's first president.

The First Indian Campaign. Without hesitation Washington used his powers as commander in chief to order a military campaign against the Indians. He selected General Josiah Harmar in 1790 to lead some 1,500 men from the vicinity of Cincinnati into the Maumee Valley to crush all opposition. The Indians were forewarned, however, and faded into the forests; Harmar's men searched in vain for the main tribes. Then, while marching south, Harmar hoped to surprise the Indians by sending a detachment of troops doubling back to the Maumee. The tribes waited in ambush, and the detachment was badly mauled, their losses totaling 183 dead and 31 wounded. A court of inquiry vindicated Harmar's actions as "honorable" and meriting "high approbation." He then resigned from the army.

The Second Indian Campaign. The second commander Washington chose was Major General Arthur St. Clair, who was instructed to build a fortification at Miami Village (Fort Wayne, Indiana), and then to "seek the enemy" and "endeavor by all possible means to strike them with great severity." Washington personally warned St. Clair to beware of Indian deceptions and to be alert to sudden attacks and ambushes, but he proved as incompetent as his predecessor. On November 4, 1791, St. Clair camped with 1,400 men near the site of Harmar's defeat, without adequate guards posted, and with tents pitched haphazardly. All through the night Indians led by Chief Little Turtle slipped into the camp, until the Americans were completely surrounded, and then at dawn fell upon their victims. St. Clair suffered the stunning total of 632 men killed and 264 wounded. The rest fled, leaving behind their cannon, and strewing the forest paths with abandoned arms. The troops had spent 10 days marching into Maumee country; their retreat to safety, covering the same ground, took 24 hours. St. Clair, Washington roared, allowed his army "to be cut to pieces, hacked, butchered, tomahawked. He is worse than a murderer! How can he answer to his country?" Yet an investigation absolved St. Clair of blame. He then resigned his commission, but was retained as governor of the Northwest Territory.

The Third Indian Campaign. The confidence of the Indians soared. Settlers left their homes and sought the refuge of frontier posts at Marietta and Cincinnati. Several officers sent to negotiate with belligerent Indians were murdered. Several previously neutral tribes decided to join the belligerents. Spanish agents in the Southwest, hoping to capitalize on these disasters, began to incite the Creeks to attack American outposts; the British did the same in the Northwest, fueling the fires of Indian expectations by promising them aid. A new British fort was constructed in 1794 at Fort Miami (near Toledo), clearly within American territory.

Meanwhile, the third commander picked by Washington, Major General "Mad Anthony" Wayne, thoroughly trained and properly equipped his soldiers. He was determined not to repeat the blunders of Harmar and St. Clair. During the winter of 1793–94 Wayne built Fort Greenville, and he remained there drilling and disciplining his men in preparation for a spring offensive. Indian warriors were also gathering, 2,000 strong, waiting for the Americans, convinced that with British aid victory would be theirs. Chief Little Turtle saw the uselessness of resisting Wayne's army, but his counsel to seek peace was rejected. On August 20, 1794, in a fight which lasted no more than two hours—the Battle of Fallen Timbers—the Indians were decisively beaten. Yet, only 50 were killed. What really shattered their spirit was the refusal of the British commander at Fort Miami to help his allies. Wayne then dictated terms, signed by the Indians in 1795, which brought peace to the Northwest for a generation, and opened a new stretch of territory for American expansion.

Indians continued to fight in the nineteenth century, delaying actions which could not stem the flow of white settlers. "If we want it," wrote Thomas Hutchins, meaning the West, "I warrant it will soon be ours." Indians were invisible men to those who dreamed of America's continental destiny. Even as Wayne opened the Northwest, the New

Disheartened and defeated, the Indian chiefs readily accepted the terms of peace dictated by General Anthony Wayne in 1795. One of Wayne's soldiers is assumed to have painted this scene of the meeting at which the Treaty of Greenville was signed. (Courtesy of the Chicago Historical Society)

England poet, Timothy Dwight, rhapsodized on the blessings of western expansion in *Greenfield Hill:*

> All hail, thou western world! by heaven design'd
> Th' example bright, to renovate mankind.
> Soon shall thy sons across the mainland roam;
> And claim, on far Pacific shores, their home;
> Their rule, religion, manners, arts, convey,
> And spread their freedom to the Asian sea.

RELIGION IN AMERICA

"One can make a good living here, and all live in peace," wrote a young Jewish housewife from Petersburg, Virginia, to her parents in Germany in 1791. "Anyone can do what he wants. There is a blessing here: Jew and Gentile are as one." Her words were extravagant. Religious prejudice never vanished—it has always been a contrapuntal theme of American development—but necessity proved stronger than bigotry in the New World. An unusual idea began to emerge in the colonial period, imperfectly realized and frequently violated, that religious persuasions were personal matters that should be untrammeled by government. The idea of religious liberty was fed by three sources: one practical, one theological, and the other philosophical.

The Practical Reason: Religious Diversity. Long before, and well into the seventeenth century, political obedience and religious conformity went hand in hand. Both were deemed vital to national unity. Dissenters felt the lash of persecution, be it directed against Hussites in Bohemia, Catholics and Puritans in England, or Huguenots in France. The first American colonists carried with them the germs of this prejudice. Toleration was a rare concept, championed by a few exotics and eccentrics. Roger Williams' colony of Rhode Island, which accepted religious fugitives, was quickly dubbed "the latrine of New England" by Puritans. The very idea of toleration was considered heretical to those who were certain they fought for the Lord, and all others served the devil. "To allow and maintain full and free toleration of religion to all men," said Edward Winslow in 1645, "would make us odious."

What made America different from Europe was the profusion of faiths, for with ethnic variety went religious diversity. The multiplicity of creeds served to checkmate each other, and made it difficult for colonial founders to establish and maintain rigorous church-state systems. The ideal of Puritan and Anglican, imitating European practice, was coercive unity. They certainly had no intention of permitting dissenters the free practice of heretical notions. But settlers were needed in every part of America, especially on the frontiers. Religious principles had to give way to economic interests. Four colonies— Rhode Island, Pennsylvania, Delaware, and New Jersey—had no state church. In five others—New York, Maryland, the Carolinas, and Georgia—the established church was too weak to impose its will upon dissenters. The rulers of South Carolina, for example, passed laws in 1704 excluding all non-Anglicans from the legislature, and creating an ecclesiastical court. An uproar ensued, since Anglicans were far outnumbered by dissenters, and these acts were annulled by Parliament. Anglicanism was strongest in Virginia, as persecuted Baptists and Presbyterians could testify, yet it was disestablished after the American Revolution. Only in Massachusetts and Connecticut did the Congregational structure remain powerful enough to endure into the nineteenth century. Even there, however, though rather grudgingly, a degree of religious liberty prevailed despite the intentions of Puritan leaders. This was partly the result of pressure from England, where

Protestant dissenters had finally cracked the wall of Anglican authority in 1689. Thus, the Royal Charter of Massachusetts in 1691 guaranteed that "there shall be liberty of conscience allowed, in the worship of God, to all Christians (except Papists)." With so many Quakers, Baptists, and Anglicans settled within its borders, Massachusetts Puritans were forced to compromise still further by the 1730's, permitting some dissenters to pay taxes to the church of their choice.

The Theological Reason: The Great Awakening. Periodically, bursts of religious enthusiasm swept through many congregations in the colonial period. An epidemic or other natural calamity, for example, would often bring frightened souls before the altar in large numbers. When fear receded, so did the religious fervor of the communicants. Particular ministers became adept at stirring audiences with evangelistic sermons. Thomas Prince, a famous Puritan divine, collected evidence of many local revivals in New England from 1660 to 1720. Jonathan Edwards, pastor at Northampton, Massachusetts, sparked a revival movement in the 1730's of such proportions, he reported, that "scarcely a single person in the whole town was left unconcerned about the great things of the eternal world." Usually it was a matter of time before the level of enthusiasm waned and the revival quietly passed away. At Northampton several residents who became despondent because they thought their souls were endangered, including Edwards' uncle, committed suicide. That ended the Northampton revival.

The Great Awakening of 1740–41 did not break unexpectedly upon an unsuspecting people. Many were already attuned to religious emotional stimuli, having experienced previous "mini-revivals." Nevertheless, despite some successful preaching, there had been numerous complaints of religious lassitude. Too many stayed away from church. Too many attended without a sense of commitment. Too many sermons were tedious, stylized, and repetitive. Too many churchmen were content to stress tradition, form, and proper standards while the spiritual core was moribund. Samuel Blair noted the "dead formality" of church life in Pennsylvania. Jonathan Edwards commented that people "do not so much need to have their heads stored as to have their hearts touched." Edwards brought theological distinction to the Great Awakening. His brilliant expositions defended the Calvinist doctrines of human depravity and predestination. Man was indeed a sinful creature, without redemption, Edwards taught, unless God chose to touch him with religious fire in the form of a

Preaching in fields, since the doors of churches were closed to him, George Whitefield drew huge crowds both in the colonies and in England. Even some of the skeptical reacted favorably. Benjamin Franklin listened to one of his sermons in 1740 and noted: "I perceived he intended to finish with a collection, and I silently resolved that he should get nothing from me. I had in my pocket a handful of copper money, three or four silver dollars, and five pistoles in gold. As he proceeded I began to soften and concluded to give the copper. Another stroke of his oratory made me ashamed of that and determined me to give the silver; and he finished so admirably that I emptied my pocket wholly into the collector's dish, gold and all." The regular clergy disliked the fanatical enthusiasm Whitefield's preaching evoked, and in England there were numerous examples of persecution and violence against evangelists. Pictured above is an artist's conception of Whitefield addressing followers in England in 1742. (Courtesy of the Periodical Department, Boston Public Library)

"saving" experience. The foremost preacher of the Great Awakening, however, was George Whitefield, whose sermons were "scaled down to the comprehension of twelve-year olds." Renowned in England, Whitefield became more so in America, preaching to enormous crowds in all parts of the country. Some listeners "were struck pale as Death," a contemporary wrote, "others wringing their hands, others lying on the ground, others sinking into the arms of their friends, and most lifting up their eyes toward heaven, and crying out to GOD." Whitefield himself reported that "the groans and outcries of the wounded were such that my voice could not be heard."

In one sense the Great Awakening was divisive. More conservative clerics deplored its excessive emotional displays. To men like Charles Chauncy, pastor of the First Church in Boston, individual salvation could not be achieved through an orgasm of religious frenzy. Such a person "mistakes the workings of his own passion for divine communication, and fancies himself immediately inspired by the spirit of God," wrote Chauncy, "when all the while, he is under no other influence than that of an overheated imagination." Many congregations split over the issue of revivalism. Departing members, known as "New Lights" (Congregationalists) or "New Sides" (Presbyterians), formed their own churches or joined the Baptists. These schisms, while bitter, were less significant than the deeper ecumenical effects of the Great Awakening upon American Protestantism. Revivalism may have been anti-intellectual, but it forced a degree of sober introspection and reformulation that shattered the old molds of religious thought. Seventeenth-century sects were narrow and intolerant, each jealously guarding the keys to heaven for its own membership. Now sects vanished and denominations began to sprout, less arrogant, less exclusive, and each following its own form of worship while recognizing the validity of others, for all promoted a common faith. As the idea of religious freedom blossomed, at least for Protestants, so the separation of church and state seemed to follow logically. "Establishments may be enabled to confer worldly distinctions and secular importance," James Manning told the Massachusetts delegates to the Continental Congress in 1774. "They may make hypocrites, but cannot create Christians." No denomination possessed the sole truth. No denomination should receive preferred political treatment. Despite its controversies and schisms, the Great Awakening, according to one scholar, "ended by establishing more firmly than ever the plurality of forces that made increased toleration, and finally full religious liberty, the most amenable solution for civic life."

The Philosophical Reason: Deism. Religious revivals were of psychological interest only to intellectuals who worshipped at a different shrine, that of science. Just as pietistic evangelists never doubted divine revelation, and trusted in "no creed but the Bible," so enlightenment thinkers were equally certain that human reason was the sole gateway to truth and knowledge. The findings of Galileo, Kepler, Descartes, Sir Isaac Newton, and others had unlocked the secrets of planetary movement, revealed the workings of gravity, and reduced motion itself to a formula. Eighteenth-century philosophers came to believe that the universe and all it contained was a giant mechanism, governed by immutable laws which could be discovered by man. If some traditionalists saw no conflict between science and scriptures, many rationalists found the two incompatible. "The indissoluble connection between earth and heaven," wrote John Quincy Adams, "is palpable and unquestionable." Thomas Paine, on the other hand, could not see how science and traditional Christianity could be "held together in the same mind." God to the rationalists was not an omnipotent and wrathful deity to whom one prayed, but a master mechanic; not a Trinitarian miracle worker in the human image, but a God of nature who had created an ordered and structured world yet did not interfere with its operation.

Such beliefs, called deism, circulated mainly among the educated classes. Some, like Paine, were distinctly anticlerical. In 1794 Paine wrote a blistering attack upon what he considered the fictions and fables of organized religion in *The Age of Reason*. Most American deists, however, were men of moderation and practicality. They might agree privately that Paine was right, but publicly they remained discreetly silent. First of all, they found Christian teaching, stripped of its superstitions, an admirable ethical code for society to emulate. Thomas Jefferson was profoundly influenced by Joseph Priestley's *An History of the Corruptions of Christianity*. Yet he attended church, and advised his grandson to read the Bible as one would read Tacitus or Livy, with critical detachment and moral purpose. In other hands deism became a form of skepticism, a step toward atheism, but to Jefferson natural law, moral law, and religious law were complementary. Second, many deists feared that militant attacks upon organized religion would promote upheavals by destroying an effective institution for the social control of the common people. Deism was fine for the elite, but dangerous for the masses. "Talking against religion," Benjamin Franklin warned, "is unchaining a tiger; the beast let loose may worry his liberator."

Since deists believed in no church, yet saw merit in all, they championed religious liberty. Moreover, as enlightenment intellectuals they concluded that freedom of conscience was a natural right, not subject to the demand or will of government. Thus, for a brief historical moment, two forces with opposite thrusts—a pietistic movement with faith in divine revelation, and a philosophical movement with confidence in human reason—combined to effect the same ends. Their triumph was contained in the opening words of the first amendment to the Constitution: "Congress shall make no law respecting an establishment of religion, or prohibiting the free exercise thereof."

"It is impossible not to be sensible," Thomas Jefferson wrote, "that we are acting for all mankind." If one does not include several million defeated Indians and enslaved blacks, his words had the ring of truth. The United States was "a bold, sublime experiment" to see whether white men could live harmoniously in a society founded on liberty and equality. America as yet had little culture of its own—no painters to match Goya, no composers like Mozart, no legal philosophers to equal Blackstone, no sculptors as accomplished as Thorvaldsen—nor did America possess an established church, a titled aristocracy, a large standing army, or monarchical government. The Americans had jettisoned the institutional machinery of European authoritarianism to test, for the first time in history, the possibility of a working democracy.

SUGGESTED READINGS

*Bernard Bailyn, *The Ideological Origins of the American Revolution*
*Barton J. Bernstein, *Towards a New Past*
*Carl Bridenbaugh, *Myths and Realities*
*Carl Degler, *Neither Black Nor White*
*Evarts B. Greene, *Religion and the State*
Richard M. Gummere, *The American Colonial Mind and the Classical Traditions*
*Marcus L. Hansen, *The Atlantic Migration*
Richard Hofstadter, *America at 1750*
*Marcus W. Jernegan, *Laboring and Dependent Classes in Colonial America*
*Winthrop Jordan, *White Over Black*
*Michael Kraus, *The Atlantic Civilization*
*Leonard W. Labaree, *Conservatism in Early American History*
Aubrey Land, *The Dulanys of Maryland*
Lawrence Leder, *Robert Livingston*

*Jackson T. Main, *The Social Structure of Revolutionary America*
Robert Middlekauff, *Ancients and Axioms*
*Perry Miller, *Jonathan Edwards*
Roy H. Pearce, *The Savages of America*
Donald L. Robinson, *Slavery in the Structure of American Politics*
*Max Savelle, *Seeds of Liberty*
*Marshall Smelser, *The Democratic Republic*
*Abbot E. Smith, *Colonists in Bondage*
William W. Sweet, *Religion in Colonial America*
Oscar Zeichner, *Connecticut's Years of Controversy*

* Available in paperback

PROBLEMS OF A
NEW NATION
1789/1815

5

AN AGE OF ARGONAUTS

Twentieth-century African and Asian nations emerging from colonial status to independence have problems which the United States did not face in 1789: a lack of trained personnel, overpopulation, immense poverty, linguistic conflicts, tribal warfare, even foreign invasion. By comparison the new American nation was rapidly recovering from the dislocations of the postrevolutionary period. Her economic potential was vast. Her geographical isolation afforded security. Her British ancestry and colonial experience had prepared her for the rigors of self-government. And her political leadership was magnificent. No other period of American history contained such an array: George Washington, John Adams, Alexander Hamilton, Thomas Jefferson, James Madison, and many lesser figures invested their political quarrels with philosophical dignity.

Washington. As commander in chief of the revolutionary armies and again at the constitutional convention in Philadelphia he had served the nation well. Though he longed to remain at Mount Vernon, he accepted the presidency in 1789 out of a sense of duty. Neither an original thinker nor daring innovator nor administrative reformer, he was dedicated, incorruptible, and the one person that Americans venerated. "If the President can be preserved a few years," wrote Jefferson in 1790, "till habits of authority and obedience can be established generally, we have nothing to fear." By serving as chief executive for eight years, by rejecting opportunities to convert the government into a constitutional monarchy or a military regime, and by avoiding foreign wars and stifling domestic insurrections, Washington contributed the one ingredient indispensable to the success of the infant republic: time.

Hamilton. Although he would have preferred a different document, Hamilton signed the Constitution at Philadelphia, supported its ratification at the New York convention, and defended its contents as co-author of *The Federalist.* Hamilton had no particular affection for local and state interests. He thought only in national terms, and throughout the 1790's he labored to strengthen the central government. Critics accused him and his Federalist supporters of authoritarian inclinations. But Washington trusted Hamilton, valued his opinions, and appointed him America's first secretary of the treasury. In that post Hamilton performed brilliantly. His recommendations, implemented by Congress, provided economic stability for the new government by restoring public credit.

Madison. More than any other man, he deserved to be called the "father of the Constitution." After 1789 he sat in the lower house and was instrumental in devising the Bill of Rights. But Madison's constitutional creations, when put into operation, did not function as he thought they would. Parts of Hamilton's financial program upset him. Their effect, he thought, would be to enrich speculators at the expense of honest taxpayers, and to increase federal powers at the expense of state's rights. If the Constitution could be so perverted, Madison concluded, perhaps Hamilton's real aim for America was monarchy. Thus, he attempted to block the Hamiltonian system by working to form a party of opposition, the Democratic-Republicans. By choosing peaceful and legitimate means of dissent—not blood, but ballots—Madison added a vital dimension to the development of American democracy.

Adams. Although he served the public long and faithfully, Adams felt both unappreciated and misunderstood. Many interpreted his love of titles and fancy dress, and his concept of the aristocrat's role in society, to be nothing more than a veiled admiration of monarchy. When Adams suggested that Washington be called "His Majesty, the President," a wag responded by labeling Adams "His Rotundity." Actually, Adams's political position was between those of Hamilton and Jefferson. As president after 1797 he proved to be a leader of remarkable fortitude, one who placed country before party. He contributed the lesson of moderation when America was wracked by political dissension.

Jefferson. Of the early American statesmen, Jefferson was the most western-minded. He conceived of America as a unique experiment, destined for greatness as long as it faced westward and avoided European infection. When Jefferson served as George Washington's secretary of state, the French minister commented: "Jefferson . . . is an American, and as such, he cannot sincerely be our friend. An American is the born enemy of all the peoples of Europe." The Federalists pictured Jefferson as a doctrinaire radical, an impractical and abstract theorist, even worse, a philosopher of revolution. Nothing could have been further from the truth. The right of revolution, to Jefferson, was the last resort of an oppressed people. Where legal and political means of redress were open, revolution was unnecessary. Certainly Jefferson was idealistic and introspective, but he was also eminently practical. "I can never fear that things will go far wrong," he once wrote, "where common sense has fair play." Jefferson's sacrifice of theoretical opinions to common-sense solutions became an essential part of the American political process.

THE GROWTH OF POLITICAL PARTIES

Although the Founding Fathers understood factions, they had not envisioned the growth of political parties. In 1789 Americans abhorred parties as the tools of unscrupulous politicians, serving only to divide the people. "If I could not go to heaven but with a party," Jefferson said, "I would not go there at all." Washington warned the people "against the baneful effects of the spirit of party" in his Farewell Address. Nevertheless, parties continued to develop. By the close of the century there were two national organizations, the Democratic-Republicans and the Federalists. Political campaigning became socially acceptable in most regions. Voters were asked to support party tickets. Candidates who had previously boasted of their independence now stressed their partisan loyalties. There were even signs that Americans were beginning to appreciate the role of parties in representative government. "Perhaps," Jefferson wrote in 1798, "party division is necessary to induce each other to watch and relate to the people the proceedings of the other."

The two-party system developed outside the Constitution, primarily in response to two events: Hamilton's financial program, and the French Revolution. One issue touched the pocketbooks, and the other the loyalties of all Americans. As a result partisan passions ran fever high in the 1790's. Some doubted that the country could survive.

HAMILTON'S PROGRAM

Hamilton's program was contained in a series of reports delivered to Congress. Summarized and simplified, his major proposals were as follows:

1. The national government would pay its revolutionary war debt, both principal and interest, by means of funding—that is, the government would by selling bonds take on a *new debt*, and the money collected would be used to pay the *old debt*.
2. The national government would also assume the revolutionary war debts of the states. The combined national and state indebtedness totaled about $79 million.
3. A system of excise taxes would be enacted to supplement tariff revenues. These funds would be used to meet the interest payments and part of the principal of the new debt.
4. A sinking fund would also be created, to buy the new bonds whenever their market value fell below their par value.
5. A semipublic Bank of the United States would be chartered by Congress.
6. Manufacturing would be stimulated by a protective tariff, by government subsidies, by awards for inventions, by quality controls, and by encouraging foreign artisans to emigrate to the United States.

The revolutionary war debt, Hamilton argued, "was the price of liberty." Its prompt payment was not only morally indisputable but economically indispensable if the credit of the country was to be maintained. Equally important to Hamilton, however, was the new debt. He did not think that the Constitution would endure if it depended upon the goodwill and shaky nationalism of the population. If the rich and powerful were given an economic stake in the government, he felt, their loyalty would be ensured. By selling government bonds and bank stock—which only the wealthy could afford—the purchasers would be committed to support the federal government out of the strongest motive, economic self-interest. The new public debt, he hoped, would be a blessing, acting to bind together the Union.

BEGINNING OF DISSENSION

Madison did not doubt that the debts of the Revolution should be paid —but to whom? Many patriots who had invested their savings in the revolutionary cause, or who had earned bonds by service in the army, were forced during the recession years of the 1780's to part with them at a fraction of their face value. Even while Hamilton's program was being debated by Congress, speculation was rampant. Should not the original purchaser receive some share of the payment, instead of giving it all to "unconscionable speculators"? Madison wanted the payments divided, but Hamilton insisted that the government was bound to pay only the current holders of the debt. Adoption of Madison's proposal, explained Hamilton, "would tend to dissolve all social obligations—to render all rights precarious and to introduce a general dissoluteness and corruption of morals."

The morals of a good many members of Congress were already corrupted by the fact that they were speculating in these securities, and Madison's motion was defeated by a vote of 36 to 13. An angry poet commented:

> "A soldier's pay are rags and fame,
> A wooden leg–a deathless name.
> To specs, both *in* and *out* of Cong
> The four and six per cents belong!"

DEBATES OVER ASSUMPTION

Congressional nerves first began to fray over the issue of the assumption of state debts by the national government. Those in favor, representing states with heavy indebtedness—such as Massachusetts, New York, and South Carolina—alternately pled for and demanded its enactment. South Carolina, said one of her representatives, "was no more able to grapple with her enormous debt, than a boy of twelve years of age is able to grapple with a giant." Those opposed, representing states with little or no indebtedness—among them Maryland, North Carolina, and Georgia—obstinately refused to have the national government absorb these obligations. "I trust we shall not run ourselves enormously into debt, and mortgage ourselves and our children," argued the representative from Georgia, "to give scope to the abilities of any Minister on earth." The Virginia delegates also argued against assumption, contending that their constituents would be doubly penalized by the measure. Their state, using land warrants and depreciated currency, had lowered its considerable debt by some 40 per cent. Could not Massachusetts do the same? Why turn to the national government for relief? Why should Virginians be taxed to pay the debts of other—mainly northern—states? After a lengthy and acrimonious debate, assumption was defeated in April 1790, 31 to 29.

For all the laments of the losers—many of whom had been speculating in state securities—assumption was not really vital to prosperity. But it was essential to Hamilton's scheme of enlarging and consolidating national power. By assuming state debts the national government could eventually dominate the country's revenue sources. The political consequences of assumption were so significant to Hamilton that he bargained with Jefferson to reverse the congressional decision. Hamilton promised to have the national capital, after a decade in Philadelphia, moved permanently to the Potomac, if Jefferson would use his influence to change several opposing representatives' votes. The arrangement was agreed to and assumption passed. "Of all the errors of my political life," Jefferson later remarked, this bargain "has occasioned me the deepest regret."

CONFLICT OVER THE BANK

The measure to charter the Bank of the United States precipitated the sharpest sectional division Congress had yet experienced. Northern congressmen, repeating the arguments in Hamilton's report, stressed the invaluable contributions which could be made by a national bank: it would loan money to the government during emergencies; it would provide a sound and extensive currency; and it would stimulate business by increasing the fluid capital necessary for economic expansion. Southern congressmen viewed the Bank as an unmitigated evil: it would benefit capitalist and mercantile classes at the expense of agrarian interests; it would, as a financial monopoly, be capable of controlling and corrupting every operation of the government; and it was, as James Madison emphasized, patently unconstitutional, since Congress had no authority to charter a corporation. The Banking Act passed 39 to 20, but of the majority, 33 votes were northern and only 6 southern; while, of the minority, 19 votes were southern and only 1 northern.

The arguments of his three fellow Virginians—Madison, Randolph, and Jefferson—failed to convince Washington, and on February 25, 1791, he signed the act.

EXCISE AND REBELLION

Hamilton felt that Americans drank too much "ardent spirits," and in *Federalist* No. 12 he had advised that the tariff on imported liquors be trebled. The effect, he noted, "would be equally favorable to agriculture, to the economy, to the morals, and to the health of society." At that time he doubted that an internal tax on alcohol could be imposed because of America's traditional hostility to excises. Yet, scarcely three years later, Hamilton included an excise in his recommendations to Congress. The nation, he said, could not rely solely on tariff revenues. He was reluctant to suggest a direct tax on land. Thus an excise seemed the most equitable means of raising the additional funds to pay the debt. Some scholars also suspect that Hamilton realized that an excise would foment trouble in the western regions, and that he relished the idea of giving the central government an opportunity to use its yet untested powers of enforcement.

Westerners did indeed consume a good deal of whiskey. One congressman boasted that his constituents "have been long in the habit

When Hamilton recommended an excise tax on whiskey, his motive was not only to secure revenue for the government, but also to make citizens aware of a strong central authority. This cartoon indicates the antifederal feeling that developed along with the excise tax and the strengthening of the federal government. (Courtesy of Atwater Kent Museum and *American Heritage*)

AN EXCISEMAN. *Carrying off two Kegs of Whiskey, is pursued by two farmers, intending to tar and feather him. he runs for 'Squire Vultures to divide with him; but is met on the way by his evil genius who claps an hook in his nose. leads him off to a Gallows. where he is immediately hanged*

of getting drunk, and they will get drunk in defiance of . . . all the excise duties Congress might be weak or wicked enough to impose." But farmers also used whiskey for medicine and currency. It was easier to ship whiskey than grain across the Alleghenies for sale in eastern markets. After the tax passed in 1791, discontent centered in Washington County, Pennsylvania. The farmers there refused to pay the tax and intimidated those who did; collectors were harassed; a few extremists threatened to secede from Pennsylvania and the union. Having listened to contradictory opinions from his cabinet—Hamilton, of course, insisted that force must be used—Washington in 1794 ordered the militia of four states assembled to march into western Pennsylvania and suppress the "armed banditti." Led by Washington, with Hamilton at his side, 12,600 troops made the long trek west, only to find that the alleged rebellion had evaporated. Twenty rag-tag prisoners were taken. Two were convicted of treason, and though Hamilton wished a maximum punishment imposed, both were pardoned by Washington. Thus ended the Whiskey Rebellion. "An insurrection was announced and proclaimed and armed against," was Jefferson's sardonic comment, "but could never be found."

RESULTS OF HAMILTON'S PROGRAM

With one exception, the Report on Manufactures, every part of Hamilton's program was approved by Congress and endorsed by Washington. That report was greeted with indifference, even hostility. Later generations hailed it as a brilliant exposition of policy for an industrial America, but in the 1790's few statesmen possessed Hamilton's vision. The high protective tariff it proposed seemed equally detrimental to the economic interests of southern planters and northern merchants, and it was pigeonholed.

Nevertheless, Hamilton had succeeded in turning old devalued bonds into sound marketable securities, in restoring the credit of a nation verging on bankruptcy, and in providing America with a banking system vital to its prosperity. He had done so, however, at the price of considerable dissension. Aimed at enhancing the authority of the national government, his policies evoked strong opposition to it. As early as December 1790, Patrick Henry drafted a remonstrance for the Virginia legislature warning that the assumption of state debts would "produce one or other of two evils, the prostration of agriculture at the feet of commerce, or a change in the present form of federal government, fatal to the existence of American liberty." Hamilton responded that the remonstrance was "the first symptom of a spirit which must either be killed, or will kill the Constitution of the United States." But the symptoms persisted. The Whiskey Rebellion was an obvious sign of the deep sectional and economic rivalries stimulated by Hamilton's policies. Would there be still other civil conflicts? And if so, would the Constitution follow the fate of the Articles?

THE FRENCH REVOLUTION

In addition to the disagreement over financial legislation, hostility between the Federalists and their Democratic-Republican opponents was increased by their divergent attitudes toward the French Revolution. In 1789, when news of a revolution in France was announced, virtually all Americans were overwhelmingly sympathetic to its cause. But by 1793, as the revolutionaries turned to violence, conservative classes in the United States became increasingly hostile to their methods and principles.

Federalist Position. Federalists stressed the "reign of terror" which swept across France, taking hundreds of lives. They lamented the death of Louis XVI, the monarch who had supported America's liberation from England. They argued that the French had used the specious mottoes, "liberty, equality, and fraternity," as magic sounds to sequester property, annihilate religion, abandon republicanism, and instigate wars. What nonsense to compare the American and the French revolutions. "Ours," said John Adams at a later date, "was resistance to innovation; theirs was innovation itself." The Federalists preferred to follow the English example of order and stability based on a balance between aristocratic rule and democratic privilege.

Republican Position. Republicans were certain that the French were fighting for the same goals Americans sought in 1776: the overthrow of monarchy and the establishment of republicanism. The French and Americans were revolutionary brothers, rejecting the past, seeking the golden age of human freedom. The Declaration of Rights, like the Declaration of Independence, was a commitment to liberty and human equality. The bloodshed from the revolution was unfortunate. "But rather than it should have failed," wrote Jefferson, "I would have seen half the earth desolated; were there but an Adam and an Eve left in every country, and left free, it would be better than as it now is." England, to Republicans, was still the stepmother country, home of the obsolete common law, an oppressive monarchy, and an entrenched, arrogant aristocracy.

INVOLVEMENT OR NEUTRALITY?

The French declaration of war on England in February 1793 posed an immediate problem for Washington's administration. Morally, many Americans considered it simple justice to assist the French. "Remember," a New York paper told its readers, "who stood between you and the clanking chains of British ministerial despotism." Legally, the United States was bound by the Treaty of 1778 to "forever" aid in the defense of the French West Indies.

Involvement, however, would mean war with Britain, and other Americans considered such a course the ultimate calamity. Washington again sought the advice of his cabinet, and they unanimously— though for different reasons—recommended a policy of neutrality. A presidential proclamation of neutrality was issued in April, and confirmed by an act of Congress the following year. But there were few who could set aside their personal biases.

CITIZEN EDMOND GENÊT

When the first minister sent to the United States by the French Republic, Edmond Genêt, arrived in Charleston, he was accorded an enthusiastic reception. His trip to Philadelphia rang with constant ovations, and at the capital zealous Francophiles received him with patriotic speeches and testimonial dinners. Washington was displeased with Genêt's actions. At Charleston the minister had commissioned privateers to capture British ships, and had conspired with George Rogers Clark to attack Spanish territory. He continued these activities in Philadelphia, even after the neutrality proclamation, and defied Washington by directly courting public favor. The president's displeasure turned to monumental anger. "Is the minister of the French republic to set the acts of this government at defiance *with impunity?*" he raged, "and then threaten the executive with an appeal to the people? What must the world think of such conduct, and of the government of the United States in submitting to it?"

Jefferson realized that Genêt had become a liability to the Republican party. The entire cabinet decided that the French minister must be recalled. At the same time the French asked the United States to recall her minister, Gouverneur Morris, because of his royalist sympathies and intrigues. Morris returned, but Genêt, believing that he would be guillotined, remained in the United States, eventually mar-

Although the Jeffersonian Republicans gave Genêt an enthusiastic reception when he arrived in Charleston, Jefferson himself soon saw the damage Genêt could do to his party. Genêt's plottings to outfit privateers and his disregard for American neutrality antagonized Washington, who asked the French government to recall Genêt. Pictured here is an artist's conception of a disturbed Jefferson receiving Genêt in Philadelphia. (Courtesy of Culver Pictures, New York City)

ried the daughter of Governor George Clinton, and settled in the Hudson Valley to live as a rich country gentleman.

JAY'S TREATY

Washington attempted to stop the deterioration of French-American relations by appointing James Monroe, a strong sympathizer with the revolutionary cause, as the minister to France. But a Treaty of

Triumph Government: perish all its enemies.—
Traitors, be warned: justice though slow, is sure.

By 1795 the Republican press pictured George Washington as a dictator, a traitor to republicanism and an enemy to liberty, and demanded his impeachment. They compared him to Caesar and Cromwell, questioned the value of his leadership during the Revolution, and accused him of "forcing the philosophic patriot (Jefferson) who first occupied the Department of State . . . to seek an humble retirement." The Federalist press was equally scurrilous, as the above cartoon indicates. A dog lifts its leg on a Republican newspaper; Jefferson, speaking in a French accent, is seen trying to "stop de wheels of de gouvernement"; and Washington in a chariot is leading his troops to suppress an invasion of the French "cannibals." (Courtesy of the New-York Historical Society)

Commerce and Amity which John Jay, the new minister to Britain, negotiated in 1794 was interpreted by the French as an Anglo-American alliance. The "cold war" with France deepened, and eventually culminated in an undeclared naval war.

Jay's Treaty was not an alliance, but American critics considered it a disgraceful and humiliating surrender to British power. The only major gain for the United States was Britain's agreement to evacuate her northwest posts. Yet this was hardly a concession, since that land had belonged to the United States since 1783. British subjects were specifically given permission to continue fur-trading activities with Indian tribes in American territory. Britain also obtained an agreement from the United States government to pay prerevolutionary war debts owed by American citizens to British merchants; however, Britain refused to pay for slaves they had seized from Americans during the war. Most important, Jay abandoned the American position that "free ships make free goods," and accepted the British rule that enemy cargoes on neutral vessels were liable to seizure. Another provision allowed American merchants to trade with the British West Indies, but only in ships of less than 70 tons carrying capacity; in exchange the United States would prohibit, for 10 years, the export of sugar, coffee, cotton, or cacao in American vessels. This legal entry to the British West Indian market was so qualified that the American government struck it from the treaty.

Washington's decision to recommend ratification of Jay's Treaty, with all its obvious defects, has been applauded by most scholars. The only alternative seemed to be a war with Britain for which the United States was not prepared militarily, and which would have wrecked Hamilton's financial system and depressed the economy. Appeasement bought time; war would have been a catastrophe. Moreover, Jay's Treaty—together with that signed by Pinckney with Spain the following year—secured the frontier and opened the Mississippi River to American trade.

WASHINGTON RETIRES

The Democratic-Republicans tried to block the ratification of Jay's Treaty in the Senate. Failing there, they continued their opposition in the lower house. Not until May 1, 1796, by a vote of 51 to 48, did Congress appropriate the funds necessary to implement the treaty. During this period of bitter partisanship Washington was subjected to vilification in newspapers, pamphlets, and speeches. One rabid Democratic-Republican wished Washington's "hand had been cut off when his glory was at its height, before he blasted all his laurels." A Virginian offered a toast to the "speedy death of General Washington." Little wonder that the president did not wish a third term, or that his famous Farewell Address deplored the development of political parties and advised America to steer clear of permanent foreign entanglements. Although he was still revered by most Americans, Washington was happy to escape further political abuse by retiring to

Mount Vernon. "The President is fortunate to get off just as the bubble is bursting," wrote Jefferson in 1797, "leaving others to hold the bag."

NEGOTIATION AND PREPARATION

Lacking Washington's prestige and charismatic authority, without a first-rate cabinet, and winner of the presidential office over Jefferson by a scant three electoral votes, John Adams faced the problems of a divided people and aggravated relations with the French. American ships were being seized and their cargoes confiscated. American sailors found aboard British ships—whether or not they had been impressed—were threatened with hanging if captured by the French. The American minister sent to replace Monroe, Charles C. Pinckney, was insulted and ordered to leave the country.

Despite their bellicose attitude, Adams chose to continue negotiations with the French. But, lest his policy fail, he also advised Congress to prepare for war.

THE XYZ AFFAIR

John Marshall of Virginia and Elbridge Gerry of Massachusetts were selected to join Pinckney in a bipartisan delegation which Adams hoped would "by its dignity . . . satisfy France." For months Americans waited anxiously for news. Would the French attitude change? Could a satisfactory accommodation of grievances be arranged? Or would the United States go to war? "The mind of Congress as well as the rest of the world," an observer noted, "seems suspended as to the measures our nation should adopt in relation to France, upon the expectation of intelligence to be received from our Commissioners." Finally, in March 1798, Congress requested and Adams released the diplomatic papers. They told of a complex attempt at international blackmail. Instead of being officially received by the French foreign minister, Talleyrand, the Americans were greeted by his agents (labeled X, Y, and Z), who first demanded a large personal bribe, then a substantial "loan" for the French government and a public apology from President Adams for allegedly anti-French remarks. When the three Americans answered "no; no; not a sixpence," negotiations ceased. Here, said Adams, was "proof as strong as Holy Writ" of French perfidy.

The American people agreed. A wave of anti-Gallic sentiment swept the country. Addresses and testimonials supporting the administration flooded in on Adams. The Federalist party seemed rejuvenated. They had always been respected; but now, for the first time, they experienced the heady sensation of popularity. The Republicans, on the other hand, were "confounded," one Federalist gleefully reported, "and the trimmers dropped off from the party like wind-falls from an apple tree in September." Joseph Hopkinson's patriotic composition, "Hail Columbia," became an immediate success. When John Marshall returned from France he was greeted with the same wild acclaim Genêt had enjoyed a few years earlier. Adams was so moved by the emotional display that he proclaimed a day of "Public Humiliation, Fasting and Prayer throughout the United States."

THE UNDECLARED NAVAL WAR

Before the XYZ revelations Congress had taken a largely defensive military posture, appropriating funds to fortify harbors, prohibiting the export of arms and ammunition, authorizing the equipment of three frigates, and increasing the number of revenue cutters. But since there was no American navy to speak of, French corsairs boldly attacked American shipping as far north as Long Island Sound. Marine insurance for vessels trading in the Caribbean rose to an astronomical 33 per cent of the value of the ship and its cargo. The United States appeared weak and vulnerable, certainly no match for a mighty European power such as France.

However, news of the XYZ incident prompted Congress to enact positive military measures. In June 1798 all commercial relations with France were suspended. In July, the capture of armed vessels sailing under the French flag was authorized. In that same month all treaties with France were declared void and inoperative. The army was strengthened, the militia was increased, taxes were raised, and, most important, the navy was enlarged. "It is gratifying to behold the military spirit which prevails," a Federalist wrote. "When such a spirit exists our country cannot be in danger." In all but name, America was at war.

Britain agreed to protect American transatlantic shipping, thus freeing the United States navy to comb the Caribbean of French warships and privateers. The task was accomplished quickly and effectively, and American merchant vessels soon sailed the Caribbean, if not with impunity, at least with reasonable safety. Before the quasi-war was ended by the Convention of 1800, the previously untested American navy had vanquished the French in eight of their nine engagements. To many Americans this feat redeemed national honor and strengthened national confidence.

THE ALIEN AND SEDITION ACTS

The fever of the XYZ affair might have been sustained, and the naval victories utilized to the advantage of the Federalists. But in their anxiety to maintain power they blundered—and lost it.

The Federalists believed that the Republicans were carriers of dangerous revolutionary doctrines, that their criticisms of the government were tantamount to treason, and that they had to be suppressed in order to save the United States from anarchy. Particularly disturbing was the presence of aliens and immigrants from England and Ireland, and French Jacobins, who propagated radical ideas, and who invariably joined the Republican party. Between May and July 1798 the Federalist-dominated Congress enacted a series of Alien and Sedition Laws, designed to silence such political opposition.

1. The Naturalization Act extended the residence requirement for citizenship from 5 to 14 years.

2. The Alien Act gave the president authority to banish any foreigner whom he thought "dangerous to the peace and safety of the United States."

3. The Alien Enemies Act permitted the president to arrest and expel any aliens of a nation with which the United States was officially at war.

4. The Sedition Act made it a crime to say or write anything "false, scandalous, and malicious" about the president or Congress. The act specified that the truth could not be considered seditious. Since most judges were Federalist, however, the safeguard proved worthless. Dissent was equated with disloyalty. Conformity was equated with patriotism. "He that is not for us," concluded an administration newspaper, "is against us."

The effect was quite the opposite of what the Federalists intended. Jefferson believed the Alien and Sedition Acts to be a crucial test: if the American people could be duped into accepting repressive measures, then there was little hope for democracy. The task of the Republican party was to employ every legal means possible to stop what Jefferson sincerely thought to be a first step toward monarchy. As a tactical response Jefferson and Madison authored, respectively, the Kentucky and Virginia Resolutions, which declared that the Alien and

Sedition Acts violated state sovereignty and were therefore "void and of no force." As a practical response the two leaders attempted to alert public opinion to the dangers of authoritarian government. Hundreds of petitions of protest poured into Congress from Republicans in all sections of the country. While Republican editors were jailed under the Sedition Act, other Republican papers were started.

The unity of the Republican party, badly splintered by the XYZ furor, was restored. "The Alien and Sedition Acts," wrote Jefferson, "have . . . operated as powerful sedatives of the XYZ inflammation." The Federalists had handed Jefferson a significant domestic issue which diverted attention from his defense of France, and which he could use very effectively in the presidential campaign of 1800.

THE NEW MISSION

The long friendship of Adams and Jefferson, strained by political quarrels during the Washington Administration, was shattered by the Alien and Sedition Acts, the XYZ affair, and the naval war with France. Adams had contributed to the public hysteria by bellicose addresses in 1798, yet he had not requested Congress formally to declare war. Federalist extremists had exerted pressures on him to make such a recommendation. Moderate Federalists, including Alexander Hamilton, were content to keep the ill-feeling against France brewing without an official declaration of hostilities. Either way, so long as the public recognized France to be the national enemy, so the Federalists reasoned, the continuation of their political control was guaranteed.

Adams's position, however, had quietly shifted from hawk to dove. In February 1799 he announced the appointment of a new diplomatic mission to France. The entire country, reported his wife Abigail, reacted "like a flock of frightened pigeons." The Republicans were elated; the Federalists divided. Some approved, others were stunned, puzzled, mortified, or incensed. Hamilton's followers, their eyes on the ballot box, considered the peace mission "embarrassing and ruinous" to the Federalist cause. Adams had placed his country before his party. He had performed a sacrificial political act, paving the way for Republican victory in the next election, but one which he never regretted. "I desire no other inscription over my gravestone," Adams later wrote, "than: 'Here lies John Adams, who took upon himself the responsibility for peace with France in the year 1800.'"

THE ELECTION OF 1800

Despite the split in the Federalist party during the election, in which Hamilton campaigned openly for Charles C. Pinckney, the peace mission was popular and Adams was only narrowly defeated. But the result was complicated by a tied electoral vote between the Republican candidates, Jefferson and Aaron Burr. A choice between the two fell, by constitutional provision, to the House of Representatives.

Hamilton exerted all his diminishing influence to persuade Federalists to support Jefferson as the lesser of two evils. The Federalists, however, would not heed his advice, and voted unanimously for Burr. Jefferson, they reasoned, would systematically destroy the edifice they had labored to construct over the past decade; Burr, they felt intuitively, was a self-seeking politician with whom they could bargain. The Republicans in Congress just as adamantly supported Jefferson. "We are resolved," wrote a Virginia Republican, "never to yield." Thirty-five ballots were taken without either party obtaining the necessary plurality. What would happen if the deadlock continued and no choice were made? Without a constitutionally elected president by inauguration day, the Constitution must perish. Political passions soared. Attempts to bribe members of Congress were rumored. The governor of Pennsylvania threatened to march on Washington with militia if the Federalists thwarted the majority's will. Finally, a few moderate Federalists broke with their party, casting blank ballots and thereby giving the presidency to Jefferson. The precedent of a legal opposition obtaining power by persuasion and not revolution—a prime condition for successful popular government—was established.

JEFFERSON'S PROGRAM

For years the Federalists had predicted dire consequences if Jefferson were elected. He would restore state power at the expense of national authority. He would ally the United States to France, and America would suffer all the excesses of revolutionary change. To the Federalists, the Virginia radical was the political devil incarnate, who could be expected to attack the Bank, the military, the judiciary, commercial interests, even organized religion. Instead, Jefferson shocked everyone by extending the olive branch. "We have called by different names brethren of the same principle," said Jefferson in his inaugural address. "We are all republicans—we are all federalists." His words were a plea to end partisan bickering, to replace past bitterness with a spirit of trust and harmony, above all to think in terms of America, not of European conflicts.

Jefferson offered no sweeping program of remedial legislation to replace the work of the Federalists. Rather, he simply suggested removing a number of Federalist laws and practices. Personal liberty, governmental economy, and social simplicity were to be the hallmarks of his administration. Thus, the Alien and Sedition Acts were permitted to lapse. Excise taxes were abolished. The elegant levees of Washington and Adams were replaced by simple receptions. The military budget was cut. Ministerial posts in Holland, Portugal, and Prussia were withdrawn. Jefferson's secretary of the treasury, the able Albert Gallatin, was instructed to devise a plan for the gradual extinction of the national debt.

If the election of 1800 was a revolution, it was a mild one, and Federalist leaders did not know how to cope with it. Although they greeted each successive Republican move with laments and threats, the public remained unconvinced. The churches remained standing. No bloodbaths took place. The country continued to prosper. Far from the metaphysician the Federalists had pictured, Jefferson proved an enormously capable politician.

JEFFERSON AND THE JUDICIARY

Having lost control of both the executive and legislative branches, the Federalists took refuge in the judiciary. Jefferson ordered an attack upon the courts which the Federalists resisted tenaciously. Their funereal dirge turned into shrieks of frightened rage. Actually, the Republican attack was restrained, justified, and based entirely on political—not theoretical—grounds. Federalist judges, not judicial power, were the target.

In 1802 the Republicans attempted to repeal a judiciary law, enacted the previous year, which had created 16 new circuit courts, to which Adams had appointed only members of his own party. The Federalists argued that Congress had no right to repeal the act, since the Constitution specified that the salaries of judges could not be diminished, nor could they be removed from office while exercising "good behaviour." They accused Jefferson and his lieutenants of upsetting the highly sensitive federal balance of power, of destroying the independence of the judiciary, and of thereby wrecking the Constitution. The Republicans responded by quoting another section of the Constitution which explicitly gave to Congress the authority to establish—and logically thus to abolish—inferior federal courts. Were this not so, they argued, a defeated party could establish thousands of judicial sinecures to be filled by their members. The repealing act passed. Its only effect was to reduce the number of courts.

Federalist congressmen called upon Chief Justice John Marshall, asking him to outmaneuver the Republicans by persuading the Supreme Court to declare the repealing act unconstitutional. Marshall wisely refused to do so, much to their disappointment. In 1803, however, he won the esteem of his party for his masterful opinion in the case of *Marbury* v. *Madison*. William Marbury, a Federalist appointed to a minor judicial post by John Adams, had not received his commission. Signed and sealed, it had been overlooked in the rush and confusion of changing administrations. Now Marbury asked the Court for a writ of *mandamus* ordering the Republican secretary of state, James Madison, to deliver the commission. Had Marshall issued the writ, it would have been ignored. Instead, speaking for the Court, Marshall declared that the writ could not be issued, because section 13 of the Judiciary Act of 1789, which gave the Court authority to do so, was unconstitutional. Marbury's job was lost. But the precedent of judicial review of federal legislation was established.

Jefferson's response was typical. Privately he was incensed by the decision, for he never considered the Supreme Court the ultimate arbiter of constitutional issues. As president, however, not wishing to arouse ebbing partisan emotions over the question of judicial review, he did nothing.

Understandable, but ill-considered, were the Republican impeachments of two Federalist judges in 1803–05. District Court Justice John Pickering was insane and should not have been tried. Several Republican congressmen were squeamish about convicting a deranged man. By a strict party vote, however, Pickering was found guilty. Associate Justice Samuel Chase was not insane, but he had conducted cases in an outrageously biased manner, and had expressed from the bench the most prejudiced opinions concerning Republicans. To convict Chase the Senate would require construing his actions as legal crimes or misdemeanors, which clearly they were not. Several Republicans broke party ranks to vote with the Federalists, and Chase was acquitted. "Impeachment," stated Jefferson, "is a farce which will not be tried again."

THE PURCHASE OF LOUISIANA

The Federalists could not awaken any serious public discontent over the judiciary, but for a time they believed another national problem might carry them back into power. Ever since 1800 it had been rumored that Spain had ceded the Louisiana territory to France. By 1802, when the port of New Orleans was closed to American traffic, the rumors had been confirmed. Naturally, Jefferson was alarmed. A lethargic, feeble Spain on the western frontier was not to be feared; an energetic, imperialistic France was a menace. "The day that France takes possession of New Orleans," Jefferson predicted, "we must marry ourselves to the British fleet and nation." The Federalists could see only two distasteful alternatives for Jefferson. Either he must

Americans practiced "manifest destiny" long before the term was coined. "Is it not better," asked Jefferson, "that the opposite bank of the Mississippi should be settled by our own brethren and children. . . ?" From Jefferson to Theodore Roosevelt, the U.S. used methods both honorable and dishonorable to expand its borders.

EXPANSION OF THE UNITED STATES TO 1903

declare war on France to satisfy the war fever spreading through the American West; or, by continuing a pacific policy, he must risk unpopularity and a consequent Federalist renaissance.

Jefferson's political genius was equal to the problem. His public addresses took on a military tone, but secretly he requested and received from Congress an appropriation of $2 million to purchase New Orleans and West Florida from France. James Monroe was appointed as minister extraordinary to join Robert R. Livingston in Paris for the negotiations. If they failed, the American diplomats were instructed to cross the channel and sign a treaty of alliance with Great Britain. Napoleon, meanwhile, had decided to sell the entire territory. His dream of building a Caribbean empire had collapsed because of catastrophic losses in Santo Domingo trying to subdue black revolutionaries. In 1802 alone approximately 50,000 French soldiers died either in battle or from yellow fever. Moreover, war between France and England was imminent, and Napoleon could not spare troops to defend Louisiana. And he needed money. "I renounce Louisiana," Napoleon told his ministers. "It is not only New Orleans that I mean to cede; it is the whole colony, reserving none of it." Monroe and Livingston were totally unprepared and somewhat mystified by his offer, but they did not hesitate. Louisiana was purchased for the sum of $15 million, subject to ratification by the American government. "We have lived long," Livingston told Monroe, "but this is the noblest work of our lives."

Jefferson was enthusiastic, for the purchase would eradicate the perennial concern of trade on the Mississippi. It would quiet western discontent, eliminate Indian raids instigated by foreign powers, ruin Federalist hopes of regaining office, and free the United States from the necessity of an alliance with England. Most important, it would double the size of the country and open a boundless land to settlement. Jefferson was troubled by doubts concerning the constitutionality of the treaty, since the Constitution was mute on the question of how the United States should acquire territory. Jefferson was a strict constructionist, believing that the federal government could not do what was not specifically authorized by the fundamental law. He had so argued a decade earlier when Hamilton proposed the incorporation of the Bank. But the nation would benefit by possessing Louisiana, Jefferson concluded, and thus justified the violation of his principles. He submitted the treaty, asking the Senate to ratify it "with as little debate as possible, particularly so far as respects the constitutional difficulty."

From 1804–1806 Lewis and Clark explored the Missouri River and as far west as the mouth of the Columbia River. The explorers kept journals taking note of Indian customs, plant and animal life, climate, and geography. The above drawing shows an Assiniboine grave, the two bodies wrapped in blankets and placed in a tree, to keep the bodies away from prowling animals. Lewis was shocked at how the Sioux, Assiniboine, and other tribes treated the aged and infirm. "It is a custom," he wrote in 1806, "when a person of either sex becomes so old and infirm that they are unable to travel on foot from camp to camp . . . to place within their reach a small piece of meat and a platter of water, telling the poor old superannuated wretch for his consolation that he or she had lived long enough, that it was time they should die." (Courtesy of the Fine Arts Department, Boston Public Library)

REPUBLICAN DOMINATION

By 1804 the Federalists were a party of the past, keepers of an antiquated political philosophy, with no leaders of national stature, and no chance of upsetting the Republicans. Hamilton was dead, killed by Aaron Burr in a duel. Others withdrew from public life. "I will fatten my pigs and prune my trees," wrote Fisher Ames in disgust, "nor will I any longer . . . trouble to govern this country." Some Federalists concentrated on the practical work of party organization, but they could not compete with Jefferson's popularity. A few extremists talked of seceding from the union and forming a "northern Confederacy." Their intrigues never advanced beyond the planning stage. In the election of 1804 Jefferson captured every state except Connecticut and Delaware. "Never was there an administration more brilliant than that of Mr. Jefferson up to this period," the Republican, John Randolph, recalled. "We were indeed in the 'full tide of successful experiment.' Taxes repealed; the public debt amply provided for; sinecures abolished; Louisiana acquired; public confidence unbounded."

THE PROBLEM OF NEUTRALITY

During the next four years Jefferson's image became somewhat tarnished. War between England and France again bedeviled the United States. Jefferson's task was to steer a course which would convince both powers to respect American rights on the high seas, which would not commit the United States to an open conflict, and which would be acceptable to the majority of Americans. A policy meeting all these conditions was never found. Jefferson did keep the peace, as one of his eulogists stated in 1809, "through a season of uncommon difficulty and trial." Yet his policies really failed, and Madison inherited issues that had been postponed rather than resolved.

England was the master of the seas, particularly after Admiral Nelson's naval victory at Trafalgar in 1805 ruined Napoleon's plans of invading England. France was master of the continent, her armies marching from the victory at Ulm to the celebrated conquests at Austerlitz, Jena, and Friedland. Within their respective spheres the two contenders were impregnable. Not being able to hurt one another with arms, they turned to economic weapons. But it was the spectator—the United States, the world's leading neutral producer and carrier—who suffered. By the *Essex* decision in 1805 a British court declared that French cargoes on American vessels might be seized. Thereafter, British ships were stationed near key American ports, boarding and inspecting merchantmen, confiscating cargoes, and, worst of all, impressing American seamen. The English insisted that their citizenship was inalienable—once an Englishman, always an Englishman. American naturalization papers, real or fraudulent, were worthless when an English ship decided that it needed more hands. To be sure, many sailors *were* English deserters; but many were not, and the impressed sailor could anticipate only low pay, filthy quarters, brutal treatment, and possible death in naval battles. Napoleon's Berlin (1806) and Milan (1807) decrees established—at least on paper—a blockade of the British Isles. They decreed that any neutral vessel that permitted itself to be boarded by the English or touched at an English port was subject to capture. England reciprocated by Orders in Council which proclaimed that neutral vessels bound for a port controlled by France must first land in England, pay full duties, and receive permission to continue. To obey the decrees of one country was to violate those of the other.

Despite these regulations, American merchants prospered because of the war. The value of reexports of West Indian products mounted from $14 million in 1803 to $60 million in 1806. Nearly 4,000 new seamen were employed on American vessels, and shipping increased at the rate of 70,000 tons annually. Although they prospered, the merchants were irritated by England's blockades, seizures, and impressments, and they demanded that the administration take appropriate steps to defend the rights of neutrals.

THE CHESAPEAKE-LEOPARD AFFAIR

The fundamental causes for a declaration of war were present, and on June 22, 1807, an immediate provocation occurred. The British frigate, HMS *Leopard*, fired three broadsides at close range into the side of an American naval ship, the *Chesapeake*. A number of Americans were killed or wounded, and four alleged deserters removed. Two were black, two white, and only one was clearly an Englishman. War fever swept the country as news of the attack radiated from Norfolk, Virginia. "Never since the battle of Lexington," Jefferson wrote to his old friend Lafayette, "have I seen this country in such a state of exasperation. . . . And even that did not produce such unanimity."

Jefferson could have seized the moment of aroused nationalism, sent a war message to Congress, and enjoyed the enthusiastic support of virtually all Americans. Personally and politically he would have profited by such a move. But he knew that the United States was not prepared for war. And war would be an admission of diplomatic bankruptcy which he was not yet ready to concede. There was a penultimate policy Jefferson first wished to try: the economic coercion of England and France.

THE EMBARGO

Precisely six months after the *Leopard's* attack, on December 22, 1807, Jefferson signed the Embargo Act. Supplemented four times by additional legislation to enforce its provisions, the Embargo prohibited virtually all exports from the United States by land or sea, and forbade the importation of specified English manufactured goods. Only

Alexander Anderson's cartoon illustrates an attempt to smuggle to-bacco, thwarted by the snapping turtle, a symbol of governmental oppression, during the period of the Embargo Act. "Ograbme," embargo spelled backward, was just one of the ways citizens, angered by the law that forbade the export of goods, transposed the word. (Courtesy of the New York Public Library, Astor, Lenox and Tilden Foundations)

vessels engaged in the coastal trade were permitted to operate. By exerting economic pressure on the belligerents Jefferson hoped to force them to respect American neutral rights.

Theoretically the Embargo seemed a sound alternative to war; in practice it proved a costly failure for several reasons. First, Jefferson overestimated the dependence of France and England upon American products. The West Indies did run short of food, the Lancashire mills of cotton, and the Irish linen industry of flax. But in general the English economy was not seriously disrupted. And France appeared completely indifferent to the Embargo. Second, it required a considerable sacrifice on the part of the American people, which they were not prepared to make. The effect upon the economy was catastrophic: idle ships, falling prices, mounting unemployment, and bankruptcies. Exports plummeted from a value of $108 million in 1807 to $22 million in 1808. "Would to God," thundered one Federalist, "that the Embargo had done as little evil to ourselves as it has done to foreign nations." Despite the rigorous enforcement provisions, the law was widely evaded. Smuggling, mainly through Canada, became a major enterprise in New England. Nor did those involved suffer any qualms concerning their loyalty. Secessionist sentiment was openly voiced in the north, and the Federalists regained strength. After 15 months, Jefferson was forced to concede defeat. Shortly before retiring from the presidency, he signed the act rescinding the Embargo.

MADISON AS PRESIDENT

"Poor Jemmy! He is but a withered little apple-John," was Washington Irving's caustic opinion of James Madison. Though Madison's electoral victory in 1808 was decisive, he lacked Jefferson's administrative talent and political ability. New figures in Washington, like the aggressive Henry Clay and the incisive John C. Calhoun, overshadowed the drab chief executive. Madison's anxiety to preserve Republican harmony resulted in numerous party defections, and his attempts to preserve the peace resulted in a series of crucial diplomatic blunders which led finally to war.

Madison made his first mistake only a few months after he assumed office. The Embargo had been replaced by a Nonintercourse Act forbidding trade with England and France. However, the law provided that commercial relations with either country could be resumed, at presidential discretion, if their decrees against neutrals were removed. A new British minister to the United States, David Erskine, eager to improve Anglo-American relations, signed an agreement which bound England to lift its Orders in Council. "Great and Glorious News," proclaimed one newspaper, "Our Differences With Great Britain Amicably Settled." Americans were jubilant, and for weeks the event was celebrated throughout the nation. Madison immediately opened trade with England, and hundreds of American ships loaded with raw materials raced across the Atlantic. Then came news of England's repudiation of the Erskine Agreement. But the damage had been done. The cumulative effects of the Embargo and the nonintercourse measures, which had begun to pinch the British, were relieved by the American cargoes.

MACON'S BILL NO. 2

By 1810 coercion had been abandoned, and in its stead Congress passed and Madison reluctantly signed Macon's Bill No. 2, a measure which amounted to economic bribery. According to the new legislation, trade with England and France was reopened without restriction. However, the bill also stipulated that if either belligerent repealed the decrees against neutrals, the United States would enforce commercial restrictions upon the other. Napoleon was quick to take advantage of the opening. He instructed his foreign minister, the duke of Cadore, to inform the Americans that France's decrees would be removed after November 1, 1810, *if* in the interim England did the same, or *if* in the interim the United States imposed restrictions against England. Cadore's letter, carefully edited by Napoleon, was purposely equivocal. But again Madison acted precipitously. He announced that the edicts of France had been revoked, and gave England three months to suspend its orders or suffer the resumption of commercial restrictions.

It soon became obvious that Napoleon had no intention of respecting America's neutral rights. Indeed, French hostility seemed to increase after the Cadore letter. American ships and cargoes, if they were not burned at sea, were auctioned off and the proceeds were placed in the French treasury. England, naturally, refused to lift its orders as long as the French decrees were being enforced. "The Devil himself," declared the Republican Nathaniel Macon "could not tell which government, England or France, is the most wicked." Madison was not deceived by Napoleon's bad faith. Nevertheless, he insisted on maintaining commercial restrictions against England. Twenty months later, seeing that those restrictions had had no apparent effect on England, and prodded by the martial spirit of some congressmen, Madison asked for a declaration of war.

THE WAR HAWKS

In June 1812, Congress responded affirmatively to Madison's message. By a vote of 79 to 29 in the House, and 19 to 13 in the Senate, the United States declared war against Great Britain. An analysis of the congressional balloting reveals that the strongest sentiment for war originated with Westerners and Southerners, while a majority of New Englanders were opposed to it. One Boston newspaper complained: "We, whose soil was the hotbed and whose ships were the nursery of Sailors, are insulted with the hypocrisy of a devotedness to Sailors' rights, and the arrogance of a pretended skill in maritime jurisprudence, by those whose country furnishes no navigation beyond the size of a ferryboat or an Indian canoe."

The complaint was not without merit. Western and southern war hawks were usually younger men, proud and nationalistic, who regarded British violations of American rights on the high seas as a personal insult. They were tired of diplomatic procrastination, and demanded a war of conquest. But they were also motivated by other sentiments, particularly their desire for expansion. They never doubted that some day the American flag would fly over Canada. "We have heard but one word," John Randolph charged, "like the whippoorwill, but one monotonous tone—Canada! Canada! Canada!" The war hawks also wanted the British monopoly on the fur trade broken. They blamed the British for the declining prices of wheat, cotton, tobacco, and other agricultural products. They believed the British were provoking Indian attacks on American frontier settlements. *"The War on the Wabash"* (won in 1811 by William Henry Harrison at the battle of Tippecanoe) *"is purely British,"* a Kentucky newspaper announced.

Ironically, if Madison had delayed a few months, no conflict would have been necessary. The news that Britain had suspended its Orders in Council arrived after hostilities had begun.

THE HARTFORD CONVENTION

New England Federalists never supported the War of 1812 and did their utmost to stir popular discontent against the Republican administration. When Secretary of the Treasury Albert Gallatin asked for public subscriptions to finance the war, Boston businessmen refused. Federalist governors openly defied Madison, refusing to permit their militia to fight outside state boundaries. Federalist newspapers were filled with disloyal and inflammatory appeals. "Anything,

The military accomplishments of Major General Robert Ross, an urbane and courageous Irishman, were truly remarkable. The British troops he led destroyed a flotilla of American vessels in the Chesapeake River, won a victory at Bladensburg, Maryland, and marched into the capital of the United States with such speed that the conquerors helped themselves to a banquet abandoned when President and Mrs. James Madison were forced to flee along with all other inhabitants. Ross would have preferred ransoming the city rather than burning it, but he could find no one with whom to bargain. Thus, unopposed, the British burned Washington—the Capitol, the White House, the War and Treasury buildings, the federal arsenal, the offices of the National Intelligencer—*since it was the British War Office's policy to try to create war-weariness in the United States. The only reaction, however, was one of indignation, and an increased determination by Americans to support the war. (Courtesy of the Print Department, Boston Public Library)*

everything," advised one Bostonian, should be done "not to be involved in the war." Another writer suggested the formation of a league of commercial states to "defy the enmity and machinations of the slaveholders and backwoods men." The possibility of secession seemed real. Madison "looks miserably shattered and woebegone," a visitor wrote. " His mind is full of the New England sedition."

By 1814 it seemed that the United States was losing the war. The American navy was victorious in two of every three battles. But with the defeat of Napoleon the British intensified their offensive along the Atlantic coast. Parts of the United States were invaded. Washington was captured and its public buildings burned. The treasury was nearly bankrupt. At Hartford, Connecticut, a convention met to "lay a foundation for a radical reform in the National compact." Fortunately, moderates rather than extremists controlled the Hartford Convention. Instead of secession, they passed a series of proposals for constitutional amendments: abrogation of the three-fifths clause; limitation of officeholding to the native-born; a one-term limit for the president; and requirement of a two-thirds vote of Congress to admit new states, to declare war, and to pass legislation restricting commerce.

END OF THE WAR

The Hartford Convention adjourned, secure in the belief that Madison would have to concede most of their demands. Two events shattered their expectations. First, the British decided to end the war. The Treaty of Ghent, signed on Christmas Eve, 1814, ended hostilities and restored prewar boundaries. Although nothing was said of impressment or neutral rights, Americans regarded the settlement as a triumph. Mighty England had conquered Napoleon, but she could not conquer America. Second, even before news of the Treaty of Ghent, there came word of Andrew Jackson's victory over the British at New Orleans. Only 7 Americans were killed and 6 wounded, while the British counted 700 killed—including their commanding officer—1,400 wounded and 500 captured. Madison suddenly became a popular president, congratulated for his perseverance "in a season of darkness and difficulty." Victory cured the schisms in the Republican party as it depressed the Federalists. Tainted by the stigma of disloyalty, the Federalist party soon vanished entirely from the American scene.

A proud glow of nationalism suffused the American people. Only a quarter of a century had passed since the ratification of the

Constitution, and the new nation had survived political divisions, authoritarian impulses, secessionist plots, and foreign threats. Now, with a free and open land extending to the Rocky Mountains, with peace restored and prosperity assured, and with a harmonious people in full possession of liberty, no one could doubt the future of America. The time of trial was over. The time of vigorous growth was to begin.

SUGGESTED READINGS

*Henry Adams, *History of the United States of America During the Administrations of Jefferson and Madison*

James M. Banner, *To the Hartford Convention*

*Charles Beard, *Economic Origins of Jeffersonian Democracy*

*Samuel F. Bemis, *Jay's Treaty: A Study in Commerce and Diplomacy*, rev. ed.

*Morton Borden, *Parties and Politics in the Early Republic, 1789–1815*

Julian Boyd, *Number 7: Alexander Hamilton's Secret Attempts to Control American Foreign Policy*

*Irving Brant, *James Madison and American Nationalism*

*William N. Chambers, *Political Parties in a New Nation: The American Experience, 1776–1809*

*Joseph Charles, *The Origins of the American Party System*

*Harry Coles, *The War of 1812*

*Noble Cunningham, *The Jeffersonian Republicans: The Formation of Party Organization, 1789–1801*

*———, *The Jeffersonian Republicans in Power: Party Operations, 1801–1809*

*Manning Dauer, *The Adams Federalists*

Alexander DeConde, *Entangling Alliance: Politics and Diplomacy Under George Washington*

David Fischer, *The Revolution of American Conservatism*

Richard Hofstadter, *The Idea of a Party System*

Linda Kerber, *Federalists in Dissent*

*Adrienne Koch, *Jefferson and Madison: The Great Collaboration*

*Stephen Kurtz, *The Presidency of John Adams*

Dumas Malone, *Jefferson and His Time*

*John C. Miller, *The Federalist Era, 1789–1801*

Bradford Perkins, *The First Rapprochement: England and the United States*

*James M. Smith, *Freedom's Fetters: The Alien and Sedition Laws and American Civil Liberties*

Page Smith, *John Adams*

* Available in paperback

JACKSONIAN ENTERPRISE
1815/1840

6

THE LONG VIEW

The year 1815 is a natural dividing point in American history, Until that date the political fortunes of the United States had been intimately connected with those of Europe. After it Americans turned inward to face the task of exploring and conquering the West. The land had to be settled, Indians removed, lines of transportation constructed, states formed, and boundaries defined. While nineteenth-century Americans pursued their Manifest Destiny, Europeans were occupied with crushing post-Napoleonic rebellions. The spirit of industrial enterprise flowered on both continents, but in Europe (though not in England) it was a spindly growth, retarded by old concepts and autocratic governments. By the middle of the century a triangular conflict had developed in Europe between reactionary monarchists, liberal capitalists, and socialist workers. In the United States, on the other hand, enterprise was encouraged by democracy and social mobility. The future was enticing, a rich reward open to anyone with initiative. Success, measured in material accomplishment, became part of the American faith.

THE SHORT VIEW

When President James Monroe visited Boston in 1817 a Federalist newspaper announced the event as marking an "Era of Good Feelings." The phrase is apt, if limited to a relatively brief period following the War of 1812. Jackson's smashing victory at New Orleans was precisely the adrenalin needed by the American people. Divided in war, they rejoiced in triumph and united in peace. Although political bickering was vile and scurrilous, it was local and personal. Although the Federalists continued to function, it was only as a token opposition. Candidates seeking high national office had to operate within the

In terms of its economic, social, and cultural impact, there is no doubt that the cotton gin was the most significant invention made before the Civil War. The first cotton gin, pictured below in a drawing by William L. Sheppard, could do the work of ten men; later models, operated by horse power, could do the work of fifty. The mechanism was so simple that any blacksmith could build one. People began adding improvements, and receiving patents; nor was Eli Whitney successful in fighting against those who disregarded his rights. Southern juries simply would not convict the infringers. (Courtesy of the Periodical Department, Boston Public Library)

Republican structure. Economically the nation, still principally agrarian, appeared prosperous. Cotton production, stimulated by Eli Whitney's cotton gin, increased as prices in Britain soared in 1816 and 1817. Land values rose accordingly, catalyzed by easy credit and the vast quantities of paper money issued by state banks.

ECONOMIC NATIONALISM

Victory, prosperity, opportunity, and one-party rule added up to the growth of nationalistic sentiment. A Republican Congress in 1816 swallowed its constitutional scruples, enacted a second Bank of the United States, and passed a protective tariff. They answered as best they could the charges of inconsistency and adoption of Federalist measures. Clay excused his change of heart on the Bank on the grounds of differing circumstances. Madison referred to the "unassuming spirit" of Republicanism as contrasted to Federalist arrogance. Whatever the rationalization, a good many Republicans understood that the old doctrines were impotent and that adjustment was vital. Although their rhetoric remained Jeffersonian, their actions emulated Hamilton. Some Republicans, however, resisted the change and clung to states' rights. Strangely, the strongest support for the Bank and the tariff emanated from the South and West, while most New Englanders opposed the legislation.

Calhoun of South Carolina and Clay of Kentucky were the major spokesmen for economic nationalism. The Bank, the tariff, and a federal transportation network, later termed the "American System," were championed by Clay as vital elements in a program to harmonize sectional interests and free the United States from overdependence on foreign markets. Calhoun agreed. "We are great, and rapidly . . . growing," he warned Congress. "This is our pride and danger, our weakness and our strength. . . . Let us bind the republic together with a perfect system of roads and canals. Let us conquer space."

LEGAL NATIONALISM

Chief Justice John Marshall had little use for Republicans, even those who had come to appreciate and preach neo-Hamiltonian doctrines. For 35 years Marshall dominated the Supreme Court. While fashions varied and opinions shifted, he remained an unswerving advocate of nationalism. So persuasive were his arguments that, while the complexion of the Court changed as Federalists died out and Republican presidents made new appointments, his opinions prevailed. Rarely was he in the minority. In case after case, speaking for the Court, Marshall defined the federal system to enhance national and limit state authority.

When Maryland attempted to tax a branch of the Bank of the United States, the state law was struck down. Following Hamilton's logic and even paraphrasing his prose, Marshall declared that Congress had the right to use any appropriate means—such as the Bank—to exercise its legitimate powers. Those powers were supreme. A state could not be permitted to tax and perhaps thereby to destroy an instrument of the federal government (*McCulloch* v. *Maryland*, 1819). When New York granted a steamship company a monopoly to operate on the Hudson River, it was resisted by a competitor carrying goods between New York and New Jersey. Marshall declared the state law unconstitutional. The Constitution had granted Congress the exclusive power over interstate commerce, Marshall reasoned. Therefore, "the subject is as completely taken from the state legislatures as if they had been expressly forbidden to act on it" (*Gibbons* v. *Ogden*, 1824). Marshall contributed no original concepts to law. His ideas were borrowed from other more erudite jurists. But he seemed impervious to public opinions and pressures. His nationalism was principled, compelling, and exalted.

DIPLOMATIC NATIONALISM

Few statesmen have served America more faithfully or conscientiously than John Quincy Adams. The wisdom of President Monroe's decision to appoint him secretary of state in 1817 was confirmed by his accomplishments. Expert in diplomatic affairs, aloof from politics, and dedicated to the national interest, Adams made several important contributions to the foundations of American foreign policy. He believed that the "natural dominion" of the United States extended to the Pacific Ocean and his fixed purpose was to stretch the boundary across the entire continent. Two nations, England and Spain, contested American territorial rights in the West. Adams's diplomacy with each was masterful. Using persuasion or intimidation, as the case warranted, ready to compromise but unwilling to yield on essentials, he accomplished his goal in two years.

In 1818 a treaty was concluded with Britain establishing the American-Canadian boundary from the Great Lakes to the Rocky Mountains. The land beyond was left open to colonization by citizens of both countries for a 10-year period. This arrangement was continued until 1846 when a permanent boundary was set for the Northwest.

Adams's negotiations with Spain were more difficult but equally successful. By the Adams-Onís Treaty of 1819 the United States acquired Florida. To western expansionists the treaty was most significant for its definition of the Spanish-American boundary. A jagged line was drawn from Louisiana to the 42nd latitude, and then due west to the ocean. Although Adams sacrificed American claims to parts of Texas, he opened a gateway to the Pacific. "The acknowledgement of a definite line of boundary to the South Sea forms a great epoch in our history," recorded Adams with pride. "The first proposal of it . . . was my own."

CHANGING CONDITIONS

Superficially it was an era of good feelings, but fundamentally it was a period of transition and readjustment. The speculative land boom proved to be ephemeral. The Republican unity was spurious. The nationalism of some spokesmen evaporated when it no longer served the interests of their section.

Profound and disturbing changes were taking place throughout the nation. No one quite understood the nature of these changes. Many feared the consequences. Virginia was undergoing an economic and cultural decline. New England was beginning to sprout factories. The West attracted hordes of eastern migrants and, later, foreign immigrants. The lower South dreamed of diversification, but cotton became king. This economic expansion was sparking an egalitarian impulse. Socially the scale was tipping away from old aristocrats to new entrepreneurs. The good feeling was merely window dressing. Behind it lurked the beginnings of sectional conflict and the struggle between economic classes for control of the nation.

PANIC OF 1819

The panic of 1819 was the first major depression to strike America. (Others would follow, periodically, well into the twentieth century, for comparable reasons. Economists have long understood the causes. Cures are another matter.) Like the depressions that would follow, its origin was partly international: a shortage of specie due to South American revolutions, a shift in European demands for American staples, rapidly increasing world competition, and falling commodity prices. Part of the cause was domestic: enormous land speculation by those who sought quick profits. The signs of a coming depression had been present for some years, but Americans had ignored them. When cotton prices on the British market finally tumbled, land prices in the South and West plunged disastrously. The entire American economy shuddered. Tens of thousands lost their savings. Bankruptcies multiplied. Commerce faltered. Unemployment mounted. Every class was affected: bankers, merchants, planters, farmers, common laborers. Imprisonment was common for nonpayment of debt, an anachronism in a capitalist society whose very foundations rested on the concept of credit.

The depression was most acute and persistent in the urban West. In Pittsburgh, Cincinnati, Lexington, and Nashville, property values plummeted, and scores of businesses failed. Some Westerners, seeking a scapegoat, attacked the second Bank of the United States. "All the flourishing cities of the West," Thomas Hart Benton of Missouri later remarked, "are mortgaged to this money power. They may be devoured by it at any moment. They are in the jaws of the monster! A lump of butter in the mouth of a dog! One gulp, one swallow, and all is gone!" The Bank may have precipitated but it hardly caused the depression. Nevertheless, a western legacy of hatred for the Bank lingered long after economic recovery was achieved. Andrew Jackson was to become the chief executor of that legacy.

MISSOURI COMPROMISE, 1820

The nationalism of the era of good feelings was tarnished by the reemergence of sectional controversy. The territory of Missouri had petitioned for statehood in 1819. An obscure New York representative, James Tallmadge, Jr., introduced an amendment to the enabling bill which prohibited the further introduction of slavery into Missouri, and provided that the children of slaves born there were to be freed at the age of 25. Scholars have puzzled over the question of Tallmadge's motives. Was he a sincere abolitionist? Or was his amendment inspired by political considerations? Northerners had long sought a way to curb any extension of southern political power. Yet, Tallmadge's words seem to show a conscience sincerely outraged by slavery. "It is the cause of the freedom of man!" he argued. "If a dissolution of the Union must take place, let it be so! If civil war . . . must come, I can only say, let it come!" Enough Northerners in the lower house agreed with him to pass the amendment. In the Senate, where Southerners were equal in strength, the amendment failed.

Americans at this time generally avoided the issue of slavery.

Nevertheless, almost a year after Tallmadge's amendment was defeated, the subject of Missouri was again on the floor of Congress. The debates were short but bitter. Southerners were offended by what they regarded as northern hypocrisy, and pointed out that prejudice against the black man was quite common above the Mason-Dixon line. Some representatives (from the lower South) delivered impassioned orations in defense of slavery. Others (from the upper South) preferred to stand on constitutional grounds, denying the right of Congress to impose conditions on the admission of a state. Largely through the good offices of Senator Jesse B. Thomas of Illinois, a compromise was arranged. Slavery was prohibited in the Louisiana territory north of latitude 36° 30'. Missouri was permitted to enter the Union as a slave state, and Maine as a free state, thus maintaining sec-

John Quincy Adams considered the question of slavery in Missouri "a mere preamble—a title-page to a great, tragic volume." Fortunately, a compromise was fashioned which postponed the issue for three decades.

MISSOURI COMPROMISE 1820

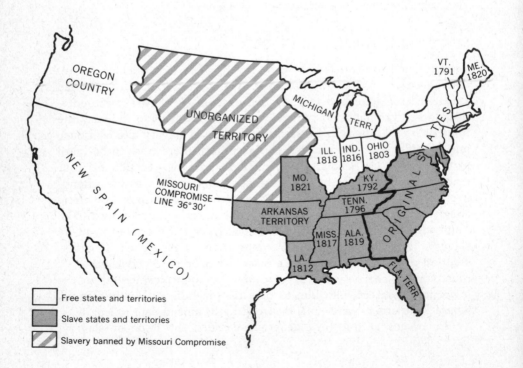

- Free states and territories
- Slave states and territories
- Slavery banned by Missouri Compromise

tional balance in the upper house. Although sectional emotions receded, the misunderstanding and distrust remained. "You have kindled a fire," a congressman from Georgia hurled at the North, "which all the waters of the ocean cannot put out, which seas of blood can only extinguish."

REPUBLICAN DIVISIONS

Still another characteristic of the era of good feelings, Republican unity, was dissipated by inept direction at the core and centrifugal pressures along the perimeter. At the zenith of its power after the War of 1812, the party began to decay because of Monroe's careless political leadership. Monroe was honest and dedicated; he was also simple and unimaginative. His reelection in 1820—in which he received all but one of the electoral college ballots—signified not Republican agreement, but popular indifference. Like Washington, Monroe wished to govern by consensus. He chose not to meddle in local affairs or to manipulate patronage or to cultivate congressmen. In effect, Monroe refused to captain the Republican vessel. His subordinates schemed and quarreled over the succession.

THE MONROE DOCTRINE, 1823

The outstanding achievement of Monroe's second term was the announcement of the "Monroe doctrine," the credit for which properly should be shared with John Quincy Adams. In 1823 the British suggested to the United States that the two governments guarantee the independence of South American countries against any invasion by European powers. The agreement was to prohibit both countries from ever acquiring any of these territories. Jefferson and Madison advised acceptance, and Monroe was prepared—if the British foreign secretary, George Canning, had not changed his mind—to conclude the arrangement. The threat of an invasion of Latin America by armies of the Holy Alliance convinced several cabinet members of the virtue of the agreement. French and Austrian troops had suppressed revolutions in Naples, Piedmont, and Spain. A Russian note stated that the intention of the Holy Alliance was the restoration of "tranquillity" everywhere. Secretary of War John C. Calhoun, certain that an army of 10,000 would sail from Cadiz, argued for cooperation with Britain.

"It would be more candid, as well as more dignified," stated Adams, "to avow our principles explicitly to Russia and France, than to come in as a cockboat in the wake of the British-man-of-war." He correctly guessed that there was little chance of an invasion of Latin

America. Even if one were attempted, he knew that Britain's navy was powerful enough alone to stop it. Nor did Adams want to restrict the possibility of American growth, as he suspected Britain intended to do by the alliance. Perhaps some day, Adams hoped, Texas and Cuba might be peacefully annexed to the United States. It is "a settled geographical element," he had informed an earlier cabinet, "that the United States and North America are identical." Adams' logic persuaded Monroe. Largely from his concepts, then, was born the doctrine of 1823, which was included in a presidential address to Congress. It contained three major points:

1. The United States would not tolerate any future colonization by European powers in the Western Hemisphere.
2. The United States would regard any foreign interference with or attempted control over any independent nation in the Western Hemisphere as an unfriendly act, "dangerous to our peace and safety."
3. The United States would abstain from European wars with which she was not concerned. "It is only when our rights are invaded, or seriously menaced, that we resent injuries, or make preparations for our defense."

THE ELECTION OF 1824

Thus the United States presented a facade of nationalistic unity. But each section of the nation was becoming increasingly aware of its own special interests. The political cement crumbled in 1824. At least five "favorite sons" sought the presidency. There were "coalitions of every description without the least regard to principle," complained Albert Gallatin. "I see nothing but . . . the fulfillment of personal views and passions." In Tennessee three men—William B. Lewis, John H. Eaton, and John Overton—plotted strategy in behalf of Andrew Jackson. In New York a shrewd politician, Martin Van Buren, decided to continue an old alliance, and joined in supporting the choice of the Virginia dynasty, William H. Crawford of Georgia. In Massachusetts the Republicans opted for their distinguished statesman, John Quincy Adams. In Kentucky the supreme politician, Henry Clay, campaigned for his "American System." John C. Calhoun, from South Carolina, also sought the main prize. However, he discerned that public opinion was in Jackson's favor. Reluctantly, but wisely, he postponed his own candidacy and joined the Jackson bandwagon.

Old Hickory—an affectionate nickname which Jackson's soldiers first used and his admirers adopted—received a plurality of both the popular and the electoral votes. Adams ran a close second. Crawford and Clay lagged far behind. Since no candidate obtained a majority the choice, by constitutional provision, fell to the members of the House of Representatives voting by states. A selection was to be made from the three front-runners.

THE "CORRUPT BARGAIN"

Rumors of intrigues and bargains, similar to those which arose during the election of 1800, were whispered throughout the capital. They centered on Henry Clay. The Kentuckian had lost the election but controlled enough western congressional votes to make his influence decisive. He ruled Crawford out on several grounds, including the Georgian's ill health and hostility to the tariff. He ruled Jackson out for other reasons, ranging from personal animosity to intellectual unfitness. "I cannot believe that killing 2,500 Englishmen at New Orleans," wrote Clay, "qualifies for the various, difficult and complicated duties of the Chief Magistrate." Adams, then, was the logical choice. The two men met together several times. An understanding was reached between them, but Jackson and his followers preferred to regard it as a corrupt bargain.

Clay's supporters in the lower house voted for Adams, who thereby won the presidency with 13 states to Jackson's 7 and Crawford's 4. A few days later, Adams announced that Clay would become his secretary of state. One scholar has termed this arrangement the result of an *entente cordiale*. Jackson used a biblical analogy: "The Judas of the West has closed the contract and will receive the thirty pieces of silver. His end will be the same. Was there ever witnessed such barefaced corruption?" The Jacksonians relentlessly and successfully rode the issue of corruption for the next four years. Their man had been cheated. It would not happen again.

JOHN QUINCY ADAMS

Adams could never convey his love of country to the people, nor could he project an exciting image. He was not a great orator. Physically he was short and plump, with a massive bald head. Jackson, by comparison, was long and lean, shaggy-haired, exuding firmness and inspiring confidence. The two would have made an unbeatable political combination. One newspaper in 1824 came out for a ticket of:

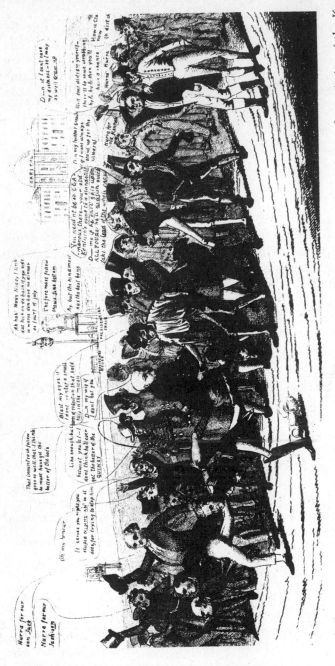

"Mr. Clay (like Judas of old it is said), sold himself and his influence to Mr. Adams, and carried a majority of the Kentuckians with him," Andrew Jackson wrote to a friend in February 1825, "for which (it was predicted), he was to receive the appointment of Secretary of State. This office has been offered to him, and it is said he has agreed to accept it. If the citizens of Kentucky submit to be thus bartered for office for a demagogue, they may bid farewell to their freedom." Jackson's followers needed no urging in condemning the "corrupt bargain," illustrated in the above cartoon. (Courtesy of The Granger Collection)

John Quincy Adams
Who can write,
And Andrew Jackson,
Who can fight.

When Adams was secretary of state he had defended Jackson's high-handed actions in Florida. In 1818, while pursuing the Seminoles, Jackson's forces had captured and summarily executed two British citizens who were suspected of inciting the Indians. Calhoun, Crawford, and other members of the cabinet wanted to punish Old Hickory by a court-martial. Adams resisted them, supported Jackson's right to invade Florida, and won Monroe over to his position. Jackson, however, did not know the details of the debate. He assumed that Calhoun had been his defender.

After 1825, the Republican party was largely in the hands of the Jacksonians, who began to style themselves "Democrats." Their representatives in Congress sought to stymie, badger, and embarrass Adams.

ADAMS'S ADMINISTRATION

Historians do not measure presidential greatness by criteria of courage or intelligence. If they did, John Quincy Adams would rank near the top. Success has been the test and Adams's administration, it is agreed, was a failure. Adams remained constant while the nation changed. He was too much the economic nationalist in an age of increasing sectional selfishness; too much the elitist in an age which apotheosized the common man; too much the idealist in an age of rising industrialism. Adams's proposals to encourage science, education, and internal improvements were largely rejected. Even his decision to have the United States participate in a Panama congress ended pathetically. "The American Union, as a moral person in the family of nations," said Adams after he left the presidency, "is to live from hand to mouth, and to cast away instead of using for the improvement of its own condition, the bounties of Providence."

THE TARIFF OF ABOMINATIONS

The failure of the Adams administration was reflected in the "Tariff of Abominations" passed in 1828. The measure was fashioned chiefly by Jacksonians and was reluctantly signed by Adams. He and Clay had long favored a high tariff to protect infant industry from foreign

*The tariff was not a significant issue in American politics until the
1820's. Gradually, however, and especially after the Tariff of
Abominations was passed in 1828, southern leaders came to feel
that the tariff penalized their section to the benefit of the North.
They viewed it as a tax imposed upon southern agriculture solely to
protect commercial and manufacturing interests. In the above cartoon the North grows fat and the South remains skinny because
of the tariff.* (From *U.S. Weekly Telegraph*, 1832)

competition. To the Jacksonians the tariff was a political "payoff."
Thomas Hart Benton of Missouri wanted duties placed on fur and
lead. Mahlon Dickerson of New Jersey asked for one on vermicelli.
Every politician wanted something. The bill at first provided for high
duties on coarse wool and other raw materials to please the growers.
A significant amendment, however, raised the tariff on finished woolen
products to please manufacturers. The tariff that emerged was impractical and jumbled. The Jacksonians, who had expected to wound
Adams, found that they had opened a fissure in their own ranks.

Textile manufacturing had advanced considerably in New England
in a decade, and now competed with commerce for economic prece-
dence. When commerce was dominant, New England had consistently
favored low tariffs; as a center of manufacturing, however, the area
wanted no competition from British goods. Daniel Webster of Mas-

sachusetts, hitherto an advocate of free trade, dramatically declared himself in favor of protection. Four other New England senators agreed with him. Their votes, completely unexpected, were instrumental in passing the Tariff of Abominations. Many Southerners had also reversed their stands. In 1816, in the first flush of postwar nationalism, southern leaders had supported protection. Since then they had learned to regard the North as an economic foe, and the tariff as an unjust tax imposed upon their section. "We of the South," wrote Thomas Cooper, "hold our plantations as the serfs and operatives of the North." The Southerners opposed the tariff almost to a man. John C. Calhoun, the ultranationalist of 1816, secretly became a spokesman of states' rights. Expecting to follow Jackson into the presidency, he felt it would not be wise to express his hostility to the tariff openly. Moreover, he and other Southerners thought that Jackson would correct the tariff inequities after the election.

ELECTION OF 1828

The tariff had no appreciable effect on the election of 1828. Jackson's charismatic personality transcended all issues. Unlike the hydra-headed race of 1824, there were only two factions. Adams represented the aristocratic past, Jackson the democratic future.

Jackson swept the election of 1828 by approximately 40,000 votes. He captured every western and southern state except Maryland, which divided its electoral vote. Pennsylvania was overwhelmingly behind him; New York gave him 20 of its 36 votes. Only in New England did Adams secure a majority.

During the inauguration ceremonies on March 4, 1829, an enormous crowd poured into the capital to celebrate the election of Old Hickory. Jackson inspired their confidence and adulation, but many older Federalists and Republicans despaired. There was a quality about Jackson which the elite distrusted. John Quincy Adams called him a "barbarian." Chief Justice Marshall's reaction was typical. "Should Jackson be elected," he had prophesied, "I shall look upon the government as virtually dissolved."

ANDREW JACKSON

Three particular qualities of Andrew Jackson initially attracted the admiration of the American people. First, he was the war hero who had conquered the haughty British at New Orleans. But he was not regarded as a professional soldier. Rather, he was idealized as the citizen-soldier, beloved by all, who had traditionally left the farm to defend their country from invasion. Second, he was the recognized head of the emerging Democratic party. But he was not regarded as a compromiser, like Henry Clay, or a self-seeking professional politician. Rather, he was seen as a selfless private citizen who reluctantly accepted a political post to restore government to the people. Third, although Jackson was actually a rich man, a slaveholder, and a plantation aristocrat, the people chose to envision him as a champion of the masses.

JACKSONIAN DEMOCRACY

The significance of Jacksonian democracy is to be found partly in the figure and personality of Andrew Jackson, partly in the way people perceived him. He represented the different, even contradictory aspirations of groups with different, even contradictory, interests in American society. Jackson was not politically astute or sophisticated enough consciously to project these various images. His judgments and decisions were mainly instinctive. Sometimes people imputed meanings to Jackson, and interpretations of the democracy he symbolized, which he could scarcely have recognized. For whom did he speak? The western farmer? The urban worker? The party stalwart? The rich planter? The new entrepreneur? The so-called common man? Jackson spoke for all. He was their demigod, created by them to serve their purposes. The fierce loyalties he evoked were understandable, but irrational. For, in 1829, no one knew Jackson's attitude toward any major issue or his philosophy of government—or even if he had one.

JOHN C. CALHOUN

The vice-president, John C. Calhoun of South Carolina, and his supporters in Congress and the cabinet, expected to steer Jackson toward the South. Calhoun had every hope of succeeding Jackson to the presidency. If Jackson were "King Andrew," as the opposition labeled him, Calhoun wanted very much to be the heir apparent. Within two years, however, a complete change took place. Jackson repudiated Calhoun and dismissed his followers. Virtually all the national influence Calhoun possessed, the result of the meticulous political labors of a decade, disintegrated. The national destiny, represented and guided by Jackson, took on a northern and western complexion. How did such a reversal come about?

PEGGY EATON

The story of Calhoun's downfall involved a saucy and reputedly promiscuous woman, Margaret (Peggy) O'Neale, whose family owned one of Washington's most renowned boarding houses. Peggy married, and Jackson in 1824 became acquainted with her as Mrs. Timberlake. He saw nothing exceptional in her behavior: evenings she entertained at the piano; Sundays she and the O'Neales accompanied Jackson to church. To capital gossips, however, Peggy had long been a subject of speculation. She was alleged, among other accomplishments, to have been the cause of a young man's suicide and of an old general's daft behavior. Timberlake was at sea as a ship's purser, and Peggy was squired by Jackson's close friend, Senator John Henry Eaton. Eaton was young, wealthy, and a widower. He helped finance Peggy's father, and she was naturally grateful. The capital in 1828 buzzed with scandalous stories of their relationship. When Timberlake died at sea, Eaton—at Jackson's insistence—married Peggy.

Eaton became Jackson's secretary of war. His wife, who looked forward to a round of pleasant parties, dinner engagements, society balls, and carriage rides with other ladies, was cruelly disappointed. The Eatons were snubbed, notably by the wives of Calhoun's supporters in the cabinet. One cabinet member who did accept an Eaton invitation, however, was Calhoun's competitor, the widower Martin Van Buren. The public humiliation of the Eatons became a major internal issue in Jackson's administration. All over Washington the question of Peggy Eaton's previous virtue or lack thereof, was debated. Evidence was collected, depositions taken. A rather unique meeting of the cabinet was held to consider the question, at which Jackson exploded. "She is as chaste as a virgin!" he shouted at a doubter, who probably remained unconvinced.

VAN BUREN'S TRIUMPH

An astute student of human character who understood Jackson's fierce loyalties, Van Buren used the Eaton affair as one of several means to ruin Calhoun, and to elevate himself in the president's eyes. Van Buren was not called the "Little Magician" without reason. His goal was the presidency, and to obtain it required no little dexterity. He had to convince Jackson of Calhoun's duplicity and of his own trustworthiness without leaving the slightest evidence of his personal political interest.

To further incriminate Calhoun, indisputable evidence of his recommendation that Jackson be court-martialed for the Florida campaign of 1818 was given to the president by Van Buren's friends. Calhoun had twice before vigorously denied insinuations to this effect. Now Jackson requested an explanation of the documents he had received. Calhoun, completely distraught, took two weeks to compose a 52-page apologia. Jackson answered curtly: "Understanding you now. . . . No further communication is necessary."

At the correct psychological moment, when Calhoun's position had badly deteriorated and the Eaton episode was deadlocked, Van Buren offered to resign from the cabinet. Convinced of Van Buren's loyalty and of the wisdom of his proposal, Jackson acquiesced. From that point each move followed Van Buren's calculations. As expected, Eaton also withdrew. Jackson then felt free to request the resignations of Calhoun's friends, which they reluctantly tendered. At last the Eaton issue was terminated. The naive president could never understand Peggy's subsequent coldness to him. In essence, Eaton had been sacrificed on the altar of Van Buren's presidential plans. With his enemies removed from high office, and his standing with Jackson never higher, Van Buren became the favorite to win the Democratic nomination and the presidency in 1836.

JACKSON'S CHOICE

Even without Van Buren's machinations, Jackson and Calhoun seemed destined to split. The Tariff of Abominations had convinced Calhoun that high tariffs were responsible for South Carolina's ailing economy. In 1828 he secretly wrote the *South Carolina Exposition and Protest*, which concluded that a state could nullify an act of the federal government it considered unconstitutional. The theory stemmed from Jefferson's Kentucky Resolution of 1798. Jefferson had advanced the doctrine as a means of defending freedom of speech and the press. Calhoun elaborated upon it as a means of preserving the national power of the southern planters.

Jackson—and Van Buren—counseled a "judicious" tariff. They also advocated restrictions on the power of the national government. But Jackson could never accept the implication of the *Exposition and Protest* that the federal government was merely the agent of the sovereign states. At a Jefferson Day dinner in 1830 that Calhoun and his friends had arranged, Jackson pointedly warned against nullification with a toast: "Our *Federal* Union—*It must be preserved.*" Calhoun

was shaken, but he responded with an opposing toast: "The Union—
next to our liberty, most dear."

NULLIFICATION

In 1832 Congress passed a tariff which the administration regarded as
a reasonable corrective to the inequities of the Tariff of Abominations.
Protection was maintained in certain vital areas, but the overall level
of duties was actually lowered. Jackson believed that the law would
pacify the lower South. Instead, aroused South Carolinians decided
not to obey the law. "He that dallies is a dastard," swore one nullifi-
cationist. "He that doubts is damned." A convention was held in
Columbia at which the "nullifiers" outnumbered the moderate "unionists." An Ordinance of Nullification was swiftly approved, to go into
effect on February 1, 1833. The ordinance stated that after that date
the federal tariff would not be collected within the boundaries of
South Carolina, and no appeals from state to federal courts would be
permitted which involved the tariff.

CRISIS AND COMPROMISE

The next move was Jackson's. Privately he was incensed. He referred
to Calhoun as demented, and threatened to hang the nullifiers for
treason. Publicly his position was remarkably tempered. A "Proclamation to the People of South Carolina" was issued, actually drafted by
Secretary of State Edward Livingston, which declared that nullification
was "incompatible with the existence of the Union, contradicted by
the letter of the Constitution, unauthorized by its spirit . . . and de-
structive of the great object for which it was formed." Each side
moved cautiously. Jackson admitted that the tariff might be reduced
further. South Carolina postponed putting the nullification ordinance
into operation.

Meanwhile, Henry Clay seized upon the issue as a perfect vehicle
to advance his political standing in the South. Despite his previous
advocacy of high protection, Clay now suggested a compromise
measure. The tariff would be lowered over a nine-year period to a general level of 20 per cent *ad valorem*. On March 1, 1833, the Compromise Tariff was completed. With it was passed the Force Act,
which permitted the president to employ military force, if necessary,
to collect the tariff.

South Carolina accepted the tariff by repealing the Ordinance of
Nullification. Then, wanting the last word, she defiantly proceeded to

nullify the Force Act. It is difficult to say who had the final victory. South Carolina, a single state, had succeeded in coercing the federal government into revising the law of the land. On the other hand, she had learned that she stood alone: no other state had openly agreed with the doctrine of nullification.

BANK OF THE UNITED STATES

The struggle over nullification was not the only melodrama of the Jacksonian administration. Concurrent with it, on another stage, with a slightly different cast of Jacksonian heroes and aristocratic villains, was portrayed the Monster Bank performance.

Act One. Congress, in 1816, chartered the second Bank of the United States for a 20-year period and thus began act one. Its first directors were undistinguished, even incompetent; its policies were injudicious. By 1818 the Bank verged on insolvency. Jealous states—including Tennessee, North Carolina, Georgia, Ohio, Maryland, and Kentucky —attempted to tax its branches. The Bank refused to pay, and the question of sovereignty was brought to the Supreme Court in the case of *McCulloch* v. *Maryland*. The greatest orators in the nation addressed the Court: Luther Martin for Maryland and Daniel Webster for the Bank. Marshall's opinion, which struck down the state tax, saved the Bank from possible ruin.

Act Two. The continued harassment of the Bank by the western states opened act two. However, the appointments of Langdon Cheves and Nicholas Biddle as successive presidents of the Bank resulted in a distinct improvement in its financial condition. Corrupt employees were dismissed. Conservative fiscal policies were applied. By 1830 the Bank was a prosperous institution, holding one third of all the deposits and specie in American banks. Biddle was everything Jackson was not: educated and urbane, he was equally at home in the worlds of poetry and business. The president was a simple man by comparison, who basically hated all banks because he did not understand their function. Henry Clay and Daniel Webster persuaded Biddle to seek a congressional recharter in 1832, four years earlier than necessary. They felt that they could persuade enough Democrats to join them to pass the bill through Congress. Jackson would have to sign it or, by a veto, lose the key state of Pennsylvania and the presidential election. The plan seemed to work well. The recharter bill was enacted, 28 to 20 in

As seen through *Martin van Buren's* newly invented *Patent Magic High Pressure* **Cabinet Spectacles**.

Andrew Jackson's veto of the bill to recharter the Bank of the United States was considered by his opponents to be economically disastrous and nationally divisive. His message, Daniel Webster said, "manifestly seeks to inflame the poor against the rich; it wantonly attacks whole classes of the people, for the purpose of turning against them the prejudices and the resentments of other classes. It is a state paper which finds no topic too exciting for its use, no passion too inflammable for its address and its solicitation." This anti-Jackson cartoon portrays him as a man who always sought personal glory and popularity, equating his military victories with his destruction of the Bank. (Courtesy of the Print Department, Boston Public Library) the Senate and 107 to 85 in the House of Representatives. Jackson then vetoed it, signaling, to Clay and Webster, his political demise.

Act Three. Jackson's ringing threat, "The Bank is trying to kill me," which he told Van Buren, "but I shall kill it," signaled the beginning of act three. He appealed over Congress to the people to support his veto. In 1832 Clay was the nominee of the National Republicans (the nucleus around which the Whig party later would develop). An Anti-Masonic party, which had originated a few years earlier in upstate New York as a protest against secret orders and exclusive privileges, entered the national political scene, nominating William Wirt. South Carolina went its separate way, isolated from the mainstream of national politics, supporting John Floyd of Virginia.

The issue was never in doubt. Wirt took Vermont, South Carolina voted for Floyd, Clay carried six other states (but not Pennsylvania), and Jackson had all the rest. Clay and Webster had badly miscalculated. Jackson had slain the Monster. But for whom? And to what purpose?

DEMOCRATIC UNITY

Disparate elements had united behind Jackson's war on the Bank.

First, eastern workingmen agreed with him in opposing all banks. Like Jackson, they were advocates of hard money. They conceived it to be immoral for a bank with only $3 or $4 million in assets to issue $30 or $40 million in paper currency. Since workingmen were, at times, cheated because they were paid in depreciated or worthless currency, their animosity is understandable. The workingmen of New York City endorsed a resolution to the effect "that more than one hundred broken banks, within a few years past, admonish the community to destroy banks altogether." Although they did not approve of Van Buren, by 1832 Jackson's attack on the Bank had won their enthusiastic support.

Second, many state bankers envied the Bank's powers and profits. As a depository for government funds, the Bank enjoyed a privileged economic position. Further, it was identified with the old aristocracy of inherited wealth and established social position. The new entrepreneurs were self-made men, the rugged individualists of nineteenth-century fact and fable, who—with Jackson—shared an antiaristocratic bias. They resented the Bank's fetters on credit and paper money. They sought to destroy the monopolistic controls of the Chestnut Street grandees. They were energetic, crass, determined, and resourceful, and they would brook no limitations—legal, moral, political, or otherwise—in their pursuit of wealth.

Third, Westerners, for contradictory reasons, joined against the Bank. Ever since 1819 speculators had chafed at the Bank's restraints on inflation. Yet other Westerners, who wanted no repetition of the land boom and bust, also viewed the Bank as an economic leech, draining off the wealth of the frontier into eastern pockets.

THE PET BANKS

Since as long as he fought the Bank he could keep the Democratic party united, Jackson would not let it rest during the concluding four years of its charter. He was determined to remove government deposits and relocate them in state banks. The secretary of the treasury, Louis McLane, refused to carry out the order and was shifted to the state department. The next secretary of the treasury, William J. Duane, also refused, and was dismissed. The next, Roger Taney, later to be rewarded with the post of chief justice of the Supreme Court, accomplished Jackson's purpose. Taney made all the government's deposits in state banks, known as "pets," and for expenditures he drew upon the reserves in the Bank of the United States.

In 1833 Biddle was forced by the dwindling reserves to curtail the Bank's operations. However, the credit contraction which Biddle ordered—a drastic reduction of loans to businessmen, and pressures upon state banks to redeem their notes and checks in specie—was probably exaggerated. Biddle frankly hoped that the economic distress would force Jackson to restore government deposits to the Bank. Hundreds of businessmen sent petitions to the president, requesting some form of relief. Others called on him. "Go to the monster, go to Nicholas Biddle," Jackson stormed. "I never will restore the deposits." By 1834 Biddle relented, reversed his policy, and ended the artificial shortage of credit.

THE SPECIE CIRCULAR

Credit expanded rapidly—too rapidly—once the Bank of the United States was stripped of its power and could no longer act as a restraining influence. Hundreds of new banks were formed. The amount of bank notes in circulation, without adequate reserves of specie, jumped from $82 million in 1835 to $120 million in 1836. People borrowed recklessly to speculate in real estate. The value of town lots increased astronomically. Federal income from the sale of public lands, which amounted to $2.6 million in 1832, climbed to $14.8 million in 1835, and then to $24.9 million in 1836. Alarmed at the speculative frenzy, and urged on by "Old Bullion" Benton of Missouri, Jackson in the summer of 1836 issued the "Specie Circular." The order directed government land agents to accept only hard money in payment for public lands.

Unfortunately, the circular came too late and too abruptly, bringing about a rapid deflation. Politically it destroyed Democratic party unity. The radical wing, itself a conglomeration of older Jeffersonian agrarians and urban workers who were dubbed "locofocos," supported Jackson. The conservative wing of bankers and entrepreneurs pressed for its repeal. Moreover, the circular unsettled the international money market. English financiers feared overinvestment in the American economy. If the United States government did not trust Yankee money, why should they? British firms with heavy American commitments collapsed. Secondary explosions rocked the cotton trade as well. In 1837 merchants in both countries were squeezed into bankruptcy. Ironically, the western speculators derived some benefits from the circular, since they could more easily acquire gold and silver from eastern sources than the ordinary settler.

VAN BUREN'S DILEMMA

The Panic of 1837 was not over until 1843. A large number of banks, including some "pets," temporarily suspended specie payments. Many others defaulted, never to reopen. Since there was no national bank to blame for the depression, guilt centered on banks in general. Van Buren, who was elected president in 1836, faced an excruciating problem. Radical Democrats demanded that the government withdraw its funds from all banks. Jackson's letters from the Hermitage constituted a ringing endorsement of their position. Conservative Democrats, with whom Van Buren was closely allied, wanted the deposits maintained. The radicals had the votes; the conservatives had the organization. Only a political magician like Van Buren would attempt to bridge the dilemma.

THE INDEPENDENT TREASURY SYSTEM

Van Buren's solution was masterful. In 1837 he summoned a special session of Congress and there publicly flayed the malefactors of wealth. Locofocos cheered. Jackson's faith in Van Buren was confirmed. The specific proposal Van Buren placed before Congress called for an independent treasury system to divorce the national government from banking entirely. Only gold and silver would be accepted and disbursed by the treasury. Public funds would be housed in government vaults in Washington and in subtreasuries in other cities.

The plan was too ingenious to unite the Democrats. The business world could see only the short-term losses, not the long-term gains. In fact, Van Buren's system offered them the culmination of laissez-faire. "The less government interferes with private pursuits," he stated, "the better." Without government regulation, or legal interference, or public supervision, enterprise would be completely free. But businessmen did not grasp the opportunity. To them the fact that government deposits would be removed from state banks was sufficient evidence of Van Buren's betrayal. They left in droves to join the Whig opposition.

The independent treasury was twice defeated in Congress, passed in 1840, repealed in 1841, and reenacted in 1846. The robber barons of a later age reaped the benefits of the system. The free enterprise Van Buren espoused was to become an eleventh commandment for the American businessman. And the common man suffered from the absence of a central banking system until the twentieth century.

ELECTION OF 1840

The crowning paradox of the Jacksonian period was unveiled in the election of 1840. For years an assemblage of oddly assorted interests, bound only by their mutual antipathy toward Jackson and Van Buren, had been coalescing into the Whig structure. Adherents of Clay and his "American System," ex-Democrats disillusioned with the administration's financial policies, states'-righters who followed Calhoun, educated classes disturbed by the anti-intellectual tone of Jacksonianism—all joined to overthrow the Democratic machine. In 1836 the Whigs had nominated no single candidate, but ran "favorite sons," making Van Buren's victory all the easier. In 1840 they decided to change their strategy. Knowing that their party was considered by the public to be high-toned and aristocratic, the Whigs purposely selected a candidate, William Henry Harrison, whom they could dress in the image of Jackson. Harrison was already known as the hero of Tippecanoe. The Whigs pictured him as a simple and honest Ohio farmer, born in a log cabin, a man of unswerving principle. To complete the irony, the Whigs identified Van Buren as a spendthrift politician who perfumed his whiskers, drank champagne, and reclined on satin cushions. Although the campaign developed no issues, free liquor, torchlight parades, and incendiary speeches excited popular emotions.

Harrison won by a small popular majority. More significant, the election of 1840 represented a crest of the democratic tide which had commenced decades before. An immense number of people voted, nearly 25 per cent more than in any previous presidential election.

A NATION ON THE MOVE

The economic landscape of the United States was changing as rapidly as its political practices. "The American flies at everything," a nineteenth-century Scottish traveler observed. " 'Go ahead anyhow,' that is his motto. . . . The American people diffuses itself, its energy, and its capital over a whole continent." Unlike the Europeans, steeped in history, and bound by the traditions of class and craft, Americans were at this time enormously mobile, wonderfully adaptive, and relatively classless. "Machines, not men, became specialized" in America, one scholar has commented. Eli Whitney produced muskets for the United States government, manufacturing each part separately but uniformly. This "uniformity system" or "Whitney system" provided the foundation of the concept of interchangeable parts, upon which the twentieth-century American miracle of mass production would be built. Another such foundation was the "factory system." Samuel Slater, an Englishman with a photographic mind, had built from memory the machinery for the first American textile factory at Pawtucket, Rhode Island, in 1790. Cotton textile factories thereafter expanded in number—particularly at Lowell, Massachusetts, and later at Utica, New York—and in size and sophistication, uniting all aspects of production under one roof. In 1800 only 2,000 spindles were in operation; by 1840 there were 2,250,000. Other industries did not develop quite so spectacularly, nor did household production disap-

A former employee of an Arkwright factory in England, Samuel Slater came to America in 1789 and accepted an invitation by Moses Brown of Rhode Island to set up a cotton textile mill in exchange for a half interest in the business. Shown here is the mill in Pawtucket, Rhode Island, from an old book published in 1824. (Courtesy of the Rare Books Department, Boston Public Library)

pear, but scores of factories were constructed near the waterfalls of New England and New York, manufacturing a variety of goods such as woolens, furniture, nails, cutlery, clocks, firearms, and machine tools.

In little more than a generation following the War of 1812, sleepy New England communities were transformed into thriving production centers. The territory of the United States nearly doubled, expanding from the Mississippi to the Pacific; population trebled; national wealth multiplied fivefold. Eastern cities, swelled by immigrants, began to bulge in size and in problems. But the most spectacular growth was in the West. Hundreds of thousands of land-hungry Americans

ECONOMIC REGIONS OF THE UNITED STATES 1840

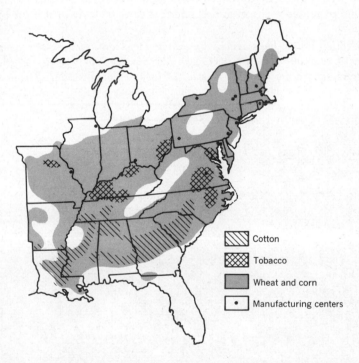

Cotton

Tobacco

Wheat and corn

Manufacturing centers

Except for the production of cotton gins, the South depended largely upon the North for farm implements and other manufactured goods, as well as for capital loans. As long as cotton and tobacco prices stayed high the South refused to diversify economically and remained essentially rural, while the North experienced a remarkable urban growth and increase in population.

poured into Alabama and Arkansas, Mississippi, Michigan and Missouri, Ohio, Indiana and Illinois. Whitney's cotton gin—a device which could remove the seed from short-staple cotton mechanically—accelerated the western expansion of southern planters, who sought fresh soil. The steamboat also hastened the opening of the Mississippi Valley by drastically reducing freight charges. In 1812, when Nicholas Roosevelt sailed his $30,000 steamer into Louisville, the inhabitants were startled. Most had never seen and some had scarcely heard of such a phenomenon. By 1820 there were 60 steamboats operating on the Mississippi; by 1830 there were over 200, and more were to come.

New Orleans, tapping the commerce of the Mississippi Valley, became one of the world's leading ports, and might have eclipsed New York City were it not for an engineering marvel of the age: the 350-mile Erie Canal. Completed in 1825, at a cost of $7 million, the Erie Canal provided a cheap and efficient means of transportation between

The Erie Canal, built solely by horsepower and manpower, joined the Great Lakes with the Atlantic Ocean. Pictured is Lockport, just northeast of Buffalo, where the need for a series of locks created a difficult construction problem. (By W. H. Bartlett in *American Scenery*, 1838, by N. P. Willis)

The Baltimore and Ohio Railroad, chartered in 1827 and carrying revenue traffic in 1830, was the first railway in the United States to carry freight and passengers. "The Railroad March," inspired by the beginning of a new railway and the 4th of July, was sold in Baltimore on July 4, 1828. (Courtesy of Harry Dichter, Musical Americana)

the Hudson River and the Great Lakes. New York City, as De Witt Clinton predicted when he sponsored the canal, became the principal gateway to the Northwest. The undertaking proved so successful that the merchants of other cities pressed their state legislatures to finance similar ventures. By 1840 Pennsylvania had almost a thousand miles of canals, the major system extending from Philadelphia to Pittsburgh. Ohio joined the Great Lakes and the Ohio River by two routes: Cleveland to Portsmouth, and Toledo to Cincinnati. In Indiana the Wabash and Erie Canal ran from Terre Haute to Fort Wayne, and then connected with the Ohio system.

Eventually the canal-building boom declined, particularly after the superiority of railroads became evident. But, because of the revolutions in transportation as well as in manufacturing and politics, the face of America had been altered.

CONSEQUENCES OF AN AGE

In the age of Jackson, then, politics became popular and enterprise became free. Both became passions of the American people, and were assiduously pursued and recklessly consummated. Pursuit meant progress, to which most Americans (outside the South) were committed. But consummation bore some bitter fruit, to which other Americans objected.

Administratively, a distinct lessening in the quality of public officials was apparent. Jackson and his aides, in the name of reform, created the "spoils system." Wholesale removals of civil servants did not take place. In fact, Jackson in eight years dismissed only one tenth of all federal officeholders, a proportion comparable to Jefferson's record. However, the replacements were judged on party fidelity and personal loyalty to Jackson. Jefferson conceived of office as a service. Under Jackson it became a reward. "Office-seeking and office-getting," one Democrat commented in 1838, "was becoming a regular business, where impudence triumphed over worth."

Politically, more people than ever before participated as voters. Candidates had to affect simplicity. As America moved away from its agrarian roots, Americans insisted that their leaders possess rural or frontier origins. A log-cabin birth became imperative, for it symbolized virtue and independence. Daniel Webster had to admit that he was not so fortunate. "But," he added, "my elder brothers and sisters were born in a log cabin." Jeffersonians had tried to cultivate and educate the public. Jacksonians and Whigs tried to manipulate opinion. Duplicity and cynicism became part of the political system. Yet, the system functioned, the people approved, and the democratic volcano Jacksonianism had activated occasionally spewed up political leaders of remarkable ability.

Economically, the United States was afflicted with all the evils of rapid and unplanned industrial growth. In comparison with other nations, the American standard of living was high. Nevertheless, 65 per cent of those employed in cotton mills were women and children who worked 12 hours a day for bare subsistence wages. Their lives were regimented. Malcontents were blacklisted. Strikes were forbidden by the judiciary. Some mills set aside "whipping rooms." Outside of New England education was for the rich. In 1833, it is estimated, a million children between the ages of 5 and 15 attended no school whatsoever. In the larger cities the poverty-stricken were crowded into slums. Periodic unemployment bred crime and prostitution. It was commonly remarked that a slave in Kentucky or Virginia was better compensated in terms of food, housing, and even personal treatment than a northern worker.

The Americans were impatient with the present, never doubted the future, yet looked longingly to the past. The more his character was stained in the pursuit of wealth, the more he sought purity at home. The more his civilization seemed mechanical, the more he displayed affection for the natural. Slums, bread riots, and multiplying urban problems evoked romantic memories of his rural past. Rapid economic growth and social movement made him acutely conscious of the need for social order. Politics continued to fascinate, a national game in which all whites could participate, but the quality of his leaders caused him to yearn for the incorruptibility of Washington. Acquisitive, he sought lost innocence. Materialistic, he wallowed in sentimentality. Beset by conflicting localisms, he became increasingly chauvinistic. He built bridges and railroads, sent clipper ships to the far reaches of the world, transformed prairie towns into thriving commercial centers—or categorically promised to do so. Truth was measured by success, and success measured by economic growth. If that growth proved an illusion—as it did in hundreds of small towns which failed—the American moved on to where it would become a reality. For all his business confidence, there persisted an uncertainty, a confusion, and a vague dissatisfaction about the meaning and the purpose of the nation. Had men died in revolution and war so that America might become nothing more than a vast countinghouse? Did economic progress mean that humanitarian values must be sacrificed? An army of reformers rose to correct abuses, to combat evils, to rectify inequalities, to amend America's institutions, and redirect its historic mission to something more than capital accumulations. "We are to revise the whole of our social structure," Ralph Waldo Emerson advised in 1841, "the state, the school, religion, marriage, trade, science, and explore their foundations in our own nature."

SUGGESTED READINGS

Thomas P. Abernethy, *From Frontier to Plantation in Tennessee*

Samuel F. Bemis, *John Quincy Adams and the Foundations of American Foreign Policy*

*Lee Benson, *The Concept of Jacksonian Democracy: New York as a Test Case*

Albert Beveridge, *The Life of John Marshall*

Van Wyck Brooks, *The World of Washington Irving*

William N. Chambers, *Old Bullion Benton: Senator from the New West*

*George Dangerfield, *The Era of Good Feelings*

*Clement Eaton, *Henry Clay and the Art of American Politics*

*John Hope Franklin, *The Militant South*

*Bray Hammond, *Banks and Politics in America from the Revolution to the Civil War*

*Walter Hugins, *Jacksonian Democracy and the Working Class: A Study of the New York Workingmen's Movement*

*Marquis James, *Andrew Jackson*

Shaw Livermore, *The Twilight of Federalism*

*Marvin Meyers, *The Jacksonian Persuasion: Politics and Belief*

Nathan Miller, *The Enterprise of a Free People*

*Russell Nye, *The Cultural Life of the New Nation, 1776–1830*

*Dexter Perkins, *History of the Monroe Doctrine, rev. ed.*

Robert Remini, *Martin Van Buren and the Making of the Democratic Party*

*Arthur Schlesinger, Jr., *The Age of Jackson*

*George R. Taylor, *The Transportation Revolution, 1815–1860*

*Frederick J. Turner, *Rise of the New West, 1819–1829*
*Glyndon Van Deusen, *The Jacksonian Era: 1828–1848*
*John W. Ward, *Andrew Jackson: Symbol for an Age*
Charles Wiltse, *John C. Calhoun: Nullifier*

* Available in paperback

LIFE IN AMERICA
The Early Nineteenth Century

7

AWARENESS OF EVIL

The evils did not originate with industrialism. Farmers had always labored from sunup to sundown. Their children were hardly pampered; their women worked as hard as men. Schooling was perfunctory. Rural slums were common. Sanitation was rudimentary. Hard times were frequent. The agrarian life was neither as innocent nor as idyllic as romantic novelists and national legend proclaimed. What industrial and urban growth did was to *concentrate* the evils, and thereby make them visible. The shock of recognition, in turn, evoked a variety of responses. Some questioned the foundations of capitalism. A few offered panaceas designed to correct all social ills. Most aimed at reforming particular grievances.

OWEN AND FOURIER

The first voices raised in criticism of capitalism came from across the Atlantic. There the dichotomy between rich and poor was more strik-

Since the apparatus for living already existed, Owen was able to establish quickly his utopian community on the banks of the Wabash. Shown is a picture of New Harmony, drawn after nature. His experiment failed, but a decade later dozens of others were attempted. "Not a man you meet," noted Emerson, "but has a draft of a new community in his pocket." (Courtesy of Culver Pictures, New York City)

ing, and the conditions of the working class more appalling. Long before Karl Marx and Friedrich Engels wrote the *Communist Manifesto,* dozens of socialistic proposals were formulated. The theories of two men in particular, a Welshman named Robert Owen, and a Frenchman, Charles Fourier, were given a limited trial in the United States.

Owen was a successful industrialist whose cotton mills and company town at New Lanark, Scotland, attracted worldwide attention for their advanced educational facilities, humane treatment of employees —and profits. Despite his own example, Owen became convinced that wealth was not created by entrepreneurial wizardry, but by science and society. Before 1820 he shifted from social reformer to socialist. Fourier's career and personality were radically different. An economic casualty of the French Revolution, he became an impoverished eccentric. For 30 years he patiently awaited the arrival of a rich patron to finance his socialist dreams. Both men envisioned a series of village utopias where people, isolated from the debilitating effects of competitive struggle, could develop intellectual independence and true social equality. Cooperation was to be the motivating force, harmony the result. Both men hoped that if the communities functioned as planned, the idea would spread until, gradually, capitalism would be replaced entirely by socialism. The United States was an ideal place to attempt the experiment. Land was cheap. Americans already possessed the requisite political freedom. Religious communitarianism had long been practiced by fundamentalist sects, mainly the German pietists.

NEW HARMONY

Owen's chance came first. He purchased the land and buildings of a Rappite settlement in Indiana, and invited settlers. The response was heartening. More arrived in 1825 than could be accommodated, including several eminent scientists and educators imbued with the teachings of the European pedagogist Johann Pestalozzi. Owen's son described the colonists as "a heterogeneous collection of radicals, enthusiastic devotees to principle, honest latitudinarians, and lazy theorists, with a sprinkling of unprincipled sharpers thrown in." But dedication and faith were not enough to operate a backwoods utopia. Largely because skilled workers were in short supply, the collapse of New Harmony was quick.

On July 4, 1826, Owen issued a "Declaration of Mental Independence." It proclaimed his hostility to a trinity of "monstrous evils": private property, organized religion, and marriage. Although a year before he had been invited to address a joint session of Congress, he was now pilloried in press and pulpit as a whoremonger and his colony was described as "one great brothel." Bitter fights and ugly recriminations rocked New Harmony. By 1827 Owen withdrew, with $200,000 lost and New Harmony practically extinct. For the next dozen years, with one minor exception, no new secular communitarian experiments were attempted.

BROOK FARM

Fourier's philanthropic millionaire never appeared, but he had several disciples, one of whom—Albert Brisbane—carried his gospel to the United States. Brisbane converted Horace Greeley, publisher of the New York *Tribune,* and the two propagandized for Fourierism with considerable success. Marx's later "scientific" socialism rested on what he saw as the natural enmity between labor and capital, the growing class consciousness of the former, and the ultimate overthrow of the latter. Fourier's "utopian" socialism, on the other hand, rejected class struggle as well as revolution. He aimed instead "to content all classes, all parties."

Dozens of Fourierist communities, called "phalanxes," were opened after 1840. They all existed briefly and died quietly. Contrary to Brisbane's advice, the phalanxes were founded with inadequate capital. The most prestigious was Brook Farm in Massachusetts, an established community of New England Transcendentalists which adopted Fourierism in 1844. Transcendentalism was different from Fourierism in its roots, its spirit, and its method, but both seemed to share similar goals. The Transcendentalists believed that mankind was corrupted by mass society and materialism. Their utopian objective, wrote George Ripley, was "to combine the thinker and the worker, as far as possible in the same individual." Nathaniel Hawthorne labored at Brook Farm with a pitchfork and manure pile. Afterwards he mocked the Transcendentalists in his book, *The Blithedale Romance.* But even Hawthorne testified to Brook Farm's "scheme of a noble and unselfish life. . . . I feel we struck upon what ought to be a truth. Posterity may dig it up and profit by it."

The heady optimism of Brook Farm's members had already started to wane when they decided to convert to Fourierism. If successful, they felt, Brook Farm could continue to operate and could become a center of the Fourierist crusade to proselytize America. Debts, fire, and smallpox, however, drained the resources and spirit of the members. In 1847 Brook Farm closed down.

SOME PET PANACEAS

The quest for social justice was not the exclusive prerogative of utopian socialists. Other reformers sought to cure the cancers of enterprise by rapid surgery. In the early 1830's, for example, the New York City workingmen organized politically to gain better hours and wages, to destroy banks, to abolish the practice of imprisonment for debts, to end compulsory militia service, and to obtain a workers' lien law for the protection of wages. Their demands were largely practical; some of their leaders were not.

Thomas Skidmore considered it a fatal mistake on the part of Thomas Jefferson to have based democratic government on only the rights of man. For democracy to be meaningful, said Skidmore, there must be economic equality. Property must be redistributed and inheritance laws altered. Skidmore's crude communism was outlined in his book, *The Rights of Man to Property! Being a Proposition to make it Equal among the Adults of the Present Generation: and to Provide for its Equal Transmission to every Individual of Each Succeeding Generation, on Arriving at the Age of Maturity.* The workingmen at first followed Skidmore, then rapidly disowned him when public opinion became hostile. "We have no desire or intention," their journal announced, "of disturbing the rights of property."

Frances Wright and Robert Dale Owen (son of the utopian socialist) exerted a considerable influence on the New York workingmen after Skidmore's decline. Their ideas were equally exotic and, to the general public, just as outrageous. Frances Wright's public expressions of atheism and her intemperate attacks on organized religion shocked society. One newspaper called her "the Red Harlot of Infidelity." Robert Dale Owen audaciously suggested birth-control measures to alleviate the miseries of the indigent. The major panacea of both Wright and Owen, however, involved education. "I believe," wrote Owen, "in a National System of Equal, Republican, Protective, Practical Education, the sole regenerator of a profligate Age, and the only redeemer of our suffering country from the equal curses of chilling poverty and corrupting riches, of gnawing want and destroying debauchery, of blind ignorance and unprincipled intrigue." According to their plan a state school system would be created, to be maintained at government expense, in which every vestige of class distinction would be obliterated. All children were to receive identical food, clothes, board, and instruction. Only then could they enter the competitive world on an equal basis, as "useful, intelligent, virtuous citizens." The scheme was rejected by some as too radical and idealistic, by others as unnecessary and inappropriate. Working-class distress, the New York Typographical Society commented, "is caused not by anything Owen could reform, but by the introduction of labor-saving machinery during the last thirty years. Has Owen any remedy to propose? Far from it."

George Henry Evans believed he had the remedy for mechanization. As early as 1833, and for the rest of his life, Evans championed free western land grants to bona fide settlers. Man had a natural right to land, said Evans, as he had to air or sun or water. A farm boy himself, he toiled for years in a drab New York printing shop, nearly destitute, composing eloquent arguments to convince eastern workers that happiness and independence could be found only in agriculture. The first Homestead Bill, providing for free western land grants, was introduced in Congress by Andrew Johnson of Tennessee in 1846. Every year thereafter the legislation was reintroduced and defeated. Evans' theories were united with abolitionism in the slogan of the Free

Soil party: "Free Soil, Free Land, Free Labor, Free Men." Not until 1862, after Evans' death, was the Homestead Act passed. Then the fallacy of his panacea became obvious. Agrarianism was no cure for the evils of industrialism. Workers did not have the capital, the knowledge, or even the desire to go West and become farmers. Whatever the merits of the Homestead Act, it failed to act as an avenue of escape for discontented eastern workers.

FREEDOM'S FERMENT

If Americans repudiated all panaceas, their rejection did not signify approval of social conditions. A ferment for reform, a crusade to eradicate evils, touched thousands of literate people throughout the North. Its particular focus was in New England, but its vision was national. Its leadership was largely clerical, but its goals transcended the narrow interests of denominationalism. It was essentially nonpolitical, but not exclusively so. It was zealous, but not violent; radical, but not revolutionary. It was optimistic, naive, and urgent, believing no challenge insuperable, all triumphs close at hand. And it was comprehensive. Every institution and every practice of larger and lesser importance was questioned, investigated, and debated, be it liquor, slavery, dietary habits, penal institutions, marriage, money, state power, war, or women's rights. One reformer called for a Convention to Emancipate the Human Race from Ignorance, Poverty, Division, and Misery. All good causes were related, and reformers made up an interlocking directorate, serving several movements simultaneously.

Unfortunately, and perhaps inevitably, cranks and crackpots were attracted to it, as well as obnoxious extremists who Emerson called "narrow, self-pleasing, conceited men." A number of Transcendentalists were food faddists; social revisionists and physiological reformers often went hand in hand; and, while some hooted, other intellectual progressives were intrigued by the "science" of phrenology. Thus, William Alcott, widely known for his household manuals, moral guides, and physiology handbooks, cautioned against tea drinking as a dangerous sexual stimulant. "The female who restores her strength by tea, the laborer who regains strength by spiritous liquors, and the Turk who recruits his energies by his pill of opium," warned Alcott, "are in precisely the same condition." Horace Mann, who single-handedly launched an educational renaissance in New England, advised young men to undergo a phrenological examination before deciding upon a career. Lewis Hough thought everyone should eat fruit and whole grain wheat, take no fluid, sun themselves in the nude,

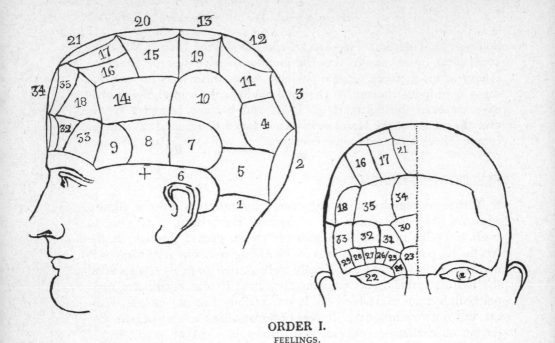

ORDER I.
FEELINGS.

The general characteristics of the feelings or affective faculties are, in the language of Dr. Spurzheim, as follows: "They have their origin from within, and are not acquired by any external impressions or circumstances. They must be felt to be understood, for they cannot be taught: in themselves they are blind and without understanding: they do not know the objects of their satisfaction, and act without reflection."

Genus I.
Propensities.

There are nine distinct Propensities, each having its specific nature and independent sphere of action: they are all common to man and animals.

1. Amativeness.   The feeling of physical love.
2. Philoprogenitiveness.   Love of offspring and children generally.
3. Concentrativeness.   It gives the desire for permanence in place, and for permanence of emotions and ideas in the mind.
4. Adhesiveness.   Attachment: friendship and fondness for social intercourse result from it.
5. Combativeness.   Courage to meet danger, to overcome difficulties, and to resist attacks.
6. Destructiveness.   Desire to destroy. It is very discernible in carniverous animals.
7. Secretiveness.   It gives the disposition and the power to conceal. It disposes to be secret in thought, word and deed.

and engage in sexual intercourse no more and no less than once a year. Sylvester Graham's program for mental and physical health included frequent baths, hard mattresses, the whole wheat cracker he made famous, and chastity. At Brook Farm a dietary table was kept for the Grahamites.

PRACTICAL REFORMERS

There were numerous other men and women who cared enough to devote themselves to practical social reforms, and whose accomplishments were substantial. "Every creature in human shape should command our respect," wrote Samuel Gridley Howe. "The strong should help the weak, so that the whole should advance as a band of brethren." Howe practiced what he preached. He fought for Greek independence in the 1820's, and returned to America to work selflessly for the blind. For 44 years he directed the Perkins Institute in Boston, training teachers of the blind in new techniques which he had developed. Charles Dickens, who saw little to admire in America during his tour, thought Howe's system a model other countries should emulate. Dorothea Dix, a Boston schoolmistress, investigated the appalling treatment of the insane in Massachusetts and submitted her findings to the state legislature in 1843. "Insane persons confined within this commonwealth," she reported, "are in cages, closets, cellars, stalls, pens! Chained, naked, beaten with rods, and lashed into obedience!" Before the Civil War, because of her efforts, more than a dozen states passed corrective legislation. She even went to Europe, where conditions for the insane were equally heinous, and enlisted the support of Queen Victoria and Pope Pius IX. Thomas H. Gallaudet had gone to Europe years earlier to study techniques of teaching deaf-mutes.

Phrenology, or bump-fingering, was regarded as a science by hundreds of thousands of Americans. Elisha Barrett, a professor at Transylvania University, wrote that "I am well satisfied of the truth of the general principles and doctrine of the phrenological physiology of the brain." Henry Ward Beecher, while a student at Amherst, kept a phrenological bust in his study. A fellow student, Orson Fowler, did bump-readings at two cents a head. Fowler went on to become the leading exponent of phrenology, turning it into a theology, maintaining that "it is sweeping into oblivion those old theories, unnatural customs, and erroneous institutions, by which past ages have been enthralled, and even the present is yet spellbound. So great is its moral power, that it will prostrate and ride over whatever religious doctrines, forms, or practices conflict with it." (Courtesy of the Boston Public Library)

While in England he found that one family had for generations monopolized the field, and they preferred to keep their methods a profitable secret. Gallaudet received a better reception in France, where he studied with Abbé Sicard; he then returned to establish the first free school for the deaf in Hartford, Connecticut. Like Howe's, it became a model for the nation.

Orphanages, poorhouses, and correctional homes for juveniles all had their groups of reformers alerting the public conscience to social abuses. John Sargent attempted to eradicate prostitution. Josiah Quincy, a pioneer in municipal reform, also fought prostitution, and made a remarkable address to the Suffolk grand jury on the effects of jailing younger offenders with hardened criminals. James Russell Lowell spoke out against capital punishment. Louis Dwight headed a society dedicated to the improvement of prison conditions. Robert Rantoul successfully argued for the legitimacy of unions and labor's right to strike. His logic helped persuade Chief Justice Lemuel Shaw of Massachusetts to overturn previous court decisions by recognizing that unions were not criminal conspiracies (*Commonwealth* v. *Hunt*, 1842).

PEACE AND TEMPERANCE

Other attempted reforms, such as peace and temperance, generated much verbal heat and few satisfying results. Both causes had dedicated leaders, national organizations, and significant clerical support, though liquor was considered a more serious evil than war. Temperance was the largest and strongest, and peace the smallest and weakest, of the reform movements.

Peace. If all agreed on the desirability of peace, still there were bitter arguments among pacifists about methods of achieving it. Some sought to devise legal techniques to settle disputes between nations. "It is high time," wrote William Ladd, founder of the American Peace Society, "for the Christian world to seek a more rational, cheap, and equitable mode of settling international difficulties." An ex-sea captain and farmer, Ladd led the pacifist crusade for two decades. His program for a congress of nations to formulate international law, and a court of justice to enforce it, was admired in the abstract but disregarded in practice. In the twentieth century it would be resurrected as Wilsonianism.

Equally ineffective was another wing of the pacifist movement which was uninterested in international conferences and unwilling to honor laws or agreements contrary to their rigid ideas. Precursors of

Gandhi rather than Wilson, these pacifists championed nonresistance. They held that neither nations nor individuals should use physical force under any circumstances whatsoever. In 1838 the abolitionist, William Lloyd Garrison, formed the New England Non-Resistance Society, and wrote its Declaration of Sentiments. In it he included the following radical statement:

> We register our testimony, not only against all wars, whether offensive or defensive, but all preparations for war; against every naval ship, every arsenal, every fortification; against the militia system and a standing army; against all military chieftains and soldiers; against all monuments commemorative of victory over a fallen foe, all trophies won in battle, all celebrations in honor of military or naval exploits; against all appropriations for the defence of a nation by force and arms, on the part of any legislative body; against every edict of government requiring of its subjects military service. Hence, we deem it unlawful to bear arms, or to hold a military office.

Henry David Thoreau sympathized with but did not participate in the reform movement. Though influenced by the passive resistance philosophy, he carefully disassociated himself from its anarchist conclusions. "Unlike those who call themselves no-government men," wrote Thoreau in his famous essay, *Resistance to Civil Government*, "I ask for, not at once no government, but *at once* a better government." Thoreau was a majority unto himself, individualistic to the point of selfishness. He objected to the Mexican War, and refused to pay taxes as a protest, but would not cooperate with other pacifists. Elihu Burritt, on the other hand, was completely selfless and cooperative, motivated by no ambition except a desire to aid humanity. With Ladd's death the peace movement came to depend upon his exertions. Between 1848 and 1852 he organized four international conferences: each was well attended, but produced no visible effects. Pacifism collapsed rapidly as nations went to war on both sides of the Atlantic— the Crimean War, revolution in Poland, unification struggles in Italy and Germany, and civil war in America. Torn between their hatred of war and hatred of slavery, most reformers adjusted their antiwar philosophy in order to support the North. "I think we should agree about war," wrote Theodore Parker. "I hate it, deplore it, but yet see its necessity. All the great charters of humanity have been writ in blood, and must continue to be for some centuries." Burritt also supported the Union; though he returned to pacifism as soon as it ended, this time advocating massive resistance, a worldwide strike of workingmen for peace. "We hope the day will come," Burritt declared, "when the working men of Christendom will form one vast Trades

Union, and make a universal and simultaneous *strike* against the whole war system."

There were temperance parades, temperance songs, temperance plays, and temperance conventions. "Dear Father, Drink No More," and "Mother, Dry That Flowing Tear," were sentimental favorites sung at their meetings, as was "Father, Dear Father, Come Home With Me Now." Lucius Sargent's Temperance Tales *were widely read; and Timothy Shay Arthur's play,* Ten Nights in a Bar Room, *was a commercial success. Famous reformers, such as William Lloyd Garrison, Elihu Burritt, Lyman Beecher, and Frederick Douglass journeyed to London to participate in a World Temperance Convention in 1846. Women were active in the movement, though barred from membership in some societies. Children, also, as the above cartoon indicates, were expected to take the pledge to renounce all liquor. (Courtesy of the New-York Historical Society)*

Temperance. Physicians, evangelical ministers, students and scholars, renowned theologians, reformed drunkards, and even children all marched together for temperance. There were literally thousands of organizations devoted to the task, such as the American Temperance Union, the Independent Order of Rechabites, the Washingtonians, the Congressional Temperance Society, the Carson League, "Father Mathew" societies, and the Cold Water Army. Over a million people took the pledge of sobriety, including children:

We, Cold Water girls and boys,
Freely renounce the treacherous joys
Of brandy, whiskey, rum and gin;
The serpent's lure to death and sin.
Wine, beer and cider we detest,
And thus we'll make our parents blest;
So here we pledge perpetual hate
To all that can intoxicate.

Temperance was the one reform to permeate the South. Senator Robert B. Rhett of South Carolina and Governor Henry H. Wise of Virginia were prominent in the movement, and General John Cocke of Virginia became president of the American Temperance Union. A number of states tried to control the worst effects of excessive alcoholic consumption by various licensing and tax laws. Massachusetts in 1838 passed the "Fifteen-Gallon Law," which forbade the sale of less than that amount at one time. The governor who signed the law, Edward Everett, was defeated for reelection, and it was repealed in 1840. Gradually more radical reformers came to the conclusion that mere temperance was not enough, and they sought total abstinence, to be enforced by complete legal prohibition. Wherever it was tried— first in Maine, and then in a dozen other states—there was fierce resistance. A crowd in Salem, Massachusetts, pelted a prohibitionist clergyman with eggs. Another in St. Paul, Minnesota, attacked the local sheriff. In some states the laws were declared unconstitutional; in other states they failed to perform as expected. Observers pointed out that though all the grogshops in Maine were closed, people there were drinking more liquor than ever before. But prohibitionists were notoriously persistent, urged on by a sense of religious fervor and moral certainty, and the issue continued to bedevil America well into the twentieth century.

WOMEN'S RIGHTS

North or South, women were not easily admitted to participation in reform activities. In fact, most did not respond to the call from leaders of their own sex to fight for equality in education, in marriage, in law, or in politics. Pioneer women shared the full burden and responsibilities of homesteading. Working-class women labored in mills and factories. But a woman of the middle and upper classes was expected to stay at home, to be pure, pious, submissive, and totally domestic. Virginity, not intelligence, was her proudest possession, the marriage night the greatest event in her life, and bearing and raising children her sole contribution. Any girl foolish enough to part with her virginity before marriage, Thomas Branagan warned in *The Excellency of the Female Character,*" will be left in silent sadness to bewail your credulity, imbecility, duplicity, and premature prostitution." The home was the stabilizing core of a fluctuating society, to be maintained and safeguarded by women. In return for that sovereignty she was expected to renounce all others. "Noble, sublime, is the task of the American mother," one author proclaimed. Those who left the hearth for the lectern "are only semi-women, mental hermaphrodites." Virtuous women possessed the most sublime and divine "rights" at home:

> The right to love whom others scorn,
> The right to comfort and to mourn,
> The right to shed new joy on earth,
> The right to feel the soul's high worth . . .
> Such women's rights, and God will bless
> And crown their champions with success.

Women who dared rebel against the prevailing social code required extraordinary fortitude. At every step their actions were greeted with public derision, taunts, and insults. "Mind," Hannah Crocker observed, "has no sex," but males feared making this dangerous concession. Emma Willard submitted a plan for improving female education to the New York legislature, and opened a female seminary in 1821. One paper commented that "the most acceptable degree" for young ladies was "the degree of M.R.S." Elizabeth Blackwell's applications to enter medical school were repeatedly denied. "You cannot expect us," a male dean told her, "to furnish you with a stick to break our heads with." She was finally admitted to a small medical college in Geneva, New York. The townspeople, she reported, theorized that she was either "a bad woman, whose designs would gradually become evident, or that, being insane, an outbreak of insanity would soon be apparent." Elizabeth Cady Stanton, Lucretia Mott, and scores of other women were enthusiastic abolitionists. Yet those women who journeyed to London in 1840 to attend the World Antislavery Convention were not permitted to participate. The males who excluded them "would have been horrified at the idea of burning the distinguished women present with red-hot irons," wrote Elizabeth Stanton, "but the crucifixion of their pride and self-respect, the humiliation of their spirit, seemed to them a most trifling matter." Women had stalwartly supported temperance reform since its inception. Yet, when Susan B. Anthony attempted to address a temperance society convention in Albany, she was informed that "ladies" could listen but take no part in the proceedings.

THE ORATOR OF THE DAY DENOUNCING THE LORDS OF CREATION

The women who fought for equal rights had to be tough, tireless, and courageous, for they were scorned by the great majority of men who preferred to treat women sentimentally and, at the same time, keep them second-class citizens. Note, in the above illustration of a women's convention, the few friendly men on the floor and the jeering crowd in the balcony. (From Harper's Weekly, *June 11, 1859)*

A sense of solidarity united feminists who had suffered male rebuffs and male condescension. At Seneca Falls, New York, in 1848, a women's rights convention adopted its own declaration of independence, a paraphrase of the original, which demanded that women "have immediate admission to all the rights and privileges which belong to them as citizens of the United States." Other conventions followed in Massachusetts, Ohio, Pennsylvania, and Indiana, though males scorned and ridiculed their efforts. At a women's meeting in Akron, Ohio, unsympathetic clergymen invaded and dominated the discussion until Sojourner Truth—an old but fiery black female abolitionist—rose to speak, dramatically reminding her audience that women's rights were not meant for whites only:

Dat man ober dar say dat womin needs to be helped into carriages and lifted ober ditches, and to hab de best place everywhar. Nobody eber helps me into carriages, or ober mud-puddles, or gibs me any best place! And a'n't I a woman? Look at my arm! I have ploughed, and planted and gathered into barns, and no man could head me! And a'n't I a woman? I could work as much and eat as much as a man— when I could get it—and bear de lash as well! And a'n't I a woman? I have borne thirteen chilern, and seen 'em mos' all sold off to slavery, and when I cried out with my mother's grief, none but Jesus heard me! And a'n't I a woman? Den dat little little man in black dar, he say women can't have as much rights as men, 'cause Christ wan't a woman! Whar did your Christ come from? Whar did your Christ come from? From God and a woman! Man had nothin' to do with Him!

In practical terms their gains were modest. More schools were open to women. Elementary teaching positions became almost a female monopoly (though they were paid considerably less than men). Massachusetts and Indiana liberalized their divorce laws. New York in 1860 gave women the right to sue as well as control of their own wages and property. Most important, a slight breach had been made in the wall of male chauvinism, and examples of female courage sustained later feminists in their struggle for equality.

ANTI-CATHOLICISM

The humanitarian impulse and Christian love of reformers had distinct limits. It scoffed at the pretensions of women who thought themselves equal to men. And it balked altogether at the idea of equating Catholicism with other faiths. Reverend Lyman Beecher thought that "if it had been the design of Heaven to establish a powerful nation in the full enjoyment of civil and religious liberty. . . . where should such an experiment have been made but in this country!" Beecher helped heaven's design by espousing the good causes of abolition, temperance, and educational reform. He also wrote, in 1835, *Plea for the West*, a nativist attack upon Catholicism whose policies would "inflame the nation, break the bond of our union, and throw down our free institutions." On one occasion Beecher's anti-Catholic sermons helped inflame a Boston mob which attacked and burned a Ursuline convent.

Anti-Catholicism was an old and familiar prejudice of Protestants in America, but never before had it flared into full-scale bigotry. In 1830 there were 318,000 Catholics in the United States, making up only 3 per cent of the population; shortly before the Civil War there

RIOT IN PHILADELPHIA
JUNE 7th 1844.

As early as 1844 the anti-Catholic "Native Americans"—predecessors of the Know-Nothing party—provoked a series of riots in eastern cities. The above cartoon shows the nativists in tall beaver hats fighting the state militia in Philadelphia. Two old and famous Catholic churches were burned, and more than twenty people were killed in the city of brotherly love before the riot abated. (Courtesy of the Library of Congress)

were 3,100,000, some 10 per cent of the population. The huge Irish immigration had made Catholicism the largest single religion in America. They are "crowding our cities, lining our railroads and canals," a worried critic observed, "and electing our rulers." Samuel F. B. Morse, promoter of the telegraph, spread the alarm in his book, *Foreign Conspiracy Against the Liberties of the United States*. Maria Monk's lurid fiction, *Awful Disclosures of the Hôtel Dieu Nunnery of Montreal*, was taken as truth, and it spawned dozens of imitations. There were, of course, numerous rebuttals. If many Protestant intellectuals included anti-Catholicism in their roster of reforms, there were others such as Parke Godwin in New York and Henry Wise in Virginia who denounced the tissue of lies and humbug directed against

Catholics. Benedict Webb, a Kentucky Catholic, wrote: "The man who impugns my patriotism on account of my religious opinions, is either an insane bigot who claims my pity, or a foul-mouthed slanderer who has my contempt." The defense was less effective than the slander. Because they were frightened by irrational fears of "papal influence," and believing they were fighting to save their country, nativists rioted in cities such as Baltimore, St. Louis, Louisville, and New Orleans.

The Order of the Star Spangled Banner, organized in 1849, combined with other nativist groups and entered politics as the American or Know-Nothing party. They scored impressive victories in 1854–55, carrying at least seven states (mainly northern), and gaining substantial support in seven others (mainly southern). Then, for several reasons, quickly as it had blossomed, the Know-Nothing party faded. It had accomplished nothing of substance where it held power. (In Massachusetts, for example, committees spent inordinate sums investigating nunneries and convent schools.) Moreover, it lacked effective leadership. Most important, the Know-Nothing party anticipated that it might achieve victory by uniting a majority of Americans on the basis of anti-Catholic and antiforeign prejudice, only to find its ranks split over the issue of slavery. Thousands of members deserted the nativist cause to join the major parties. By 1856, Millard Fillmore, the Know-Nothing presidential candidate, could garner no more than eight electoral votes.

VARIETIES OF RELIGIOUS EXPERIENCE

A resurgence of religious spirit, a second Great Awakening, crossed over the land in the early nineteenth century. The fastest growing faiths were evangelical, which rejected elaborate theological structures understood by the few for emotional appeals appreciated by the many. This movement was in keeping with the temper of the times. The age of deference had passed, replaced by an age of mass participation, of equalitarian values, which sought simpler, more democratic paths, including the path to heaven. There could be no exclusivity in politics, economics, or religion. Old-fashioned Calvinism, with its emphasis on predestination, finally lost its hold upon the New England mind. Unitarianism took its place, at least among the intellectual elite. For the masses, however, Unitarianism was too cold, too cerebral, and too lacking in essential piety. They preferred fiery, declamatory sermons which stirred the soul. "Young men," Lyman Beecher advised prospective ministers, "pump yourselves brim full of your subject till you can't hold another drop, and then knock out the bung and let nature caper." Revivalism became the central element of the Protestant structure. All churches were affected, though the Methodists and Baptists reaped the richest rewards in numbers of converts.

Revivalism seemed to fulfill the psychological needs of society. Men and women under the spell of itinerant preachers twitched their bodies, rolled on the ground, shrieked in agitation (or religious ecstasy), barked like dogs, suffered hallucinations, and often fell unconscious. "Jerking" was a common symptom of their camp meetings. "The hands of the jerking patients flew with wondrous quickness, from side to side in various directions," a witness to a Kentucky revival noted, "and their necks doubled back like a flail in the hands of the thresher. Their faces were distorted and black, and their eyes seemed to flash horror and distraction." All kinds of religions proliferated in America, particularly in rural and frontier areas, including some rather strange and short-lived cultists who followed self-proclaimed seers. Vermont and upstate New York, along the main route of New Englanders journeying westward, was especially "burnt-over" by the fires of religious excitement. Here there originated the Millennial movement of William Miller, who in the 1820's predicted that the second coming of Christ would occur in 1843, then revised the date to 1844. Millennialism spread phenomenally, into the urban East and as far west as Iowa. A million converts were claimed, mainly poor and uneducated farmers, workers, and shopkeepers, who accepted Miller's prediction and prepared accordingly. Some disposed of all their material possessions. Some went berserk when the appointed day passed without Christ's appearance. Miller continued to believe, supported by a handful of Adventists; but the rest, terribly disillusioned, abandoned their faith in Millennialism.

The "burnt-over" district also spawned a variety of spiritualists. Perhaps because they were not zealous holy rollers, yet claimed to offer direct communion with divine forces, many educated people were attracted by clairvoyants. The Fox sisters of Rochester became nationally famous for their alleged ability to contact the spiritual world. "We are convinced beyond a doubt," testified Horace Greeley, publisher of the New York *Tribune*, "of their perfect integrity and good faith." Though some mediums were exposed as charlatans (including the Fox sisters), prominent figures such as James Fenimore Cooper, Edgar Allan Poe, and Harriet Beecher Stowe, the historian George Bancroft, the Workingmen's party advocate Robert Dale Owen, the scientist Robert Hare, and the transcendentalist preacher Theodore Parker either endorsed the authenticity of or experimented with seances and other spiritualistic nonsense. Every town seemed to have a renowned local medium. Spiritualism as part of religious faith was very widespread. It was an integral component of Shaker religious life, and of Swedenborgianism, which several Brook Farm residents took seriously. Andrew Jackson Davis, known as the "Poughkeepsie Seer," swore that he talked with Swedenborg's ghost, as well as with Benjamin Franklin and St. Paul. Adin Ballou, a respected reformer and leader of the Hopedale Community in Massachusetts, was a spiritualist. So was Warren Chase, founder of a Fourierist commune in Wisconsin.

THE MORMONS

The most astonishing success story in American religion originated in the "burnt-over" district. In 1830 certain golden plates dug up by Joseph Smith, and deciphered by him with the aid of magic stones, had been published in Palmyra, New York—the *Book of Mormon*. Within two decades, despite Protestant hostility, which drove Smith's supporters from New York to Ohio to Missouri to Illinois, and finally to Utah, Mormonism became the ninth largest religion in the United States. The governor of Missouri declared Mormon residents to be "public enemies," who must be "exterminated or driven from the State, if necessary, for the public good." At Carthage, Illinois, a wild mob of 200, unrestrained by the militia, killed Joseph Smith and his brother. Under the leadership of Brigham Young the Mormons moved on to the valley of the Great Salt Lake in Utah. Here they hoped to build, as did the Puritans two centuries before, a Zion in the wilderness. Here there was virgin land and the promise of salvation. "In this place," wrote a Mormon convert from England, "there is a prospect of receiving every good thing both of this world and that which is to come."

Even in that isolated region hostility pursued the Mormons. Emigrant groups on their way to California complained of the outrageous prices Mormons charged for goods. Brigham Young's autocratic rule conflicted with the authority of territorial judges appointed by the federal government. But most criticism was directed at the Mormon practice of polygamy, which many reformers equated with slavery as barbaric evils not to be tolerated in America. An agent of the American Bible Society described the Mormon colony as a "bedlam, brothel, sink of iniquity, Hades, and vortex of moral ruin." Anti-Mormon feeling reached a pitch when a wagon train of 120 emigrants was murdered by a combined force of Indians and Mormons. One eastern newspaper demanded that the "beastly heresy" of Mormonism be crushed. "This is the first rebellion which has existed in our territories," President Buchanan declared, "and humanity itself requires that we should put it down in such a manner that it shall be the last." His order dispatching federal troops to Utah territory might have led to war were it not for the good sense of peace negotiators on both sides. Thereafter the Mormons nominally accepted "gentile" governors from Washington, continued to obey Joseph Smith, and set an example of thrift, industry, and piety which attracted many converts and did much to earn the respect of all Americans.

All told, the cause of religion prospered in the nineteenth century, if one judges by its free expression, its amazing assortment of creeds, its vitality, and its growth. However, theology went bankrupt. In this

THE TABERNACLE AT SALT LAKE CITY.—[From a Photograph by Burr & Mogo.]

"Mormonism," writes a scholar member of that church, William Mulder, ". . . is as native to the United States as Indian corn and the buffalo nickel. We have to specify an American Judaism or an American Catholicism, but Mormonism is American by birth." Most Americans, outraged by the doctrines of Mormonism, were reluctant to accept that honor. Even at the time the above engraving of the Mormon tabernacle in Salt Lake City was made, in 1858, federal troops were prepared to do battle against Mormon forces, and a war was barely averted by intelligent mediation. (Courtesy of the Periodical Department, Boston Public Library)

respect it bore a striking parallel to political developments. No group of political leaders emerged to match the stellar array of intellectual talent that guided America during the revolutionary and federalist eras. And no Protestant theology or theologians of the first order were produced during the century of its greatest expansion.

CULTURAL INDEPENDENCE

A country as energetic and bustling as America was emphasized practicality rather than theology, and applauded material achievements rather than philosophical systems. People interested in either building or reforming had no time for metaphysical hairsplitting or recondite reasoning. One might expect, therefore, that America had little to contribute culturally, that the leveling effects of a democratic society would drive out intellectual creativity. There were authors and artists, disillusioned by and disengaged from the American scene, who fled to Europe. There were those who spoke rather bitterly, and with much truth, about the crudity and vulgarity of their own land, with its lack of opportunities for the serious writer. "The utmost any American author can look for in his native country," Charles Brockden Brown told his brother, "is to be reimbursed his unavoidable expenses." James Fenimore Cooper spent much time abroad, and complained of the imaginative poverty of America. "There are no annals for the historian; no follies . . . for the satirist; no manners for the dramatist; no obscure fictions for the writer of romance . . . nor any of the rich artificial auxiliaries of poetry," Cooper wrote contemptuously in *Notions of the Americans*. It was an indictment to be repeated by many other American authors at a later date. Yet Brown and Cooper were distinctively American, their works marking a shift from the classical stress of the eighteenth century to the romantic qualities of the nineteenth century. Cooper published more than 50 books and pamphlets in 30 years, frequently using the American wilderness as a setting to spin out his themes of conflict between the civilized and the primitive.

As early as 1778 Noah Webster called for a declaration of cultural freedom. "America," he wrote, "must be as independent in *literature* as she is in *politics*, as famous for *arts* as for *arms*." This nationalistic appeal was echoed many times over, but without too much success. In Boston the Anthology Club and in New York the Friendly Club were formed to encourage American authors to cast off fashionable English styles and to create a national literature. Few agreed with Cooper that the United States was a land of dull uniformity. Rather, it was endlessly diverse, and it required authors of sagacity and skill to exploit the rich materials it afforded. Ralph Waldo Emerson in his Phi Beta Kappa address, "The American Scholar," delivered at Harvard University in 1837, exulted that "our day of dependence, our long apprenticeship to the learning of other lands, draws to a close. The millions that around us are rushing into life cannot always be fed on the sere remains of foreign harvests. Events, actions arise, that must be sung, that will sing themselves." Walt Whitman responded wholeheartedly, setting himself the task of consciously joining democracy to literature, of becoming the poet Emerson envisioned singing of America. "The drama of this country," he once wrote, "can be the mouthpiece of freedom." If Cooper saw mainly contradictions and ambiguities in America which soured him, Whitman loved the expansive multiplicity of democratic forces at work in the land. As a young reporter on the Brooklyn *Daily Eagle* he asked for "American plays, fitted to American opinions and institutions." "The United States themselves," he once noted, "are essentially the greatest poem." Whitman set the type for *Leaves of Grass* with his own hand, 12 poems in free verse, coarse, uneven, sensuous, and mystical, yet emphatically and authentically American.

The essays of Emerson and Thoreau and the poetry of Whitman mark a turning away from Europe. The trend was equally apparent in the novels of Nathaniel Hawthorne and Herman Melville. Between 1850 and 1855 there appeared *The Scarlet Letter* and *The House of the Seven Gables* by Hawthorne, *Moby Dick* by Melville, *Walden* by Thoreau, and *Leaves of Grass* by Whitman. "You may search all the rest of American literature," according to one critic, "without being able to collect a group of books equal to these in imaginative vitality."

MASS CULTURE

In the end the American public reviled Cooper for his criticisms. Thoreau was little appreciated in the United States, though hailed as a genius elsewhere. Hawthorne enjoyed some success, as did Whitman, but Melville was too profound to be popular, and he died in obscurity. The masses, then as now, preferred reading sentimental novels that stirred the emotions but did not tax the intellect.[1] Their tastes ran to what was practical or patriotic or moral or pornographic posing as moral. For example, the leading male writer in America was George

[1] In 1818 Thomas Jefferson wrote: "A great obstacle to good education is the inordinate passion prevalent for novels, and the time lost in that reading which should be instructively employed. When this poison infects the mind, it destroys its tone and revolts against wholesome reading. Reason and fact, plain and unadorned, are rejected. . . . The result is a bloated imagination, sickly judgment, and disgust towards all the real business of life."

Lippard, a religious charlatan, pseudoradical, and superpatriot. His novel, *The Quaker City; or, The Monks of Monk Hall* (1844), was filled with sinister Jews, hulking blacks, corrupt clergymen, and grasping bankers who raped virgins and killed old women. The combination of sex and social protest was irresistible. The book sold 60,000 copies the first year of publication, and half that number annually for the next decade. Lippard's patriotic writings were made up of whole cloth. His *Washington and His Generals; or Legends of the American Revolution* (1847), another best seller, began the myth of the "Liberty Bell" being rung to announce the signing of the Declaration of Independence.

Heartrending stories of poor orphans, ravished innocence, and blighted love—forerunners of the modern soap opera—were favorites of American readers. The fiction of Sir Walter Scott and Charles Dickens was much in demand, and American female authors joined in, virtually monopolizing the "domestic" novel. Mary Jane Holmes's lachrymose books became classics, selling over a million copies. Maria Cummins' *The Lamplighter* was an instant success. Probably the best-known single volume was *The Wide Wide World* by Susan Warner. Her characters, one reviewer commented, "are distinguished for the union of purity, sweetness, and admirable sense. . . . They display a naturalness and beauty of conduct which never fails to touch the moral sensibilities." Little wonder that Hawthorne remarked in anger: "America is now wholly given over to a damned mob of scribbling women, and I should have no chance of success while the public taste is occupied with their trash."

Above all, Americans loved oratory, especially if it was inspiring and educational. A lyceum movement—an association providing public lectures—spread so rapidly that by 1835 there were 3,000 in existence in 15 states. By 1859 *Harper's Magazine* observed that "the lyceum has now become a fixed American institution." For a modest fee one could attend and hear a talk on "The Life of Mohammed," "The Honey Bee," "The Education of Children," "The Memoirs of Count Rumford," or "The Progress of Democracy." Emerson was a great favorite on the lyceum circuit, as were Daniel Webster and Horace Mann. The lyceum was undoubtedly a more significant cultural force than formal academic institutions. Besides spreading knowledge to all age groups, lyceums encouraged the establishment of public schools and libraries as well as scientific collections. A Swedish visitor to America, P. A. Siljeström, was so impressed that he advised Europeans to copy the lyceum if they wished to avoid either despotism or revolution.

With the development of more efficient printing techniques, such as the Hoe rotary press, newspapers became inexpensive educational instruments for the masses. To be sure, the "penny press" thrived on sensationalism, emphasizing the three r's of rape, riot, and robbery. And many remained political sheets of no particular distinction. But by the 1840's reputable metropolitan dailies, such as Horace Greeley's *Tribune*, helped form American cultural tastes. Political news came first, of course, as well as commercial items, yet one could find book notices, synopses of lyceum lectures, editorials espousing reforms, travel accounts by distinguished journalists, and extended analytical essays by foreign correspondents. Karl Marx, in fact, was the "London correspondent" for the *Tribune* before the Civil War.

THE DEIFICATION OF WASHINGTON

One aspect of the American character dominated all others. An aggressive people, Americans were also incurably sentimental; inclined to materialistic goals, they made a fetish of piety; culturally chauvinistic, still they harbored the idea that Europeans could do it better; if most were boosters and boasters, others were dissatisfied reformers. In this complex of opposites, Americans sought unity in patriotism. Local jealousies and sectional tensions might prevail, but all could unite in veneration of the past—if only the past could be sterilized and sanctified. The figure of George Washington was an obvious and inevitable choice, to be mythologized by a public who yearned for an incorruptible father image to glorify.

The process of glorification whereby Washington was converted from a fallible human to a faultless saint began early and was exceedingly rapid and thorough. Even while Americans still mourned his death in 1799, an itinerant book peddler and evangelist, Mason Locke Weems, decided to enrich himself (financially) and the nation (morally) by penning a series of mainly spurious anecdotes revealing the "Great Virtues" of Washington. The work of this clever fraud, which first appeared in 1800, had an enormous impact, probably greater than that of any single volume in American history. It satisfied the public need to hear homilies of his life and accounts of his piety, wisdom, and dedication. Other heroes might possess blemishes, but Washington, as "Father of His Country," needed to appear spotless. So he was presented by Weems and by dozens of imitators, and so he was envisioned by Americans.

There were a few who resisted the unqualified acclaim. Emerson remarked that people bored with such unstinting praise were apt to

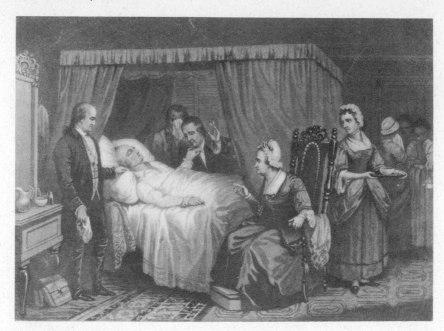

This engraving by H. S. Sadd of George Washington on his death bed, which appeared in the Columbian Magazine *of 1846, is typical of the veneration Americans accorded their first president. Another favorite picture showed him kneeling, at prayer in the snow, at Valley Forge. All other heroes were quite secondary. The typical American believed that Washington was a devout Christian, that he never lied, and that the spurious tales of Parson Weems were gospel truth.* (Courtesy of The Granger Collection)

remark in private, "Damn George Washington." Artemus Ward poked fun at the image: "G. Washington was abowt the best man this world ever sot eyes on. . . . He never slopt over." Hawthorne wrote derisively: "Did any body ever see Washington nude? It is inconceivable. He had no nakedness, but I imagine he was born with his clothes on, and his hair powdered, and made a stately bow on his first appearance before the world." Yet those who refused to join in the deification of Washington, who insisted that men, while good enough, are far more complex and fascinating than mere divinities, were in a distinct minority. More typical were the words of Abraham Lincoln, who owned the tenth edition of Weems, and learned its lessons well. "To add brightness to the sun or glory to the name of Washington is alike impossible," he proclaimed on February 22, 1842. "Let none attempt it. In solemn awe pronounce the name and in its naked deathless splendor leave it shining on."

All the patriotic reverence of Washington, together with all the Fourth of July speeches, could not make the issue of slavery disappear. The reforming energies directed against the money power turned to combat the slave power. Movements for social equality, economic justice, peace, and suffrage expansion were swallowed by abolitionism, and then lost in the whirlpool of Civil War. What remained was a cynicism, a frustration, which would linger for decades before the impulse for reform could be reawakened.

SUGGESTED READINGS

*Irving H. Bartlett, *The American Mind in the Mid-Nineteenth Century*

*Arthur Bestor, *Backwoods Utopias*

*Carl Bode, *The American Lyceum: Town Meeting of the Mind*

*———, *The Anatomy of American Popular Culture, 1840–1861*

*Daniel J. Boorstin, *The Americans: The National Experience*

E. Douglas Branch, *The Sentimental Years*

Fawn Brodie, *No Man Knows My History: The Life of Joseph Smith*

*Henry S. Commager, *The Era of Reform*

*———, *Theodore Parker*

*Whitney Cross, *The Burned-Over District*

*Marcus Cunliffe, *The Nation Takes Shape*

Merle Curti, *The American Peace Crusade*

Arthur A. Ekirch, *The Idea of Progress in America*

*Leslie Fiedler, *Love and Death in the American Novel*

Octavius B. Frothingham, *Transcendentalism in New England*

*Joseph R. Gusfield, *Symbolic Crusade: Status Politics and the American Temperance Movement*

John A. Krout, *The Origins of Prohibition*

*F. O. Matthiessen, *American Renaissance*

Sidney E. Mead, *The Lively Experiment*

Clara Sears, *Days of Delusion*

*Andrew Sinclair, *The Emancipation of the American Woman*

*Henry N. Smith, *Virgin Land: The American West as Symbol and Myth*

*Alice F. Tyler, *Freedom's Ferment*

*Bernard Weisberger, *They Gathered at the River*

* Available in paperback

FREEDOM AND SLAVERY
1840/1865

8 THE AMERICAN TRAGEDY

Slavery had existed long before the South was thought of as a slave power. The climate and soil conditions below the Mason-Dixon line favored the institution. Wherever staples could be grown —first tobacco and rice, then cotton—slavery flourished. When Eli Whitney's gin made short-staple cotton an important money crop, slavery spread with the cotton belt across the lower South.

Until the second quarter of the nineteenth century, however, slavery was not a major issue to white Americans. Northerners were not oblivious to it. Advertisements for runaway slaves appeared regularly in the northern press. Occasionally a Quaker petition recommending the abolition of slavery raised a flurry in Congress. Americans, North and South, were well aware of the dichotomy between preaching liberty and practicing slavery. But the North was preoccupied with economic development. The southern attitude was both firm and apologetic. If they would not tolerate interference with slavery, neither would they build any elaborate arguments to defend it.

Slavery has been America's greatest tragedy. By the time enough people cared about the problem, it was beyond compromise and civil war resulted. Nor is the tragedy over. "The grapes of wrath," one historian has noted, "have not yet yielded all their bitter vintage."

THE SOUTHERN DEFENSE

Partly as a reaction to northern abolitionism, the South began to devote its collective intellectual abilities to proving that slavery was a wise and beneficial practice. Southern ministers cited the gospel as a theological defense. Southern economists asserted that slaves were better treated than many northern workers. Southern politicians reproached Northerners for criticizing an institution recognized by the Constitution. Southern scientists concluded that blacks were intellectually inferior to whites and therefore best suited to be slaves. Southern historians pointed to the existence of slavery in ancient and contemporary cultures. Southerners may once have questioned the profitability of slavery and speculated about its deleterious effects on whites. But such reservations were swept away by the 1840's. Contrary views were not permitted. Discussion was not tolerated. Slavery was deemed essential to the economic system and the social stability of the South. Indeed, Southerners boasted that through slavery they had created a unique civilization, superior to all others. So zealous was the South's attempt at justification that for decades it produced few enduring works in art, literature, philosophy, or science.

Lurking behind this self-assurance was the gnawing fear of slave insurrection. "We regard our Negroes," one Southerner commented, "as the *Jacobins* of the country, against whom we should always be on our guard." The black slave was not the docile, contented, loyal servant romantics like to imagine. Nor was he the rebellious firebrand some authors have portrayed. Statistically many more conspiracies were plotted than the small number of open rebellions that were actually attempted. Nevertheless, at times the fear of a "Black Terror" led southern whites to the point of hysteria. Repression and white supremacy became the distinguishing hallmarks of the antebellum South, to be passed on to future generations.

THE ABOLITIONIST ATTACK

"Everybody is opposed to slavery," wrote William Lloyd Garrison sarcastically, "O, yes! There is an abundance of philanthropy among us." The question of what to do about it, if anything, divided the

Although the underground railroad was neither underground nor a railroad, it helped approximately 50,000 slaves escape between 1840 and 1860. Some scholars have suggested that the underground railroad acted as a safety valve for slavery, since the most dangerous slaves, the natural leaders of rebellions, fled to freedom. Portrayed above is a group of fugitive slaves fleeing from Maryland to the Delaware "depot." (Courtesy of Historical Pictures Service, Chicago)

Northerners into bitterly antagonistic camps. At one extreme were those abolitionists who followed the lead of Garrison, preaching that slavery was a sin to be atoned only by instantaneous repentance—the immediate and uncompensated emancipation of all slaves. Like other zealots, Garrison had little patience with those who questioned his methods. His newspaper, the *Liberator,* established in Boston in 1831, never attained a circulation greater than 3,000. Nevertheless, to most contemporaries and to many later scholars, Garrison symbolized the antislavery crusade.

Actually, a second center of abolitionism existed in upstate New York, western Pennsylvania, and Ohio. This movement stemmed from and borrowed the techniques of religious revivalism. It was at once more practical, more moderate, more influential, and more politically oriented than the Garrisonians. A volume by one of their better-known leaders, Theodore Weld's *Slavery As It Is,* sold over 100,000 copies the first year. Weld advocated the doctrine of gradual immediatism: to begin the process of emancipation of slaves immediately and to achieve complete freedom gradually.

Abolitionists alternately cooperated and quarreled among themselves, yet they shared a common martyrdom. Most Northerners, although they might admit that slavery was evil, professed that it was not their affair. Abolitionist speeches pricked Northerners' consciences and aroused furious reactions. In 1835 Garrison was tied with a rope and pulled through the streets of Boston by an enraged mob which threatened to lynch him. Elijah Lovejoy was less fortunate. He was killed in 1837 in Alton, Illinois, defending his printing press against a rampaging mob. Nor were these isolated examples: literally hundreds of incidents occurred in which abolitionist homes were sacked, or their meetings disrupted, or their offices destroyed, or bodily harm inflicted. Then, in less than a decade, northern opinion shifted. Abolitionism was still hardly popular, but abolitionists came to be tolerated by the masses and toasted by the intellectuals.

THE "GAG" RESOLUTION

The obtuseness and intransigence of southern congressmen helped the abolitionist cause. For some time the abolitionist societies had been flooding Congress with petitions to emancipate slaves, or to forbid the slave trade in the District of Columbia. These petitions had no practical effect and served only to impede the consideration of other business. But they occasionally provoked discussions of slavery which the Southerners wanted to block. Some northern members agreed that the subject was dangerous and should be silenced. Thus, in 1836, the lower house passed a "gag" resolution to receive and automatically table all such petitions. Technically the "gag" rule was not an abridgement of the right of petition, but in effect it constituted a denial of that right.

Massachusetts' most famous congressman, old John Quincy Adams—ex-minister, ex-secretary of state, and ex-president—single-handedly took up the cudgels for free discussion. Adams was friendly to the antislavery movement, though he was no abolitionist. Indeed, he had voted to maintain slavery in the capital. But the right of petition transcended immediate issues. At stake, Adams told his constituents, was "your freedom of thought and of action, and the freedom of speech in Congress of your representative." For eight years Adams scored Southerners in debate, enduring their taunts, their intimidations, and even their attempts to pass resolutions of censure, until the rule was finally repealed in 1844. By that time a solid core of northern congressmen, mainly from the Whig party, had joined Adams. And by that time events in Texas had pushed northern congressmen further toward the antislavery position.

THE TEXAS REBELLION

Early American migrants to the Mexican territory of Texas did not journey there with a view to rebellion and the hope of eventual annexation to the United States, though Mexicans, with good reason, came to believe such was the case. Like the movement across the boundary into Canada, migration into Texas was impelled by land hunger. Many were prepared to serve a different flag. A few were outlaws who defied all flags. When a group of Texas settlers revolted in 1826 and established the Fredonian Republic, Americans led by Stephen Austin cooperated with Mexican troops to suppress the uprising.

In the next decade, however, Americans in Texas became increasingly dissatisfied. The Mexican government was unstable, inept, corrupt, and despotic. Slave property was not secure. Political and economic grievances over the tariff, immigration, and representation were in turn aggravated by cultural clashes between the proud Texans and the aristocratic Mexicans. Ultimately a short but decisive revolution resulted. On March 2, 1836, Texan independence was declared; on March 6, the Alamo fell; on April 21, at the battle of San Jacinto, the Mexican army of General Santa Anna was routed. Thereafter the Texans quickly ratified a constitution, legalized slavery, made Sam Houston their president, and voted by the overwhelming ratio of 60 to 1 to abandon their recently acquired sovereignty if the United States would agree to annex Texas.

THE ANNEXATION QUESTION

Abolitionists interpreted American expansion into Texas as part of a southern conspiracy to extend the boundaries of slavery. John Quincy Adams echoed the charge and added some vivid reminders of what annexation of Texas would entail: a costly and bloody war with Mexico. Northern politicians were alarmed at the political weight that would be added to the South if Texas, carved into perhaps five states, were admitted. Eight northern states passed resolutions of opposition. Even if Andrew Jackson wanted annexation, he could not act without jeopardizing the election of his successor, Martin Van Buren. Just before retiring from the presidency Jackson received the minister from the Lone Star Republic, and the United States officially recognized the independence of Texas.

During the administrations of Martin Van Buren, William Henry Harrison, and, after his death, John Tyler, the annexation question agitated American politics. Andrew Jackson urged Tyler to some decisive action. Britain was making serious overtures to the Texas Republic. "To prevent Great Britain from getting it, or an influence over it," warned Jackson, "we must have it, *peaceably if we can, but forcibly if we must.*" Some Northerners, who had purchased Texas bonds and thus had an economic interest in the area's future, strongly advised annexation. Tyler needed little encouragement. One of his main purposes in appointing John C. Calhoun as secretary of state in March 1844 had been to fashion a treaty which would bring Texas into the Union. The attempt failed. In addition to the indefatigable Adams, but for different reasons, a bipartisan group which included Thomas Hart Benton and Henry Clay voted to defeat the treaty Calhoun submitted. After nine years of fruitless effort in Congress, expansionists turned to the people. The election of 1844, it was hoped, would finally decide the issue of Texas.

THE ELECTION OF 1844

Rejecting Martin Van Buren, the Democratic party nominated a "dark horse" candidate, the first in American history, James K. Polk of Tennessee. Their platform promised the "reannexation" of Texas and, to satisfy northern Democrats, the "reoccupation" of Oregon to the latitude of 54° 40'. Carrying out either plank could well mean war with Mexico or Great Britain. Were a majority of American voters willing to risk it? Democratic orators whipped up sentiment for expansion. The United States was pursuing a divine destiny to attain its natural geographic limits, Democrats proclaimed, a movement at once glorious, inevitable, irresistible—and manifest. The "peace" candidate of the Whig party, the venerable Henry Clay, was also confident of victory. Clay had declared plainly enough that he would annex Texas if it could be accomplished "without dishonor, without war, with the common consent of the Union, and upon just and fair terms." Would a majority respect Clay's experience and trust his cautious judgment? The result was close—and cruelly ironical. Clay lost the election by losing New York state; he lost New York because the abolitionist Liberty party candidate, James Birney, attracted enough antislavery Whig votes to give Polk the edge. Out of a total of 2,636,000 votes cast for the two major candidates, Polk won by only 38,000.

Despite the narrow margin, President Tyler considered the results a popular mandate for the annexation of Texas. Before his office passed to Polk, Tyler suggested that Congress pass a joint resolution to annex Texas. The strategy was constitutionally questionable but undoubtedly shrewd, for a resolution needed only a simple majority while a treaty required a vote of two thirds. The final ballot was nevertheless close: 120 to 98 in the House of Representatives and 27 to 25 in the Senate.

WAR WITH MEXICO

Had Polk been content with the incorporation of Texas, war with Mexico might have been avoided. To be sure, annexation ruptured relations between the two countries. The offended nationalism of the Mexicans clashed with the expansive nationalism of the Americans and stirred martial feelings on both sides. Still, to say that the war was inevitable excuses responsibility for it. War was inevitable because Polk made it so. He wanted California as the basis of an American empire fronting on the Pacific, and one way or another he was determined to wrest the land from Mexico.

Polk was no swashbuckling militarist. He preferred peaceful solutions and was willing to compromise. He had done so with Great Britain over the northwestern boundary between the United States and Canada. In 1846 a settlement had been arranged at the 49th latitude which, despite the opinions of some extremists and disgruntled politicians, was heartily approved by the people of both countries. To Mexico Polk had dispatched a minister, John Slidell, to offer money for California. The mission failed. "Be assured," Slidell reported, "that nothing is to be done with these people until they shall have been chastised." Polk then ordered American troops commanded by General Zachary Taylor to enter disputed territory between the Nueces and Rio Grande rivers. The results of this deliberately provocative act were all that Polk could ask. Shots were fired; Taylor reported 16 Americans killed or wounded; and Polk coolly asked Congress to declare war on the grounds that Mexico had commenced hostilities.

TREATY OF GUADALUPE HIDALGO

An American military victory was never in doubt, though the Mexicans fought courageously against what a later generation would call invading imperialistic forces. Polk's main problem, in fact, was to keep the war small while continuing it until its chief purpose—the acquisi-

*Ordered by President Polk to capture Mexico City, General Winfield Scott—
undeniably pompous yet quite competent in military matters—sailed from
New Orleans and captured Vera Cruz after a siege of eighteen days. His
army of ten thousand men then began the long tortuous journey to the
capital, over steep mountain passes, fighting engagements against the
troops of the Mexican leader, Santa Anna. The expedition took six months
before the Americans stormed the last barrier to the capital, the hill of
Chapultepec; then burrowed under the stone walls of the fortified city and
swept through the streets. On September 17, 1847, Santa Anna raised the
white flag of surrender, and the conquerors led by Scott—shown below—
marched into Mexico City. (Courtesy of the Rare Books Department, Boston Public Library)*

tion of California—was attained. He was embarrassed, one scholar
has written, by "an ephemeral enemy that continued to lose all the
battles but refused to ask for terms of peace." At home a substantial
number of Americans disapproved of "Mr. Polk's war." Abraham
Lincoln, a young Whig congressman from Illinois, received national
attention when he demanded to know the precise spot upon which
American blood was first spilled. As the war progressed some leading
Democrats joined the Whigs in requesting that it be speedily terminated.

By accident as much as by design, the war ended as Polk had
wished. Nicholas Trist, the chief clerk of the state department, had
been sent to Mexico to negotiate. Although recalled by Polk, he

ignored the order and stayed to sign the peace treaty of Guadalupe Hidalgo. According to the terms Mexico ceded virtually all its northern half, including New Mexico and California, and in return the United States agreed to pay $15,000,000 and to assume American claims that totaled $3,250,000. Polk asked the Senate to ignore the circumstances surrounding the transactions and to vote on the merits of the treaty. Thus, one observer commented, the peace "negotiated by an unauthorized agent, with an unacknowledged government, submitted by an accidental president to a dissatisfied Senate, has, notwithstanding these objections in form, been confirmed."

POLK'S ACCOMPLISHMENTS

Polk was no less triumphant in his other presidential objectives. Besides settling the Oregon boundary with Great Britain and seizing California from Mexico, he achieved a reduction of the tariff and engineered the reestablishment of the independent treasury system. An eminent nineteenth-century historian called Polk "one of the very foremost of our public men and one of the very best and most honest and most successful Presidents the country ever had." Yet, two problems resulted from the Mexican War which Polk had clearly foreseen but which he had been powerless to avoid.

One was political. The generals in charge of the Mexican War, Zachary Taylor and Winfield Scott, were both Whigs. Scott was a bit pompous. But Taylor, affecting simplicity, became a popular hero known as "Old Rough and Ready." He fully appreciated the value of the press and conducted each military campaign, though bravely enough, with an eye to the next presidential election. Polk could not have removed him from command without arousing a storm of public protest. As a result Taylor went on to obtain both the Whig nomination in 1848 and then the presidency, defeating the Democrats' choice, Lewis Cass of Michigan.

The other problem was more significant. During the war Congressman David Wilmot, a Pennsylvania Democrat, attached a rider to an appropriation bill that specified that "neither slavery nor involuntary servitude shall ever exist" in any lands acquired from Mexico. Wilmot's proviso passed the lower house repeatedly but each time met defeat in the Senate. There the South Carolinian John C. Calhoun introduced resolutions—despite ample precedents to the contrary—denying the congressional right to prohibit slavery in any territory of the United States. These were also defeated. In and out of Congress suspicions and jealousies between Northerners and Southerners created an atmosphere of misunderstanding. The two sections had long coexisted by means of cooperation and compromise, but as the 1840's closed each was regarding the other with increasing distrust and animosity.

SLAVERY IN THE WEST

Few issues in American history have been more persistently divisive than that of slavery, particularly slavery in the West. Many observers claimed that the latter problem was essentially theoretical. A special set of geographic and climatic conditions were necessary, they insisted, to raise the kinds of crops upon which slave labor could profitably be employed. Since those conditions were not present in the Great Plains, the Rocky Mountains, or the southwestern deserts, slavery could not possibly spread there. Others agreed, but maintained that a principle was involved, one that was worth fighting for. And still others regarded the question as neither specious nor academic. They felt that the lush valleys of California could conceivably support a thriving slave economy. California was growing swiftly because of the discovery of gold in 1849, and had in fact already applied for admission to the union as a free state. Theoretical or not, the problem of slavery was ominous for the American future.

Three major Protestant churches—Presbyterians, Methodists, and Baptists—had split over slavery (and would remain divided until the twentieth century). The issue also crossed party lines. In the North, "Conscience Whigs" and "Barnburner Democrats" abandoned their traditional political allegiances and joined with ex-Liberty party members to form the Free Soil party. In the lower South a Southern Rights movement was initiated which ignored the old partisan loyalties. Gradually the institutional cement of nationalism was crumbling beneath the weight of aroused sectionalism. Most Northerners were not abolitionists, but they considered slavery as a moral wrong; they wanted it kept out of the territories by congressional law, and they wished to admit California as a free state. Most Southerners were not secessionists, but they believed the western territories belonged to all Americans and that each citizen had a constitutional right to bring slave property there. They reasoned that, since California had been won, in the main, by Southern soldiers, it should come in as a slave state or not at all, and they were incensed at Northerners who made a mockery of the Constitution by blocking the return of fugitive slaves. Clearly the question of slavery had to be resolved or the consequence would be disunion.

COMPROMISE OF 1850

The spirit of concession, which had so often and so effectively operated in past crises, was invoked once again by Henry Clay. A master politician in the best sense of that term, Clay had long espoused the concept of sectional balance. Now, in the winter of 1850, and in the twilight of his life, he rose in the Senate to plead once again the cause of moderation. "I hold in my hand," he said, "a series of resolutions which I desire to submit. . . . Taken together, in combination, they propose an amicable arrangement of all questions in controversy between the free and slave states, growing out of the subject of Slavery." By Clay's proposals California would enter the Union as a free state; the southwestern regions would be organized into territories by legislation that neither permitted nor excluded slavery; the Texas boundary with New Mexico would be drawn in the latter's favor, and Texas compensated by federal assumption of its preannexation debts; the slave trade, though not slavery itself, would be prohibited in the District of Columbia; and a new and more powerful fugitive slave law would be enacted, guaranteeing Southerners the return of slaves who fled north.

Compromise, by its very nature, is abhorrent to idealists who reason in terms of ethical absolutes. "I think all legislative compromises radically wrong and essentially vicious," Senator William H. Seward of New York declared in speaking against Clay's plan. How could there be compromise on a subject as morally reprehensible and outrageous as human slavery? Southerners were equally vehement in their denunciation of a settlement they regarded as unjust. "The South asks for justice, simple justice," charged Calhoun, "and less she ought not to take." Physically emaciated and near death, Calhoun sat in gloomy silence as his opposition speech was read by a fellow Southerner. One particular voice, however, no longer resonant but nevertheless spellbinding, rose in defense of compromise. Daniel Webster, on the 7th of March, addressed the Senate "not as a Massachusetts man, nor as a Northern man, but as an American. . . . I speak," said Webster, "for the preservation of the Union. Hear me for my cause."

Although Webster was cruelly and at times vilely abused by New England radicals, his speech was instantly acclaimed by the vast majority of Northerners. Piece by piece the acts making up the Compromise of 1850 were skillfully maneuvered through Congress by Senator Stephen A. Douglas of Illinois. President Taylor had threat-

COMPROMISE OF 1850

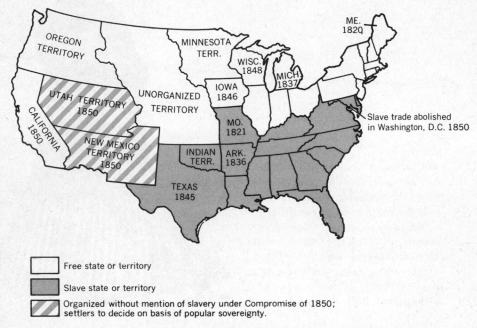

Free state or territory

Slave state or territory

Organized without mention of slavery under Compromise of 1850; settlers to decide on basis of popular sovereignty.

In 1850 it appeared that the American genius for compromise had settled the issue of slavery in the territories. President Pierce expressed the hope "that no sectional or ambitious or fanatical excitement may again threaten the durability of our institutions or obscure the light of our prosperity."

ened to veto any compromise measures. His unexpected death, caused by overeating and quack medical remedies, removed executive obstruction. Taylor's successor, Millard Fillmore, one of Senator Seward's bitterest enemies, fully agreed with and facilitated the adoption of each bill. Finally, Calhoun's death significantly weakened the southern extremists. In Georgia, Alabama, and Louisiana, even in Mississippi and South Carolina (though by narrower majorities), unionist candidates who endorsed the Compromise of 1850 triumphed over secessionists in statewide elections. One could almost sense the national relief: war had been averted.

THE FUGITIVE SLAVE ACT

But relations between Northerners and Southerners did not improve because of the Compromise of 1850. Americans were torn between an

A woman of immense courage, Harriet Tubman, born into slavery in Dorchester County, Maryland, escaped to freedom in 1849. Nineteen times she made hazardous journeys into the South to help lead other slaves to freedom. She tolerated no cowardice, telling the faint-hearted she would use her revolver: "Dead niggers tell no tales, you go on or die." (Courtesy of the Rare Books Department, Boston Public Library)

awareness that the compromise had averted a national tragedy, and a sheer inability to live up to its terms. Agitators in both sections, momentarily subdued when the compromise was first announced and applauded, returned to foster distrust among receptive audiences.

Northerners found the Fugitive Slave Act impossible to swallow. The act allowed the fugitives no jury trial, or even a hearing before a judge. A federal commissioner was authorized to certify the immediate return of an accused slave. Any deputy who refused to carry out the law could be fined $1,000. Any citizen who hid a fugitive could be fined the same amount, imprisoned for six months, and compelled to pay civil damages. Hundreds of panic-stricken free blacks, alarmed at the potential abuses, left their northern homes for Canada. The severity of the law invited popular resistance. A mob in Syracuse broke into a building to free a captured slave. Another in Boston rescued a slave from deportation. In Pennsylvania a slave hunter was murdered. The Supreme Court of Wisconsin absolved a newspaperman who had violated the Fugitive Slave Act, by declaring it unconstitutional: a decision which was not reversed by the United States Supreme Court until 1859 (*Ableman* v. *Booth*). Statistically the number of such incidents was small, but each one further strained sectional tensions.

THE WHIG DEMISE

The national problem was epitomized in the election of 1852. No important difference separated Whig and Democratic party platforms. Both endorsed the Compromise of 1850. Both labored at the task of maintaining party unity. The Democrats in convention balloted 49 times before selecting a nonentity, Franklin Pierce of New Hampshire, as their candidate. The Whigs hoped to win with another hero of the Mexican War, General Winfield Scott. Pierce carried all but four states, and, while his popular majority was not extraordinary, his electoral victory amounted to 254 to 42. The Whigs never recovered. Like their Federalist predecessors they soon vanished as a national party.

But why? How could one defeat spell political oblivion for the Whigs? First, the Whig party had received its direction from political leaders of ability and stature. Those spokesmen of an older generation were gone, and the party fell to men of small talents and limited imaginations. Second, southern Whigs, alienated by the antislavery proclivities of northern members who helped fugitive slaves, deserted the party by the thousands. The lessons of the Whig demise should have been clear to Democrats, but they were not. Pierce was followed by Buchanan. Both men were incapable of providing the nation with direction. More vitally, instead of seeking ways to moderate sectional grievances, the Democrats blundered by reopening the question of slavery in the territories.

THE KANSAS-NEBRASKA ACT

Senator Stephen A. Douglas of Illinois, known as the "Little Giant" because of his small size and commanding appearance, bore responsibility for the blunder. Douglas had far more initiative and intelligence than Pierce, Buchanan, or other Democratic chieftains. A fine orator, a clever politician, a rabid expansionist and dedicated nationalist, Douglas was immensely popular with northern voters. He had every reason to anticipate becoming president. His chance was considerably lessened, if not destroyed, the Democratic party was ultimately splintered, and the nation was pushed along the road to war all because Douglas—believing it was most democratic to allow the settlers themselves to decide on slavery—introduced legislation that specifically repealed the Missouri Compromise of 1820.

Because Douglas would benefit economically and (he thought) politically, he wanted the federal government to support the construction of a transcontinental railroad from St. Louis to San Francisco. Because the route would pass through Nebraska, it was essential to organize that area into a territory. Southerners, for obvious reasons, favored making New Orleans or Memphis the eastern terminus. In addition, southern congressmen had previously defeated territorial legislation for Nebraska since that region was north of 36° 30′ and would be formed into free states. A new Kansas-Nebraska Bill, sponsored by Douglas, divided the territory in two, explicitly declared the Missouri Compromise void, and left the settlers to decide whether or not slavery would be permitted. Southerners, recognizing an opportunity to expand the boundaries of slavery, supported it. For the same reason Northerners besieged their legislators with pleas to oppose it. Douglas, however, exerted considerable political pressure. Enough northern congressmen succumbed to make the Kansas-Nebraska Act the law of the land in May 1854.

A substantial portion of northern opinion was so enraged that effigies of Douglas were burned all across the plains of Indiana and Illinois. So irate was a Chicago audience that Douglas could not speak above the uproar. "Abolitionists of Chicago!" Douglas is alleged to have shouted, "It is Sunday morning. I'll go to church, and you may all go to hell." Chicagoans called him the "Benedict Arnold of 1854." In Boston thousands of United States soldiers and marines, as well as the state militia, were needed to enforce the deportation of one fugitive slave. Douglas had opened a Pandora's box. The railroad was all but forgotten.

BLEEDING KANSAS

Douglas had argued that letting the settlers decide on slavery—a system called popular or "squatter" sovereignty—was the most democratic of all methods. In theory, he may have been right; in practice, he was definitely not. The act turned Kansas into a bloody battlefield. Most settlers were neutral, but from New England came a number of emigrants carrying rifles and ammunition, sworn to keep Kansas free. Funds were collected at church services and public meetings, and funneled through various emigrant aid societies to assist the freedom fighters. From the South also came settlers, though not as many, determined to legalize slavery in Kansas. "Border ruffians," as Horace Greeley termed them, crossed over from Missouri with no real intention of remaining, to spread terror or to jam the ballot boxes for

slavery. Atrocities were committed on both sides, but the most celebrated was John Brown's wanton massacre and mutilation of five men
at Pottawatomie. Brown considered slavery a form of murder, and he
felt no remorse. Emerson, Thoreau, and other northern literati idolized
Brown as a man of action. European philosophers regarded him as an
authentic American national hero. Brown's role in Kansas was insignificant, but he became a symbol—a just and wrathful prophet—to
his admirers and to posterity.

The conflict in Kansas was mirrored in Congress: there also the
dispute turned from harsh words to physical violence. Senator Charles
Sumner of Massachusetts, a devoted but sharp-tongued abolitionist,
surpassed his previous vituperative efforts in a two-day speech entitled "The Crime Against Kansas." Some of his most pointed insults
were aimed at Senator Andrew P. Butler of South Carolina, who was
not present to defend himself. Three days later, while Sumner was
seated at his desk in the Senate chamber, he was assaulted by Butler's
nephew, Representative Preston Brooks. Brooks beat Sumner unconscious with his cane, and then bragged that he made the Northerner
bellow "like a calf." Brooks became a southern hero, praised in the
press, banqueted, and rewarded for striking back against northern
insults.

THE REPUBLICAN PARTY

The issue of Kansas gave birth to the Republican party. In 1854, in
the old Northwest (various localities claim to be the birthplace) antislavery Whigs combined with old Liberty and Free Soil partisans, dis-
sident Democrats, land reformers, and temperance men to raise the
banner against slavery's extension. The new organization incorporated
several groups with antithetical interests. For example, many German
political refugees from the unsuccessful European revolutions of 1848,
generally idealistic, liberal men to whom slavery was an abomination,
joined the new party. Yet most northern members of the Know-
Nothing movement—a secret, superpatriotic, anti-Catholic, and antiforeign group which flourished briefly—also joined the Republicans.

The party was completely sectional, representing the mainstream
of northern opinion. It took no stand against slavery in the South,
and abolitionists faced the choice of either going their own ineffective
way or staying with the party to exercise what influence they could.
Nor did the Republicans pretend to be any special friend of the black
people. Their press repeatedly called them the "White Man's Party."
None of the states in the old Northwest, for example, permitted blacks

to vote. Illinois even prohibited their entering the state. The Republican party platform in 1856 was concerned primarily with the West. It denounced proslavery voting frauds in Kansas, and called for congressional action to forbid "those twin relics of barbarism, [Mormon] polygamy and slavery" in the territories.

ELECTION OF 1856

The Republicans became an immediate threat to the Democrats. In 1856 they nominated, in the Whig tradition, a romantic military figure, John C. Frémont. The son-in-law of Thomas Hart Benton, Frémont was nationally known for his exploits in California. Their alliterative songs and slogans asked voters to support "Freedom, Freemen, and Frémont." The Democrats rejected Pierce and Douglas and nominated James Buchanan, an experienced but inoffensive politician who, though from Pennsylvania, had markedly southern inclinations. Their platform reaffirmed the concept of popular sovereignty contained in the Kansas-Nebraska Act.

Buchanan won by taking all the slave states except Maryland (which voted for Fillmore, who ran on the remnants of the Know-Nothing movement), plus Pennsylvania, New Jersey, Indiana, Illinois, and California. The campaign was exciting and, in retrospect, alarming. Southerners, including those who had supported the Union in 1850, had made it plain that if Frémont had won, they would not have submitted. In the next election Republicans would concentrate on the four northern states they lost in 1856. By winning these, they could win the national election. Did the Southerners mean what they had said? Would they in fact secede in the event of a Republican triumph?

THE DRED SCOTT DECISION

Two days after Buchanan took his oath of office the United States Supreme Court announced its decision in the case of *Dred Scott* v. *Sanford* and radically altered national perspectives on the question of slavery in the territories. According to the Court, the Missouri Compromise of 1820, which had been repealed by the Kansas-Nebraska Act of 1854, had never been constitutional. Congress, said the Court, had no authority to keep slavery out of any territory. Then, and ever since, scholars have criticized the Dred Scott decision as one of the most poorly reasoned and subjective judgments in Supreme Court history. Northerners were chagrined, angry, openly defiant. The decision confirmed their belief that the five southern judges, headed by Chief

Justice Roger Taney of Maryland, were hopelessly biased. The Court, wrote one New York journalist, has "draggled and polluted its garments in the filth of pro-slavery politics." Republicans proposed a variety of constitutional amendments to upset the Dred Scott decision. Southerners, of course, were delighted, for the Court's finding confirmed their belief that slaves should be transportable to any territory. To Stephen Douglas and the Democratic party, however, the Dred Scott ruling spelled disaster.

DOUGLAS AND BUCHANAN

The decision drove a wedge between northern and southern Democrats. Party unity had largely depended upon the agreement to uphold popular sovereignty. Many Southerners saw no reason to do so when the Supreme Court had ruled otherwise. Moreover, President Buchanan urged the American people to accept the Court's ruling as a final settlement; Douglas, on the other hand, was not yet ready to abandon his doctrine.

This opening rift in the Democratic ranks was widened by developments in Kansas. There a rump body of proslavery delegates meeting in the town of Lecompton had composed a state constitution legalizing slavery. The Lecompton constitution was submitted to the people in a manner so unfair that it made a mockery of popular sovereignty. Even the territorial governor of Kansas, Robert J. Walker of Mississippi, who had been appointed by Buchanan, denounced the maneuver and advised that the Lecompton constitution be rejected. Nevertheless, Buchanan decided to recommend it to Congress as the basis for Kansas' admission to the union. Douglas objected, and the two men exchanged heated words. "No Democrat ever yet differed from an Administration of his choice without being crushed," Buchanan warned Douglas. "Mr. President, I wish you to remember that General Jackson is dead!" Douglas snapped back. Buchanan did try to crush Douglas by depriving him of patronage, but Douglas' strength among northern Democrats in Congress was enough to prevent acceptance of the Lecompton constitution. Kansas did not enter the union until 1861, and then as a free state.

Republicans began to court Douglas. Horace Greeley's New York *Tribune*, a newspaper of considerable influence throughout the country, admired his stand against the forces of slavery. Any chance of an alliance, however, was killed by the pronounced hostility of Illinois Republicans toward Douglas. They aimed at gaining his senatorial seat in 1858. To do so they were promoting the reputation of a lawyer from Springfield, a tall, angular, awkward politician whom the people intuitively trusted, named Abraham Lincoln.

DOUGLAS AND LINCOLN

The Illinois senatorial contest between Douglas and Lincoln attracted huge crowds. They met seven times in debate, covering the state from north to south. Never in American history has a public debate surpassed that of these two masterful and articulate speakers.

Douglas was the more consistent debater. When, in the town of Freeport, Lincoln challenged him to defend popular sovereignty, which seemed a farce in the light of the Dred Scott case, Douglas did so. "Slavery cannot exist a day or an hour anywhere," explained Douglas, "unless it is supported by local police regulations." In other words, the people of a territory could, if they wanted, ban slavery by the simple expedient of not enacting legislation protecting it. The "Freeport Doctrine" was repudiated by southern Democrats as heretical, but remained a viable principle to northern members. Lincoln shaded his speeches depending upon the area in which he spoke. In Chicago, where antislavery sentiment was strongest, he cited the Declaration of Independence: "Let us discard all this quibbling about . . . this race and that race and the other race being inferior. . . . All men are created equal." Two months later in the town of Charleston, where many Southerners had settled, Lincoln changed his tune: "I will say, then, that I am not, nor ever have been, in favor of bringing about in any way the social and political equality of the white and black races. . . . I am not nor ever have been in favor of making voters or jurors of Negroes, nor of qualifying them to hold office, nor to intermarry with white people. . . . I as much as any other man am in favor of having the superior position assigned to the white race."

If Douglas was more consistent, he was blind to the moral implications of slavery—and Lincoln was not. The difference was crucial. Lincoln felt that slavery was a blight upon the land which must eventually be extinguished. "I do not expect the Union to be dissolved—I do not expect the House to fall—but I do expect it to cease to be divided," he said in his most famous speech of the 1858 debates. "It will become all one thing or all the other." Lincoln planned no assault on slavery in the states. He made it quite plain that abolitionism had no place in the Republican party. But by confining slavery to the old South Lincoln hoped to promote its gradual attrition and disappearance. Douglas drew no moral distinction between slavery and freedom. "Every sentiment he utters," said Lincoln, "discards the idea that there is any wrong in slavery." While Douglas emphasized that Lincoln's stand could mean only war, Lincoln countered by portraying Douglas as a proslavery conspirator. Let Dred Scott stand, warned Lincoln, and there would soon follow "another Supreme Court decision, declaring that the Constitution of the United States does not permit a *State* to exclude slavery."

Douglas won the election, but Lincoln established a reputation which two years later made it possible for him to gain the Republican nomination for the presidency.

JOHN BROWN'S RAID

The sore festered, and the poison ran through the body politic. At what point the disease became incurable, no one can say. Surely a

Pictured is an illustration of a slave auction which appeared in Harriet Beecher Stowe's Uncle Tom's Cabin, *published in 1852. While living in Cincinnati, a favorite crossing place on the Ohio River for fugitive slaves, Mrs. Stowe had come into contact with slavery. Her book, an instant success, sold over 300,000 copies in its first year of publication. (From* Uncle Tom's Cabin, *1852)*

crisis of some kind seemed imminent. A United States senator from California was killed in a duel with a Southerner. Many Northerners, having read the immensely popular *Uncle Tom's Cabin*, believed everyone south of the Mason-Dixon line to be a Simon Legree. Many Southerners believed everyone north of it to be an irresponsible abolitionist agitator or sympathizer. Even a northern accent aroused suspicion anywhere in the South. Republican attempts to disassociate the party from the extremists failed to persuade Southerners. If some were not yet fully convinced, in 1859 an act of northern fanaticism took place that removed any lingering doubts.

John Brown had no trouble raising money in the North. Men of the highest social distinction contributed tens of thousands of dollars to finance his guerrilla warfare. Six men in particular—the so-called Secret Six—who represented the cream of northern society, knew that Brown planned an audacious raid into the South itself, to arm slaves and to incite them to rebel against their white masters. Brown planned to establish a revolutionary government in the South, with himself as military dictator, and he carefully composed a "Provisional Constitution and Ordinances for the People of the United States." The Secret Six—a philanthropist, a financier, a surgeon, a professor, a minister, and a philosopher—had diverted funds collected for use in Kansas to support Brown's invasion. Lest they become too deeply implicated, however, they asked Brown not to tell them the precise time and place of the attack.

Brown struck on a Sunday evening, October 16, 1859. His expedition numbered 18 men, including five blacks, enough to capture the unguarded federal arsenal at Harpers Ferry, Virginia. But thereafter nothing worked out as Brown planned. The slaves did not rise. "It was so absurd," Abraham Lincoln later commented, "that the slaves, with all their ignorance, saw plainly enough it could not succeed." Ironically, the first to die was a free black who failed to heed a command to halt given by one of Brown's men. Four citizens of Harpers Ferry and a United States marine were killed by the insurrectionists, and others were taken prisoner. A telegraphed alarm brought government troops, headed by Colonel Robert E. Lee and Lieutenant J. E. B. Stuart. Surrounded and trapped in a locomotive roundhouse, Brown displayed the courage of a truly dedicated man. According to an eyewitness: "Brown was the coolest and firmest man I ever saw in defying danger and death. With one son dead by his side, and another shot through, he felt the pulse of his dying son with one hand and held his rifle with the other and commanded his men with the utmost composure, encouraging them to be firm and to sell their lives as dearly as they could." Ten died and a few escaped before Brown and five others were taken prisoner. The revolution had lasted a little more than 24 hours.

Brown was tried and convicted of murder, criminal conspiracy, and treason against the state of Virginia. He died on the scaffold as bravely as he had fought.

NORTHERN AND SOUTHERN REACTIONS

Republican and Democratic political leaders immediately disowned and denounced Brown's raid. "No man, North or South," said Lincoln, "can approve of violence or crime." Anti-Brown meetings in Boston and New York were exceptionally well attended. Southerners, however, heard other voices which canonized Brown. He was "not only a martyr," wrote Theodore Parker, "but a SAINT." Thoreau composed an eloquent "Plea for Captain Brown." Wendell Phillips told an audience that "John Brown is the impersonation of God's order and God's law." Emerson believed that Brown's death "will make the gallows as glorious as the cross." Little wonder that when war came northern soldiers went South singing:

> "John Brown's body lies a-mouldering in the grave,
> But his soul goes marching on."

In the South, Brown's raid touched off a witch-hunt for subversives and fellow travelers. Few were found, but hundreds of innocents suffered: a minister in Texas was lashed 70 times; a schoolteacher was ordered to leave Arkansas in 36 hours; three sailors off a Maine ship were flogged in Georgia; a Connecticut bookseller was beaten in Charleston; the northern president of an Alabama college was dismissed; an Irish stonecutter in Columbia, South Carolina, was tarred and feathered. A great fear settled over the South. Rumors of northern invasion, of slaves rioting, raping, burning, and killing, and of abolitionist conspiracies to poison all whites multiplied and spread panic.

Such was the paranoia in the nation when citizens were asked to vote in the election of 1860.

THE ELECTION OF 1860

The Democratic party held its convention in Charleston, a rich and quiet city of mansions and tree-lined streets. But the mood of the delegates belied their surroundings. Hostile and inflexible, southern delegates brought in a plank which declared it a federal duty to protect slavery in the territories. "Gentlemen of the South," an Ohioan responded, "you mistake us—you mistake us—we will not do it." Douglas' men were in a majority. When their resolution for popular sovereignty passed, the Southerners walked out. Since no presidential candidate could be nominated without a two-thirds majority, the convention adjourned. The Democrats never reunited. Several months later the convention reassembled in Baltimore and chose Douglas; the dissenting Southerners held their own meeting and selected John C. Breckenridge of Kentucky.

The Republican party met in Chicago, in a noisy carnival atmosphere stimulated in part by quantities of free liquor. John Brown's attack was repudiated, as was abolitionism, and the Dred Scott decision was declared "a dangerous political heresy." The Republicans affirmed that freedom must be national, and slavery sectional. But they were no longer a single-issue party: for the Germans there was a plank opposing any changes in the naturalization laws; for middle-western farmers and their sons, a plank recommending passage of a homestead act; for eastern industrialists, endorsement of a high tariff. The platform was carefully drawn to appeal to a variety of northern interests. Selection of a presidential nominee was spirited and caused some dissension. The front-runner was Seward, no longer the radical of 1850, but that image persisted and ruined his chances. Most Republicans wanted a middle-of-the-road figure and, after some back-room manipulations and secret political commitments, particularly of cabinet appointments, Abraham Lincoln was nominated.

The antebellum South has been described as a nation within a nation, and in 1860 southern balloting was an election within an election. No Lincoln ticket was presented in the cotton states, and Douglas was virtually ignored except by a minority of loyal adherents. The choice was between Breckenridge for the southern Democrats and John Bell as the candidate of the Constitutional Union party. The Constitutional Unionists advocated peace and union, but offered no fresh formulas. Though Bell polled a respectable 588,000 popular votes, he captured the electoral votes of only Virginia, Kentucky, and Tennessee. Breckenridge polled 849,000 votes and took every other southern state. In the North the contest was entirely between Lincoln and Douglas. Douglas received 1,377,000 votes, but they were so spread across the country that he carried only Missouri and part of New Jersey. Lincoln had every free state. His popular total was 1,866,000 votes (a minority), but in the electoral college he obtained 180 ballots (a substantial majority).

SECESSION

With Lincoln's election the lower South seceded, and it is important to ask why. For decades the South had exercised an influence in the national government far out of proportion to its population or productivity. That influence should have reached its peak and declined a generation before, but the southern cause possessed a charm which enlisted northern political advocates, and they helped sustain southern power beyond its time. Thus, the South had dominated the presidency, the cabinet, and the Supreme Court, and had maintained strength equal with that of the free states in the Senate.

Politically, southern leaders realized that Lincoln's election was the beginning of northern domination. Minnesota's entrance to the Union in 1858 gave the North a predominance in the Senate. Now, they felt, a Republican president elected entirely by northern votes was being imposed upon them. Calhoun had long foreseen this moment and had attempted to alter the federal structure to ensure southern equality in the national councils, or a southern veto over national laws. He had even suggested a dual executive. He had warned that secession would follow unless the South were protected against the tyranny of a northern majority. That moment had come.

Economically, while some southern leaders favored economic diversification, others insisted that the South could only prosper by expanding into new lands. They saw the economic gap between North and South widen steadily with each passing year. The northern wheat crop alone was worth more than all the southern cotton. Railroads built in the 1850's connected the trans-Mississippi West to eastern metropolitan centers, tying these sections to one another by mutual interest. True, the tariff had been low. But Republicans, Southerners had no doubt, would eventually raise it. They felt isolated, encircled, squeezed. They feared that exploitation would follow.

Culturally, the South was unique. Northern society was mixed and mobile; southern society was a throwback to the feudal past. The South was proud and aristocratic, vaunting superiority to cover a basic insecurity; the North was optimistic, democratic, and self-critical. Southerners were quick to duel over personal insults, real or fancied. Primogeniture was still the custom if not the law. White women were publicly venerated. Kinship and family meant much to Southerners, who were very conscious of history; less to Northerners, who counted on the future. The Southerner of means revered the traditional, the classical, the agrarian, and the graceful and leisurely way of life. He had no wish to join in the advance of Western civilization.

He wanted to preserve his social structure, including its central tenet, white supremacy. The North would not permit it. Northerners had declared slavery wrong, and the South had to resist or see its culture destroyed. "We are a people, a *nation*, with arms in our hands," wrote one Southerner, ". . . and we shall never submit the case to the judgment of *another people*, until they show themselves of superior virtue and intellect."

South Carolina was the first to secede. Six more states of the lower South soon followed. By February 1861 the Confederate States of America had been established, and Jefferson Davis was chosen as provisional president. Federal forts and arsenals were seized and declared to be Confederate property. Diplomats selected by the new government prepared to sail. Buchanan in his final month in office did nothing. A pathetic figure, he watched each secessionist move with acute discomfort and total irresolution. Eight other slave states, meanwhile, decided to wait for the next president to take his oath. Indeed, the entire nation was eager to know what Lincoln would do.

This 1860 lithograph symbolizes the beginning and the end of James Buchanan's administration. In four years the proud and defiant American eagle had been reduced to a crippled and dying bird because of secession. (Courtesy of the New-York Historical Society)

LINCOLN'S POSITION

Lincoln's position was uncompromising. Several desperate bids to preserve the Union were made, one by Senator John J. Crittenden of Kentucky and another by a Peace Convention of 133 delegates which met in Washington shortly before Lincoln's inauguration. They failed because Lincoln would accept no quarter on the question of the extension of slavery in the territories; nor would the leaders of the Confederacy bargain. In his inaugural address, however, Lincoln renewed the Republican pledge to respect slavery in the states. His words had no effect on southern extremists, who were obsessed with the idea that the president was an abolitionist. But while some Republicans, like Horace Greeley, advised letting the South secede in peace, Lincoln thought otherwise. "In your hands, my dissatisfied fellow countrymen," said Lincoln, "and not in mine, is the momentous issue of civil war. The government will not assail you. You can have no conflict without yourselves being the aggressors."

FORT SUMTER: THE WAR BEGINS

Whether North or South was the aggressor in the Civil War is still a subject of historical dispute. Lincoln's first decision as commander in chief concerned two island fortresses, Pickens at Pensacola and Sumter at Charleston. Both were held by federal troops who were running short of supplies. The Confederacy demanded their evacuation and surrender. At Charleston rebel batteries were placed in strategic positions ready to fire upon the fort. The Confederates made it clear that any attempt to send relief vessels to Sumter or Pickens would be regarded as a hostile act. Lincoln pondered, hesitated, sought the counsel of his cabinet, and weighed the consequences of his alternatives. Sending vessels could precipitate war and turn the upper South to the Confederacy. Not sending vessels could be interpreted as a sign of weakness. Seward, who had been appointed secretary of state and had a rather exalted opinion of his own ability, suggested that the United States pick a quarrel with some European power in order to rally all Americans to the flag and thus relieve sectional tensions. Seward and four other cabinet officers adamantly opposed sending reinforcements to Sumter or Pickens, but Lincoln overruled them and ordered the vessels to sail.

Confederate officers at Charleston called upon the commander at Fort Sumter and requested his surrender. Fort Sumter, he responded, still had a two-day supply of food and, as a point of honor, would not surrender until those provisions were exhausted. The Confederates would not wait. Even before the supply ship arrived, at 4:30 in the morning of April 12, 1861, Confederate batteries fired the first shots of the Civil War.

A burst of indignation swept through the North upon news of Sumter's capitulation. "The plan succeeded," wrote Lincoln. "They attacked Sumter—it fell, and thus, did more service than it otherwise could." Lincoln issued a call for 75,000 volunteers and proclaimed a naval blockade of the South. Virginia, North Carolina, Arkansas, and Tennessee seceded and joined the Confederacy. However, western Virginia seceded from Virginia and remained loyal to the Union. Delaware, Kentucky, Missouri, and Maryland also remained loyal, though Maryland did so only because it was occupied by federal troops.

LINCOLN'S MILITARY LEADERSHIP

Anyone who served as president during the Civil War would have been memorable. Lincoln, however, did not merely preside. He was the one dominant and decisive figure of the war years. Americans have turned Lincoln into a legend, enshrining him with Washington in their pantheon of demigods. However, many of his actions have been harshly criticized. Setting the myths aside, and weighing the criticisms, Lincoln still emerges an extraordinary individual.

Lincoln never attempted to evade the military responsibilities of his office. His policy of blockading Confederate ports at the very outset of the war was of fundamental importance in the defeat of the South. He also adopted the idea of fighting the war on several fronts. "We have the *greater* numbers, and the enemy has the *greater* facility of concentrating forces upon points of collision," said Lincoln. "We must fail unless we can find some way of making *our* advantage an overmatch for *his;* and this can only be done by menacing him with superior forces at *different* points, at the *same* time." The North had 2,000,000 soldiers to the South's 800,000, and an enormous preponderance in transportation, military equipment, industrial production, sea power, wealth, and population. Yet, southern soldiers, fighting in defense of their homeland, seemed to have the advantage in the early years. Lincoln's policy was sound, but he had to find a general equal to Lee to carry it out.

Ulysses S. Grant was that man. He was appointed lieutenant-general of the Union armies in March 1864. Thirteen months later

Lee surrendered at Appomattox Court House in Virginia, ending a conflict so bloody that in four years 620,000 soldiers had been killed.

LINCOLN'S POLITICAL PROBLEMS

Lincoln was a clever, adroit, and hardworking politician. He had to be. He was attacked by "peace" Democrats who campaigned for a negotiated settlement. Their strength in the southern parts of Ohio, Indiana, and Illinois was formidable. They considered Lincoln a warmonger, and the war itself unjust, inhumane, and unnecessary. Most were loyal to the Union, but a good many were southern sympathizers, known as "copperheads," and a few engaged in subversive acts. Lincoln suspended the writ of *habeas corpus* in critical regions, and permitted the military to suppress hostile newspapers and to arbitrarily arrest and try civilians—actions which the Supreme Court later declared to be unconstitutional. But Lincoln was no dictator. If he violated the law, he did so cautiously, reluctantly, and sanely, because without these violations the war might have been lost and with it the Union.

Lincoln had as much trouble with his own party as with copperheads. A radical wing of the Republicans was bent on revenging themselves on the South, and were annoyed by Lincoln's moderate attitude. The radical Republicans formed and dominated a joint congressional committee on the conduct of the war, and they badgered Lincoln to abolish slavery. To do so, Lincoln felt, would 1. Violate the Republican platform, which had promised that the federal government would not interfere with slavery in the states; and 2. Outrage public opinion in some of the border states that had remained loyal, pushing them to the Confederate side. "My paramount object in this struggle," wrote Lincoln, "*is* to save the union, and is *not* to save or destroy slavery." Nevertheless, under constant pressure from the radical Republicans, Lincoln in 1863 used his wartime presidential powers to issue the Emancipation Proclamation. Ironically, the proclamation ordered freedom for the slaves only in those areas in which Lincoln had no real authority. Some radicals thought Lincoln should have made a more courageous and forthright statement. Democrats, on the other hand, thought Lincoln had acted hypocritically by yielding to the demands of the radical Republicans:

> "Honest old Abe, when the war first began,
> Denied abolition was part of his plan;
> Honest old Abe has since made a decree,

The war must go on till the slaves are all free.
As both can't be honest, will someone tell how,
If honest Abe then, he is honest Abe now?"

The Emancipation Proclamation was put into effect by northern armies as they gradually conquered southern territory. The Thirteenth Amendment to the Constitution, which abolished slavery everywhere, was not finally adopted until after Lincoln's death, although he was instrumental in forcing it through Congress.

ELECTION OF 1864

Lincoln kept the Republicans united during his administration, no easy task in view of party bickering in the cabinet, in Congress, and among state leaders. For a while Lincoln thought he would lose the election of 1864. Radical Republicans were less than pleased with his veto of the Wade-Davis bill, a plan for postwar reconstruction of the South which Lincoln considered too harsh. Horace Greeley, on the other hand, accused Lincoln of extending the war for selfish reasons when he could have terminated it by negotiation. The radical Republican-Greeley alliance was strange, but nevertheless disturbing to Lincoln.

Pictured is Sherman's army moving out of Atlanta on November 15, 1864, at the start of the famous march across Georgia to the sea. Called a prophet of modern total war, Sherman employed the technique of destroying civilian property to break the enemy will to resist. "I have been told by dozens of men," reported J. W. DeForest a year later, that Sherman "couldn't walk up the main street of Columbia in the daytime without being shot." (From Harper's Weekly, *January 7, 1865)*

He was running on a coalition ticket of Republicans and War Democrats, the National Union party, with Andrew Johnson of Tennessee as the vice-presidential nominee. The regular Democratic organization nominated General George B. McClellan, an officer of limited ability whom Lincoln had removed from his command in 1862 for incompetence.

Sherman's march through Georgia and his capture of Atlanta, which broke the backbone of the Confederacy, abruptly altered northern political alignments. Greeley came out for Lincoln, as did the radical Republicans. The National Union party swept to victory by 212 to 21 electoral votes and a popular majority of nearly half a million. "The election," said Lincoln, "has demonstrated that a people's government can sustain a national election in the midst of a great civil war."

"With malice toward none; with charity for all; with firmness in the right, as God gives us to see the right," Lincoln said in his second inaugural address, "let us strive on to finish the work we are in; to bind up the nation's wounds . . . to do all which may achieve a just and lasting peace among ourselves, and with all nations." A month later he was dead, assassinated as he sat watching a play at Ford's Theatre. One wonders, had Lincoln lived, if he could have mastered the postwar problems as superbly as he had directed the nation in war. Or would his image have been sullied in the muddy waters of Reconstruction? While deifying Lincoln the people really forgot him. The years after his death, instead of being marked by charity and justice, were years of vengeance, corruption, and exploitation.

SUGGESTED READINGS

*Gilbert H. Barnes, *The Antislavery Impulse: 1830–1844*

Samuel F. Bemis, *John Quincy Adams and the Union*

*Ray Billington, *The Far Western Frontier: 1830–1860*

Gerald Capers, *Stephen A. Douglas*

Bruce Catton, *The Centennial History of the Civil War*

Arthur C. Cole, *The Irrepressible Conflict*

*Avery O. Craven, *The Coming of the Civil War*

David Donald, *Charles Sumner and the Coming of the Civil War*

*Dwight Dumond, *Antislavery: The Crusade for Freedom in America*

*Clement Eaton, *The Mind of the Old South*, rev. ed.

Stanley Elkins, *Slavery: A Problem in American Institutional and Intellectual Life*

*Don Fehrenbacher, *Prelude to Greatness: Lincoln in the 1850's*

*Louis Filler, *The Crusade Against Slavery, 1830–1860*

*C. S. Griffin, *The Ferment of Reform, 1830–1860*

*Holman Hamilton, *Prologue to Conflict: The Crisis and Compromise of 1850*

Allan Nevins, *The Ordeal of the Union*

———, *The Emergence of Lincoln*

*Roy F. Nichols, *The Disruption of American Democracy*

Russell Nye, *William Lloyd Garrison and the Humanitarian Reformers*

*David Potter, *Lincoln and His Party in the Secession Crisis*

Thomas Pressley, *Americans Interpret Their Civil War*

*J. G. Randall, *Lincoln, the President*

Carl Swisher, *Roger B. Taney*

Benjamin Thomas, *Abraham Lincoln*

* Available in paperback

INDEX